SOUL
PRESCRIPTION

SOUL
PRESCRIPTION
Experience True Healing and Freedom

Bill Bright & Henry Brandt
Foreword by Tim LaHaye

Pleasant Word
A Division of WinePress Group

Pleasant Word (a division of WinePress Publishing, PO Box 428, Enumclaw, WA 98022) functions only as book publisher. As such, the ultimate design, content, editorial accuracy, and views expressed or implied in this work are those of the author.

This book contains stories of people the authors met with over the years. In some cases, names and secondary details have been changed to protect the privacy of those involved.

Unless otherwise identified, all Scripture quotations in this publication are taken from the *Holy Bible, New Living Translation, Second Edition.* Copyright © 1996, 2004. Used by permission of Tyndale Charitable Trust. All rights reserved.

Scripture quotations marked NIV are taken from *Holy Bible, New International Version®.* Copyright © 1973, 1978, 1984 by International Bible Society. Used by permission of Zondervan.

Scripture quotations marked NKJV are taken from the *New King James Version.* Copyright © 1979, 1980, 1982, 1990, Thomas Nelson Inc. Used by permission.

Scripture quotations marked KJV are taken from the *King James Version* of the Bible.

Scripture quotations marked NASB are taken from the *New American Standard Bible,* © Copyright 1960, 1963, 1968, 1971, 1972, 1973, 1975, 1977 by The Lockman Foundation. Used by permission.

ISBN 13: 978-1-4141-1223-7
ISBN 10: 1-4141-1223-8
Library of Congress Catalog Card Number: 2008902641

He heals the brokenhearted and binds up their wounds.

—Psalm 147:3 NIV

CONTENTS

ACKNOWLEDGMENTS

Preparing a book for publication is no easy task, and we are grateful to many who gave invaluable assistance.

Marcus Maranto's analytical mind was a tremendous resource for us during the early, conceptual work on the book.

Robert Barnes was also a big help in the early planning and research. He was the first to begin preparing some of the text with us.

Jim Bramlett was always faithful to tap the Bright archives.

Wayne Bruce provided useful feedback throughout the process and was especially helpful in suggesting material for the "Soul Prescription" sections of the chapters in part 2.

Kimra Johnston offered valuable suggestions to improve the theory of spiritual healing.

Eric Stanford was the wordsmith who brought the project to completion. He helped us to more effectively communicate our message.

Helmut Teichert shepherded the project through from beginning to end. He, more than anyone else, is responsible for making sure this book made it out into the light of day.

Most of all, we are grateful to God for His Spirit who leads us out of our predicament of sin.

PREFACE

My old friend Bill Bright and I would often speak together at events sponsored by Campus Crusade for Christ. We had a regular procedure on such occasions. I would begin by confronting the listeners with hard truths about themselves. Many times I could be heard expounding a favorite text from Colossians: "Put off all these; anger, wrath, malice, blasphemy, and filthy communications out of your mouth. Lie not to one another." Then, after I had put our listeners in a sober frame of mind about the ways they had failed God, Bill would get up to speak. In keeping with his more winsome nature, Bill would preach about the kindness and mercy of God, especially God's offer of forgiveness. In other words, he delivered his good news as the counterpart to my bad news—two parts of the same whole.

The last time Bill and I did this kind of side-by-side preaching was some years ago, now. But in a way, this book represents one last time for Bill and me to team up in addressing the people of God about the crucial matter of sin and holiness. You, friend, are our audience as we present time-tested and biblically based principles for repenting of sin and going on in holiness. Here you will hear tough truths about the costs of sin, as well as, welcome encouragement about the grace God supplies to those who honestly seek Him. You will be presented with a prescription capable of healing the harm that sin has caused in your life.

The credit for envisioning this book goes to Bill. We got together early in the summer of 2002, more than a year before his death, and were doing some reminiscing about the old days. But, because Bill knew he was dying, his mind was more on the future—he wanted to accomplish as much as he could for Christ in the time left to him. So at one point Bill said, "Why don't we write a book together?" He explained that he had for some time been worried about the number of Christians who are living with sin in their lives—seemingly accepting the situation as the way it has to be. Then, Bill went on to explain why he wanted me involved in this project.

Bill was concerned that too much of Christian counseling today is not dealing with the core problem of sin. Counselors may know a lot about current, psychological theories and may care about people's emotional distress, but they too often neglect the need to take responsibility for wrongdoing. The fact that many patients go to counseling for months and years on end appears to be a sign that some counselors are helping people grow comfortable with a sinful lifestyle instead of getting past it. While it may sound simplistic, the truth is that if people would quit with sin, they could take a shortcut to greater spiritual and emotional well-being. Bill knew I would agree with this analysis of the situation because for decades the focus of my counseling practice has been on sin.

Today there are dozens of Christian counselors in every major city of America. But to my knowledge, when I started in the 1950s, I was one of the first two Christian counselors in the country (Clyde Narrimore was the other). You could say that I lit the fire—and to be frank with you, sometimes I am sorry I did. By and large, Christian counselors are bright, well-educated people. But in most cases they have gotten caught up in secular theories of psychology based on the idea that there is no God. These theories say that we are on our own and have to fix our problems through self-effort. It is a human-focused approach instead of a God-focused approach. Bill wanted me to bring the old-fashioned, but never more relevant, perspective of biblical counseling to this book, and I was glad to supply it.

After getting *Soul Prescription* on its way, Bill was not able to join me in seeing it through to its conclusion. Nonetheless, up to a week before his death, Bill was still working on the manuscript of this book until the wee hours of the morning. Propped up in bed and breathing through an oxygen mask, he would be holding a page up to his bedside light while other pages lay scattered across his bed. For me, this image of him in his final days reveals more poignantly than anything else how important the message of holiness really was to him.

Bill died on July 19, 2003, of complications related to pulmonary fibrosis. The world lost a great light for Christ that day, and I lost a dear friend. But if Bill were here right now, I know he would join me in praying that you will find freedom from sin with the help of the biblical truths presented on these pages. Nothing resonated more with his heartbeat. Nothing resonates more with mine.

Enough of laying the groundwork for the book. Are you sick of sin? If so, begin the healing process now.

—Henry Brandt, Ph.D.

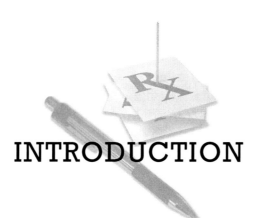

INTRODUCTION

It is truly an honor to write a small introduction to this book written by two incredibly influential Christian leaders, both of whom made major contributions to my wife Beverly's life and my own. The Biblical principles we learned from them, many of which are found in this book, not only changed our marriage and ministries, but have brought us happiness and fulfillment for over forty-five years.

Soon after accepting the call to pastor a wonderful church in San Diego, God brought Dr. Bill Bright into our lives. We caught the spirit of his lifetime passion for soul winning and evangelism which has never left us. In my opinion, Bill Bright has directly and indirectly, through teaching thousands his "Four Spiritual Laws," led more people to Jesus Christ than anyone since the Apostle Paul. And, that was even before his vision to make the movie *Jesus* which has been seen by over one and a half billion people world wide. Only, God knows how many millions of them have received Christ.

We know, personally, the first full-time worker to join the Campus Crusade for Christ staff, and who later moved to San Diego and joined our church. Today CCC has over 25,000 full-time soul winners on staff and has trained thousands more who have moved on to become pastors, missionaries, and faithful servants of Christ all over the world.

While the CCC headquarters was still in Arrowhead Springs, two graduates of the Harvard Business School offered their organizational expertise and spent two months studying Bill's rapidly growing ministry. Finally, they asked for an appointment to give him the benefit of their analytical study. They explained to him that the Harvard "experts" had discovered that the top leader or administrator could have no more than seven leaders answering directly to them, and, then, added, "Besides being CCC's leader, you have a speaking ministry, a writing ministry, and you have 21 key leaders who answer directly to you." Bill looked them in the eye and said, "You don't understand, I'm different!" With his boundless energy he kept leading, speaking, writing, and training new leaders…and God used him mightily to start even more ministries.

Bill's faith in God's leading and provision are legendary. Just four months before he went to be with the Lord we had dinner in their home. Sitting beside his faithful wife, Vonnette, he told us that early in their life he asked his mentor, Dr. Henrietta Mears, if he could ask God to give him the gift of faith. She obviously encouraged him because he learned to "believe God for whatever he called him to do." As a result, today, multiplied millions know Christ as Lord and Savior! We have met many men and women of faith–but none quite compare to Bill Bright.

In the early years we attended one of Bill's first evangelism conferences at Arrowhead Springs, California, where we were introduced for the first time to the Spirit-filled life. As a result, Beverly grew in her faith and later founded Concerned Women for America—the largest national women's organization which has had a profound affect on saving this nation from its total descent into moral and civil depravity. It was at this conference we met Bill Bright's friend and associate, Dr. Henry Brandt, the first Christian counselor with an earned PhD in psychology. At that time in history, the popular theories of humanistic psychology most often contradicted the Bible, but Dr. Brandt courageously taught that we should trust the Bible, not Freud, Skinner, or Adler. He transformed my counseling ministry and encouraged me to write my first book, *Spirit-Controlled Temperament*, for which he wrote the foreword.

God brought Dr. Brandt into our lives when Bev was a young, dedicated pastor's wife—gifted at leading elementary-aged children to Christ, but so dominated by fear that she often said, "I never speak to adults, only to children!" When she sought him out at one of his conferences, he very lovingly and gently confronted her with the cause and cure for her self-limiting fears. I watched her gradually trust the Holy Spirit to bring her out of her shell of self-protection and to speak first to 100 ladies (five of whom accepted Christ). She has never been the same. Later I introduced her to an audience of 7,000 people at the Long Beach Civic Auditorium where she spoke for 35 minutes and loved every minute of it. Still, later, I watched her speak to 40,000 cheering people in a Wichita, Kansas stadium (with 250 hostile journalists and photographers in front of the stage). Today, Concerned Women for America is based in Washington, D.C. and has over one half million members. It is amazing how God has used her Spirit-filled and fear-free life ever since!

Dr. Brandt accepted my invitation to come to San Diego several times to preach for me, and we would arrange a free Counseling Seminar for pastors in the city. There he turned us away from Carl Roger's non-directive counseling (and often non-effective counseling) to become Biblical counselors. In 1970 he helped us when we founded San Diego Christian College to incorporate the Henry Brandt School of Counseling. He also helped many other Christian colleges to turn from the godless teachings of psychology and incorporate his standard of "Biblical Counseling." Today there are over 30,000 Christian counselors and therapists in the American Association of Christian Counselors headed by Dr. Timothy E. Clinton (another of Dr. Brandt's disciples) associated with Liberty University in Virginia.

No man has done more to turn those Christians trained in humanism to become Biblical counselors than Henry Brandt, PhD.

Throughout his career, Henry taught in a number of institutes, colleges, and seminaries—including the General Motors Institute, Houghton College, North American Baptist Seminary, Trinity Evangelical Divinity School, Christian Heritage College, and Palm Beach Atlantic University. He was instrumental in founding departments of psychology for both Christian Heritage College and Palm Beach Atlantic University.

Some of you may be shrugging your shoulders as you read this, thinking, "What's so great about a Christian therapist communicating Christian principles?" You need to understand that when Henry began counseling, there really was no such thing as a "Christian counselor." After World War II, counseling was reserved for "professionals," those with PhDs from secular universities who had no use for the Bible or the truth it contains. In fact, even many Christian colleges taught what the psychology "experts" said rather than the Bible. Nobody thought of God, the Creator, as the expert in understanding the human mind and heart. Nobody, that is, but Henry Brandt.

Though Henry eventually received a well-earned PhD from Cornell University, he entered the counseling field through the back door, so to speak. He was saved as an adult in a little Baptist church where one Sunday he heard the pastor say, "The Bible has the answers to the problems of life."

Henry thought that sounded pretty good, so he shared this truth with his colleagues at Chrysler, where he worked as an engineer. Six weeks after he was saved, a man in Henry's department approached him and said, "Well, Henry, you say that the Bible holds the answers to the problems of life. What does the Bible say I should do about this problem?" And the man went on to explain the issue he was struggling with. Though Brandt was a young Christian, he had to tell the man, "I don't know, but I'll go home and study the Bible. When I've found the answer, I'll tell you."

And that's exactly what he did. He had three books at his disposal: the Bible, a Bible dictionary, and a concordance. He poured over these resources, made a list of the answers, and presented them to the man at work.

Word soon spread about Henry and his Biblical answers, and person after person approached him seeking help for various problems. Over the years, he developed a thick notebook of the answers the Bible contains, and he was spending so much time counseling, he began to feel guilty that Chrysler wasn't getting enough of his energy and effort. Little did he realize he was helping so many people at work that the department's productivity level picked up.

Shortly thereafter, he left the auto plant, and, as I mentioned, went on to earn a PhD. He told me some years later, "I now use my degree as a door opener into churches, schools, and other places where I can influence people. But I'm not teaching them psychology; I'm teaching them the Biblical principles for living I learned and used when I was an engineer."

Ever since his conversion, Dr. Brandt has been a "people-helper." Speaking for my wife and me, I know we could never repay the debt of gratitude we feel in our hearts for the investment Dr. Brandt made in our lives, marriage, and ministries. But payment was never his concern. His life's focus and dedication was to God and the truth of His Word. As he said himself, "To know God, to get acquainted with God, and to draw on the resources of God—and to know when to do it—is a long, long journey.... Some days are happier than other days, but that's the only message we've got.... Just tell me the old, old story of Jesus and His love."

Soul Prescription should be a treasure in your library. Feel free to use any thoughts from it because they really come from the Word of God, inspired by His Holy Spirit through His devoted and faithful servants of Jesus: Drs. Bill Bright and Henry Brandt. We look forward to thanking them personally after they hear our Lord say to them, "Well done, good and faithful servants; enter into the joy of your Lord—forever!"

—**Drs. Tim and Beverly LaHaye**
Authors, Public Speakers, and Fellow Servants

Part I

THE HEALING PROCESS

Chapter 1

THE HEART OF THE PROBLEM

Frank sat behind the wheel, fuming. It was bad enough that every light was red, but then the guy in the pickup had changed lanes without using his turn signal. Frank checked his rearview mirror, hit his turn signal, and whipped into the left lane, accelerating past the slow-moving truck. As he picked up speed, exceeding the limit and barely making it through the intersection before the light turned red, Frank remembered the fish on the back of his car and felt the conviction of once again losing his temper.

It had been a bad night at the slot machines. Where had the hours gone, and more importantly, where had her paycheck gone? Maria tried to come up with a believable story on her way home. But then, she realized it was no use; her husband had heard them all before. She had tried to quit gambling several times and had even gone to one of those twelve-step groups at church for a while. Nothing seemed to work. She just could not resist dropping quarters into the machines.

His face was hot, and Donald knew it was red. There was no place to hide and no use denying what had just happened. He had been checking out the new girl in the jewelry department, and his imagination was running wild when his Bible study partner, Jerry, caught him at it. Jerry and Donald both looked down, embarrassed. On the way out of the store, Donald kept telling himself that his fantasizing was harmless, but he knew better. He just could not seem to stop.

Frank, Maria, and Donald have something in common with each other and with many other Christians—they have a sin habit. They do not just slip up occasionally, in different ways, and then correct themselves. No, they all have a particular sin of mind, heart, or action that causes them to go back again and again—even though a part of them would like nothing better than to be free from the prison of their habit. Can you relate to them?

You may not have a problem with rage, gambling, or sexual fantasy, but you may find yourself in another type of sin rut and want desperately to be free. What is it for you? Do you repeatedly drink past the "safe limit" you had set for yourself and wind up drunk? Are you the prickly type of person who is always starting arguments? Are you bearing a grudge because you just could not stand to let the other person off the hook?

You do not have to admit your habitual sin to us. God knows the truth, the whole truth about who you are and what this sin is doing to your life. He also sees the problems that sinners bring upon themselves, including self-loathing, guilt feelings, discouragement, damaged health, ruined reputations, broken families, impaired relationships with God, and diminished ministry effectiveness. (And that's a partial list!)

Having learned a few things about the defeat of sin problems over the years, both in our own lives and through the experiences of those we have counseled, we wish to share our insights by the vehicle of this book. Consider what you find on these pages—the fruit of two long lives of ministry. We hope and believe that here you will find help for your sin problem, not because we are so wise, but because we will point you to the only One who offers healing to the soul.

We do not promise that this book will lead you into sinless perfection. After all, each of us remains vulnerable to temptation throughout our lives on this earth as the sinful nature we were born with strives to manifest itself in many different ways. Nevertheless, we *do* believe that we can help you if you are struggling with a particular sin, especially those that you repeat again and again almost as if it were involuntary (it really is not). This book will also be helpful to you in informally counseling a friend or loved one who is also struggling with particular sin areas.

If you are serious about healing from sin, please read carefully all the chapters in part 1 of this book. Here is where we lay out the spiritual healing process. Then, when you get to part 2, you can pick and choose among the chapters, reading the ones that most clearly apply to your own particular struggles. That is where you will be able to personalize the process for yourself.

Our primary tool throughout the book will be the unchanging Word of God, the Bible. Why? "For the word of God is alive and powerful. It is sharper than the sharpest two–edged sword, cutting between soul and spirit, between joint and marrow. It exposes our innermost thoughts and desires" (Hebrews 4:12). The use of this tool may be painful at times, but it is effective like no other.

If you have struggled mightily against sin with little to show for it and have lost hope, now is the time to hope again.

If you have struggled mightily against sin with little to show for it and have lost hope, now is the time to hope again. Victory really is possible for the Franks, Marias, and Donalds of this world. God loves us and does not want us to suffer the harm we bring on ourselves through our sin. He eagerly helps those persons who want to stop sinning. One such person was named Harry.

FEELING MISERABLE?

Harry gave every indication of being a joyful, fruitful Christian. He was active in every major event of his church and in many citywide Christian efforts. He always maintained high visibility, and because of his outgoing personality, he came across to many as a model Christian. But then one day I (Bill) got to see the real Harry.

In a private conversation, Harry confessed to me his struggles with habitual sin. He had real integrity problems. For instance, he embezzled money from a major evangelistic campaign that he served as treasurer. (He was actually pulling money out of the till while the choir was singing its altar call hymn!) He was also having an affair with his secretary.

After confessing these wrongs and others, Harry blurted out, "I'm a hypocrite—miserable, defeated, frustrated. I've lived a lie and worn a mask all my life, never wanting to reveal my true self. But I need help. I'm seriously thinking of committing suicide. I just can't live the Christian life, no matter how hard I try."

At this, I pulled out my Bible and began reading Romans 7:15–24, a passage in which the apostle Paul agonized over his own sinful tendencies in words so raw that we can almost hear the frustration in his voice:

> I don't really understand myself, for I want to do what is right, but I don't do it. Instead, I do what I hate. But if I know that what I am doing is wrong, this shows that I agree that the law is good. So I am not the one doing wrong; it is sin living in me that does it.

> And I know that nothing good lives in me, that is, in my sinful nature. I want to do what is right, but I can't. I want to do what is good, but I don't. I don't want to do what is wrong, but I do it anyway. But if I do what I don't want to do, I am not really the one doing wrong; it is sin living in me that does it.

> I have discovered this principle of life—that when I want to do what is right, I inevitably do what is wrong. I love God's law with all my heart. But there is another power within me that is at war with my mind. This power makes me a slave to the sin that is still within

me. Oh, what a miserable person I am! Who will free
me from this life that is dominated by sin and death?

Harry was nodding in agreement by the time I was done reading this passage. "That is my biography, the story of my life," he
said. "I've done everything I know to find victory—to live the
Christian life as I know I'm supposed to live it. But everything
fails for me."

In spite of Harry's evident distress, I could not help smiling
at his response. I have seen it time and again: people who feel
trapped by sin find their condition accurately reflected in the way
the Bible describes the struggle against sin. Paul's anguish is their
anguish. "Oh, what a miserable person I am!" they cry together.

Healing begins simply by knowing that God understands our
predicament. He must! The book He gave us is so realistic about
the human condition. A part of us wants to do what is right, but
we go ahead and do what we know is wrong anyway.

An important question for us to consider is, what causes us to
do wrong?

A part of us wants to do what is right, but we go ahead and do what we know is wrong anyway.

THE BLAME GAME

If we listen to the "experts," or even to the ordinary folk we live
with every day, we hear many different explanations for why
people do bad things. What most of these explanations have in
common is a tendency to say that the behavior is not really the
fault of the one who does it.

- Do you have a problem with rage? Maybe you can lay the
responsibility for it at the feet of your father, who mistreated
you when you were a kid.
- Do you feel a desire to engage in sex with persons of your
own gender? It might be that you have a "gay gene."
- Do you steal things? Maybe the fault lies less with you than
with a society that stacks the deck against the poor.
- Do you drink too much? It could be that you have alcoholism
disease.

- Do you have a hatred for men? Maybe it is all due to the date rape you suffered when you were younger.

We do not mean to make light of the hardships people endure—not in the least. Victims of abuse and misfortune deserve our concern and support. And we should recognize that they really do have to deal with the consequences of what has been done to them through no fault of their own.

On the other hand, we *do* mean to point out the ways that people tend to shift some, if not all, of the blame for their actions away from themselves. This all-too-human tendency goes back to the first couple, because when God tried to get Adam and Eve to fess up to the fruit-eating incident, Adam blamed Eve—and Eve blamed the serpent![1]

The practice of blaming bad behavior on a variety of factors other than sin is certainly understandable—who wouldn't like to avoid responsibility for their faults if they could? But it is an unfortunate manifestation of the sinful nature, nevertheless.

In some instances, the blame is completely misplaced. In other instances, the blaming does manage to identify a contributing factor to someone's poor behavior. But even in such cases, the contributing factor does not constitute the heart of the problem. The blaming misses what is really going on.

Sadly, everyone loses at the blame game. Worst of all, blaming poor behavior on secondary factors results in a reliance upon solutions that do not work.

COPING OR CURE?

People naturally seek treatments suitable to the causes they believe are driving their bad behavior. Today, people seem to rely most upon such methodologies as medical treatment, psychotherapy, and education.

Coping skills like those offered by such treatments can be effective in the sense that they may squelch the conscience and help people feel better temporarily. But a *cure*, not coping, is what you want, is it not? Certainly a cure is what we want to help you find.[2]

In *Soul Prescription* we frequently refer to sin as "sickness." But we do not mean by this that our sin is something for which we do not bear responsibility. We are not victims of our sin; we are the perpetrators. The analogy of sickness is useful because it describes the way our spiritual system becomes disordered through sin.

We are not interested in helping you live with your problem—we want you to be fundamentally transformed. And a cure like this is possible only if we get to the heart of the problem.

Long ago, when Israel's prophets and priests failed to deal with the people's rebellion against God, the Lord said of these religious professionals,

> They dress the wound of my people
>   as though it were not serious.
> "Peace, peace," they say,
>   when there is no peace.
>
> —Jeremiah 6:14 NIV

We are not interested in helping you live with your problem—we want you to be fundamentally transformed.

Learning a lesson from this, we must do more than administer superficial treatments for our chronic behavior problems expressing our sinful nature. We cannot delude ourselves into thinking we are at a place of spiritual peace when actually war is raging in our hearts.

As Jesus approached the end of His time on earth, He told His disciples, "I am leaving you with a gift—peace of mind and heart. And the peace I give is a gift the world cannot give" (John 14:27). In part, He was saying that there *is* a kind of worldly peace. This is the peace that can come through coping strategies that make us feel better for a while. But Jesus' peace is qualitatively different. It is based on real, heart-level change that can come only through the work of the Holy Spirit. In the words of one Old Testament prophet, "righteousness will bring peace" (Isaiah 32:17).

Unfortunately, it is easy to mix up the two kinds of peace: worldly and godly. I (Henry) know a Christian businessman who was furious when he lost his job. To deal with his anger problem, he took up knitting. And do you know what? He started to feel better. He has gone on to start a new business, and he credits knitting with giving him the peace of mind to do it. "Peace is peace," he says.

But is that right? Was the peace he got from knitting the kind of peace God wanted him to have?

You may find that going to a counselor or a doctor will give you some relief or help you address contributing factors to your problems. But what we are doing in this book is something much more basic and direct: we want to help you deal with the heart of your problem. And you know what that is. It is sin.

Sin really is the heart of the problem, because in the end each of us is responsible for our own behavior. Regardless of the influences that may be acting upon us, sin is an act of the will. We choose to do what we know is wrong. As John Bunyan—author of *The Pilgrim's Progress*—said, "There is no way to kill a man's righteousness but by his own consent." This is true even when the sin has become habitual.

We have to tell you (in case you do not already know) that it is never safe to try to live with a sin problem. Sin is like a cancer: it grows in seriousness over time. A little entertaining of lust, for example, can grow to encompass pornography use, adultery, and even crimes like rape. Furthermore, sin is like a contagion: it spreads from one person to another. If your problem is a quick temper, your lashing out a coworker might cause her to overreact to her child at home. Then, the child becomes upset and acts cruelly to a playmate. And so on.

This book is for people who are ready to say, "I can't do this on my own. I need God's help to deal with my sin."

If you throw a rock in a still pond, the ripples spread out and gradually die away. But if you commit a sin, the ripples it sends out may not die out; they may continue spreading within your own life or the lives of those around you. The harm they can do is incalculable. Now, we ask you, is this not a good reason to seek real healing for your sin problem and not just learn to live with it?

This book is not for people who want to dodge their sin problem, or merely cover it up, or make it better but not get rid of it. It is for people who are sick and tired of their sin problems and are filled with a drive to get rid of it once and for all. They are ready, at last, to say, "I can't do this on my own. I need God's help to deal with my sin." This approach requires courage and faith, but it has the virtue of dealing with the real problem.

THE REAL PROBLEM YOU FACE

While society looks to DNA or abuse or social conditions as causes for bad behavior, the Bible gives a completely different explanation. Why is the world so messed up? Why do people hurt themselves and others? How can an evil tendency become so ingrained in us that we cannot seem to get rid of it no matter how hard we try? It is all because at the beginning of human history, a change came over our race that marked us with sin.

Read Genesis 2 and enjoy the picture of human beings who knew the delight of living in untroubled communion with God and nature. Linger over it, because it does not last for long. By the next chapter, we see how Adam and Eve chose to violate the one restriction God had placed upon them. As a result, God decreed that they and their descendants would struggle with sin and its consequences as a captured bird struggles in a net. "Because one person [Adam] disobeyed God, many people became sinners" (Romans 5:19).

Sometimes we will hear someone say, "I believe human beings are basically good." Don't you believe it. A scan of the headlines should be enough to disabuse a person of this notion. Think of rape. Think of torture. Think of terrorism. In fact, think of your own troublesome sins. Paul had a realistic outlook on humanity:

> No one is righteous—
>   not even one.
> No one is truly wise;
>   no one is seeking God.
> All have turned away;
>   all have become useless.
>
> —Romans 3:10–12

Human nature after Adam and Eve includes a bent toward wickedness that we can never straighten out on our own.

When God formed a special nation on earth—Israel—to advance His plan of redemption, He gave the Hebrews tools for dealing with their sin problem. First, He gave them rules to live by, collectively known as the Law. We find the law preserved still today in the first five books of the Bible. Second, he gave them guidelines for burning sacrifices on an altar as a symbolic means of expressing repentance and receiving forgiveness. But, of course, the deaths of lambs and goats could not really eliminate guilt—something more was needed.

Enter the Lamb. "He is Jesus Christ, the one who is truly righteous. He himself is the sacrifice that atones for our sins—and not only our sins but the sins of all the world" (1 John 2:1–2). Since we were unable to defeat sin on our own, God became one of us in the form of Jesus and took our sins upon Himself, paying the penalty for them on the cross.

The forgiveness available in Christ does not, however, automatically go into effect. We must each individually climb off the throne of our lives and invite Christ to take His rightful place there. If you have never done this, you must do so if you ever want to be free of sin and be accepted by God. All it takes is a sincere prayer of confession and commitment to God. (For more information on becoming a Christian, see appendix A: "How to Know God Personally.")

Once we are believers in Jesus Christ, God does a remarkable thing: He accepts Jesus Christ's righteousness as our righteousness. "We are made right with God by placing our faith in Jesus Christ" (Romans 3:22). That is how we can experience God's offer of forgiveness.

But of course, in practice we are not as righteous as Jesus. We sin. Usually it is like entering a revolving door: we first entertain the idea of sinning. This is the point of temptation. At this point we can choose to enter into the sin or to keep going around in the revolving door until we exit. All too often we choose to enter. This is where individual sins and sin habits start. "Temptation comes from our own desires which entice us and drag us away" (James 1:14).

Despite our failures, however, we can work at bringing our behavior into line with our position before God. "Dear friends, let us cleanse ourselves from everything that can defile our body or spirit. And let us work toward complete holiness" (2 Corinthians 7:1).

In this we have one great advantage: we are not at the mercy of sin like we were before our salvation. Why? Because "the power of the life–giving Spirit has freed you from the power of sin" (Romans 8:2). To repeat: the power of sin over us is broken. It is a tiger with its teeth and claws removed.

At the end of the American Civil War, some African Americans kept on living as slaves. In some cases, they had not heard about the Emancipation Proclamation, because at that time news spread slowly. In other, still sadder cases, they had heard about the ending of slavery, but they would not believe it at first. They were so used to the slavery system that they could not imagine themselves as free.

That's similar to our position. We can be free from sin through the power of Christ if we will believe it—and will act on our belief.

THE ANSWER

PARENT SINS

Pride
Fear
Anger
Overindulgence
Dissatisfaction
Immorality
Deceit
Divisiveness
Rebellion
Irresponsibility

Repenting and turning to God for help are first steps toward the freedom from sin that we so desperately desire. But as we have said, that requires facing up to the fact that sin is at the heart of our problem. We have to deal with our sin head on.

Christians, in earlier centuries, identified what they called the "seven deadly sins," namely anger, sloth, gluttony, envy, greed, lust, and pride.[3] For this book, we have done something similar in defining what we call "parent sins." These are sins that seem to be widespread in the human population in every generation. If you will check out the list, chances are that you will find some of your own thoughts, attitudes, or behaviors reflected there.

Actually, each of these ten parent sins is at the head of a family of sins. For example, along with the parent sin of pride, we find the related sins of conceit, boasting, and vanity. This concept of sin families will be developed in greater length later in this book. The sin families will help you zero in on your sin problems.

For now, just begin thinking about how the different parent sins correlate with your own sin habits. Those are the areas where you will need to seek God's help to free you from the chains that bind you. And as you think about your sin, do not be discouraged! We are just beginning this journey of soul healing together. There is hope for you.

Do you remember Harry—the man who so identified with Paul's anguish over doing wrong when he wanted to do right? I (Bill) did not leave him in his quandary. I turned to Romans 7 a second time and repeated the question with which Paul concluded his cry of anguish: "Who will free me from this life that is dominated by sin and death?"(Romans 7:24). Then I went on to read verse 25: "Thank God! The answer is in Jesus Christ our Lord."

The answer for Harry—and for us—is in Jesus Christ. "This High Priest of ours understands our weaknesses, for He faced all of the same testings we do, yet He did not sin" (Hebrews 4:15). At the same time, He is God, and so He has the power to heal us of sin.

Throughout this book we will connect you with the aid Jesus wants to give you. With Paul, you can be praising Christ for supplying the answer to your tough sin problem. *Soul Prescription* will help you get there. Our next step, though, is to redirect our attention temporarily away from sin and onto its opposite: holiness.

LIFE REFLECTION

1. What sin (or sins) do you habitually commit?
2. In what ways have you tried to *cope* with your sin problem instead of seeking a *cure* for it? Do you understand the difference between coping and curing?
3. Do you have a personal relationship with God? If not, are you prepared to receive Christ today through faith? If you already know Christ, how can your relationship with Him serve as the foundation for dealing with your sin problem?

Visit www.SoulPrescription.com for more insights and resources, and to download a free leader's guide for small group Bible studies.

Chapter 2

THE SECRET TO LASTING HEALTH

If you feel yourself infected by sinful struggles in mind, body, or spirit, you are probably eager to be healed and have your life transformed. If so, your desire shows that your conscience is still alive and that the Holy Spirit is working inside you to will what God wills. What you are feeling is a godly restlessness—a dissatisfaction with the things of this world and a yearning for the things that are from above. The rest of this book is designed to help you achieve the spiritual health you desire. Before we get to the prescription for your soul, however, we want to present another key idea: *you not only need to be cleansed of your sin, but at the same time you need to be filled with holiness.*

We may get rid of a compulsive thought, attitude, or behavior, temporarily—perhaps through an exertion of willpower or by some type of therapy. That's good as far as it goes. Yet if we do not cooperate with God to supply a new thought, attitude, or behavior to take its place, the sin is likely to come back into our lives with a vengeance.[1] What a sad outcome! As Peter said, "And when people escape from the wickedness of the world by knowing our Lord and Savior Jesus Christ and then get tangled up and enslaved by sin again, they are worse off than before" (2 Peter 2:20). They are worse off than before because they have fallen more deeply into a sin habit.

In the past, have you had trouble making your resolutions to quit sinning stick? Maybe it is because you concentrated on the negative part of the equation (eliminating sin) and forgot about the positive part (adding holiness). Erwin Lutzer, senior pastor of Moody Church in Chicago, has rightly said, "We cannot say no to temptation without saying yes to something far better." It is like defeating cancer: doctors not only want to destroy the cancerous cells but also boost the body's ability to replenish healthy cells. We need to tear down sin habits in our lives and replace them with virtue habits.

We cannot say no to temptation without saying yes to something far better.

If we leave a vacancy in our spiritual lives, it *will* be filled with something. Either the same sin will return (perhaps grown more powerful) or another will come in to take its place. If you quit getting drunk, for example, you might start overeating. Instead of that kind of setback, let's allow holy qualities to flow in and fill the space vacated by a sinful practice. That is the biblical way.

DRESSED FOR GODLINESS

The Bible pairs the idea of eliminating sin with the idea of adopting holiness so consistently that we must take it to be an important principle of the Christian life. One of the clearest examples occurs in the letter to the Colossians. Here Paul used the image of taking off the old clothing of sin and putting on the new clothing of holiness (notice especially the emphasized phrases below).

> So put to death the sinful, earthly things lurking within you. Have nothing to do with sexual immorality, impurity, lust, and evil desires. Don't be greedy, for a greedy person is an idolater, worshiping the things of this world. Because of these sins, the anger of God is coming. You used to do these things when your life was still part of this world. But now is the time to get rid of anger, rage, malicious behavior, slander, and dirty language. Don't lie to each other, for you have stripped off your old sinful nature and all its wicked deeds. Put on your new nature, and be renewed as you learn to know your Creator and become like Him. In this new life, it doesn't matter if you are a Jew or a Gentile, circumcised

or uncircumcised, barbaric, uncivilized, slave, or free. Christ is all that matters, and He lives in all of us. Since God chose you to be the holy people He loves, you must clothe yourselves with tenderhearted mercy, kindness, humility, gentleness, and patience. Make allowance for each other's faults, and forgive anyone who offends you. Remember, the Lord forgave you, so you must forgive others. Above all, clothe yourselves with love, which binds us all together in perfect harmony. And let the peace that comes from Christ rule in your hearts. For as members of one body you are called to live in peace. And always be thankful.

—Colossians 3:5–15

Either we will don the shining new garments of holiness or we will put the dirty rags of wickedness back on.

Nobody in their right mind would take off their clothes without sooner or later putting clothes on again. In the same way, figuratively speaking, we cannot take off the rags of sin without putting some clothes back on. Either we will don the shining new garments of holiness or we will put those dirty rags of wickedness back on.

In case you might consider all this to be merely theoretical, let us challenge you with a few practical questions:

- Do you tend to be lazy at work, at home, or at church? If so, you need to take off the garment of sloth and put on the garment of diligence.
- Do you gripe, grumble, and complain when things do not go your way? In that case, take off the garment of dissatisfaction and put on the garment of contentment.
- Do you always bring a conversation back to yourself and what you have accomplished? If so, take off the garment of pride and put on the garment of humility.

As we all know, old clothes can sometimes be the most comfortable. And in the same way, our old habits of sin can seem easiest for us to wear. The problem is that they are morally shabby and are inappropriate attire for one who wants to enter the presence of the King. We need to judge our sin by the objective standard of Scripture, not by the temporary pleasure or comfort it might give us. Otherwise, we might not see its destructiveness until it is too late. The "comfortable" clothes always become restrictive in the end. Whatever your particular sin problem might be, therefore, you need God's grace to remove it from your life and then begin to "wear" a new, holier attitude in its place.

And how do you do this? First, you identify your sin. Then you ask God for His help in defeating the sin once for all. You also seek the Spirit's transforming power to establish new and better choices in your life. (Note: These are just the basics. We will be introducing a more thorough process for healing particular sin problems at the end of this chapter.) Of course, in practice, the putting-off/putting-on process looks a little different in everyone's life.

Years ago, when I (Henry) was speaking at a Christian conference in the Midwest, a young man named Tim LaHaye was attending the event. (This was long before Tim became well-known as coauthor of the Left Behind series of books.) He had a problem with anger and, in fact, when he sat down to listen to my message, he had just been arguing with his wife, Beverly. In my message, I happened to read the verse that says, "Put off all these; anger, wrath, malice...."

At that, Tim got up from his seat and went to a tree outside the conference hall to weep and pray to God for forgiveness of his anger problem. Though he was an angry person, his heart was still tender enough toward God that he had been convicted of his need to put off his sin of anger and put on the virtue of mercy. That's how the process worked in one life at one point in time. It may look different in your life—but it has to be there if you are to be spiritually transformed.

This biblical image of changing clothes is a memorable one. An even more familiar image from the Bible—namely, fruit bearing—makes the same point, though with a twist.

FRUITFUL FOR GOD

Many Christians would name Galatians 5:22–23—the passage about the "fruit of the Spirit"—as among their favorite verses in the Bible. But are you aware that Galatians 5 refers not to one kind of fruit but to two? The Spirit produces love, joy, peace, and all the rest, surely enough, but before that our old nature produces a welter of shameful sins.

> When you follow the desires of your sinful nature, your lives will produce these evil results: sexual immorality, impure thoughts, eagerness for lustful pleasure, idolatry, participation in demonic activities, hostility, quarreling, jealousy, outbursts of anger, selfish ambition, divisions, the feeling that everyone is wrong except those in your own little group, envy, drunkenness, wild parties, and other kinds of sin...

> But when the Holy Spirit controls our lives, he will produce this kind of fruit in us: love, joy, peace, patience, kindness, goodness, faithfulness, gentleness, and self-control.
> —Galatians 5:19–23

The fruit of the sinful nature correspond to the filthy clothing we are to remove, while the fruit of the Spirit correspond to the clean clothes of righteousness.

The twist is this: while the Colossians 3 passage about changing clothes implies that we have to make a personal effort at combating sin, the Galatians 5 passage about fruit bearing brings out more strongly the role of the Holy Spirit in our godliness. If the Spirit has control of our lives, we will live in a way that reflects the holiness of God. It is as natural as a healthy grapevine bearing big, juicy grapes.

If the Spirit has control of our lives, we will live in a way that reflects the holiness of God.

As you seek to substitute holiness for the sinful choices in your life, remember that the effort is a cooperative endeavor between you and God. Of course, you have your own part to play—you have to decide to act in accordance with God's holy commands and then follow through. But even more importantly, the Holy Spirit is at the same time working in you to help you stop doing what is wrong and start doing what is right. His help is primary and crucial to your deliverance from sin. His power is what makes it happen.

Pastor John Ortberg said, "Spiritual transformation...involves both God and us."

> I liken it to crossing an ocean. Some people try, day after day, to be good, to become spiritually mature. That's like taking a rowboat across the ocean. It's exhausting and usually unsuccessful.
>
> Others have given up trying and throw themselves entirely on "relying on God's grace." They're like drifters on a raft. They do nothing but hang on and hope God gets them there.
>
> Neither trying nor drifting are effective in bringing about spiritual transformation. A better image is the sailboat, which if it moves at all, it's a gift of the wind. We can't control the wind, but a good sailor discerns where the wind is blowing and adjusts the sails accordingly.[2]

In other words, as we head toward our destination of holiness, the Spirit will be the wind that pushes us there.[3]

Of course, all this presumes that we are filled with the Holy Spirit in the first place.

FILLED WITH POWER

Years ago, I (Bill) met a young man who had come home from the mission field in defeat. The young man described his frustration and despair. It was clear to me that he had been trying to obey God through his own efforts, not through the power of the Holy Spirit, and that this was what had led to his failure. I explained this perspective to the young man and told him that he desperately needed to be filled with the Spirit.

His response was an angry one. Had he not been serving on the mission field for years? Had he not given of himself sacrificially to reach people for Christ? He stormed out of my office.

After deeper consideration, he called me and asked for a second meeting. Of course I agreed, and at this second meeting we continued our discussion of the Holy Spirit. A few days later I heard from the young man by mail. My friend said he had invited the Holy Spirit to fill him, and he shared with me the joy and excitement of his new discovery.

Maybe you need what that young man needed. Maybe you need a new filling of the Holy Spirit so that you can reengage your enemy (your sin habit) with a powerful ally (the Spirit) by your side. In the words of P. T. Forsyth, "Unless there is within us that which is above us, we shall soon yield to that which is about us."

We all receive the Holy Spirit when we come to believe in Christ. But each of us can receive a fresh filling of the Spirit from time to time if we will seek God for it. Ask God to send His Spirit to you in greater fullness than ever, then attune your spirit to what God's Spirit is telling you. (See appendix B: "How to Be Filled with the Holy Spirit.")

Our prayer for you is the same as Paul's for the Ephesians: "I pray that from His [the Father's] glorious, unlimited resources He will empower you with inner strength through His Spirit" (Ephesians 3:16). Mighty inner strength—think about it! Wouldn't that be great to have as you seek to be healed of a sin habit and establish holiness in your life? God's power is available to you if you will ask for it.

Personal effort is part of the solution. But nothing helps in the battle to be sin-free and virtue-full more than the Holy Spirit. "For the Lord is the Spirit, and wherever the Spirit of the Lord is, there is freedom" (2 Corinthians 3:17). Indeed, freedom from sin and the freedom to be holy can be yours only through the Spirit.

In this book we will be discussing not only sins that sadden God's heart but also virtues that please God. You will find that a complete definition of victory over sin includes the institution of new, holier practices in your life that will prevent you from going back to your old, sinful ways. If your problem is with deceit, for example, cooperate with the Spirit to become a person of unshakable honesty. Or if your problem is causing conflict, seek God's help to become someone who is known for creating harmony among people.

Becoming a person of virtue means not only taking off the rags of sin but also putting on robes of righteousness. It means not only pruning away the fruit of the sinful nature but also letting the fruit of the Spirit ripen to perfection.

PARENT SINS

Pride
Fear
Anger
Overindulgence
Dissatisfaction
Immorality
Deceit
Divisiveness
Rebellion
Irresponsibility

VIRTUES

Humility
Faith
Forgiveness
Moderation
Contentment
Purity
Honesty
Harmony
Obedience
Diligence

Does that sound like something that's easier said than done? Well, you are right. But there *is* a way to do it, and it is through what I (Bill) have long called "spiritual breathing."

SPIRITUAL BREATHING

Some time ago, a young Christian came to share his problems with me (Bill). This young man was frustrated and confused, and he spoke of the constant defeat and fruitlessness he experienced in the Christian life.

"You don't have to live in defeat," I said to him.

The young man looked surprised.

"You can live a life of victory, a life of joy, a life of fruitfulness," I assured him. And I went on to tell him the lesson I have learned in more than twenty-five years as a Christian. It is "spiritual breathing."

"I have grieved and quenched the Spirit at times with impatience, anger, or some other expression of the flesh," I confessed. "But when I grieve the Spirit, I know exactly what to do. I breathe spiritually. I confess my sin to God and immediately receive His forgiveness and cleansing, and by faith I continue to walk in the fullness and power of the Holy Spirit."

Spiritual breathing is "exhaling" guilt through confession and "inhaling" grace through filling by the Holy Spirit. Whenever we have sinned, we can "breathe" in this way.

In the process of breathing, our lungs expel carbon dioxide (dangerous to our health) and take in oxygen (needed for proper tissue function). Similarly, spiritual breathing is "exhaling" guilt through confession and "inhaling" grace through filling by the Holy Spirit. Whenever we have sinned, we can "breathe" in this way.

The main difference between the two kinds of breathing is this: physical breathing is automatic, while spiritual breathing is voluntary. We *choose* to breathe spiritually. (See appendix C: "Spiritual Breathing.")

The key to spiritual breathing is stopping a sin as soon as we are convicted of it. Otherwise, we will just reinforce a sin habit. Rather than letting the sin go on, we bring it before God and ask His forgiveness. Assuming our repentance is real, we can be confident that He will forgive. "But if we confess our sins to Him, He is faithful and just to forgive us our sins and to cleanse us from all wickedness" (1 John 1:9).

But we do not stop there. We seek God further for grace to obey Him in the future. As the apostle John said, "My dear children, I am writing this to you so that you will not sin. But if anyone does sin...." (1 John 2:1). In other words, while we may be freed from habitual sins, we will never be free from temptation and human weakness as long as we live in this world. Sin always remains a possibility, and so we never outgrow the need for grace.

God is faithful. He is like a kind father who gives his children what they need.[4] Our God gladly gives us what we ask for, as long as it is in line with His will, and so of course He gives the resources we need to escape temptation. His mercy is what makes it possible for us to be filled with virtues where formerly we were full of sin.

Spiritual breathing does something wonderful for us. It helps us achieve and maintain holiness. And holiness is another name for Christlikeness.

QUEST FOR CHRISTLIKENESS

Kay Arthur begins her book *As Silver Refined* by describing a metalworker patiently refining ore to produce pure silver. He begins by crushing the lump of ore into smaller pieces, then places them in a crucible and sets it in a fire. Gradually, the impurities rise to the top of the molten metal, and the metalworker skims off this dross. He repeats the process again and again throughout the day, keeping a watchful eye over the metal. Finally, "he bends over the crucible, and this time he catches his breath. There it is! In the silver he sees what he has waited for so patiently: a clear image of himself, distinct and sharp."[5]

That is what God hopes to see in us as He purifies us of sin: an image of Himself.

Hebrews 1:3 states that "The Son radiates God's own glory and expresses the very character of God." While we sinners have had the image of God in us marred by sin, Jesus Christ perfectly reflects the image of God. This is not surprising—since He *is* God!

Meanwhile, it is God's will that we conform ourselves to Christ. He chose us "to become like His Son" (Romans 8:29). How does that happen? "So all of us who have had that veil removed can see and reflect the glory of the Lord. And the Lord—who is the

Spirit—makes us more and more like Him as we are changed into His glorious image" (2 Corinthians 3:18).

So we are back to the role of the Holy Spirit. We become holy with the help of the Holy Spirit. And as we become more holy, we become more like our Savior, Jesus Christ. Thus the process of replacing virtues for vices is a part of our God-ordained goal of Christlikeness.

Preeminent among the Christlike virtues is love.

As we become more holy, we become more like our Savior, Jesus Christ.

LOVE: THE MAIN VIRTUE

Every virtue is important, but none other is so important as love. To Jesus, love for God and love for people represented the sum of all obedience. (See Matthew 22:34–40.) When Paul talked about taking off the rags of sin and putting on new garments of righteousness, he commented, "Above all, clothe yourselves with love, which binds us all together in perfect harmony" (Colossians 3:14).

The same preeminence of love is supported in 1 Corinthians 13, where we see love split into its elements the way a prism separates light into the spectrum of color.

> Love is patient and kind. Love is not jealous or boastful or proud or rude. It does not demand its own way. It is not irritable, and it keeps no record of being wronged. It does not rejoice about injustice but rejoices whenever the truth wins out. Love never gives up, never loses faith, is always hopeful, and endures through every circumstance.
>
> —1 Corinthians 13:4–7

It has been said that the description of love in 1 Corinthians 13 is a portrait of the character of Jesus. That's true. And since for us becoming more holy means becoming more like Christ, 1 Corinthians 13 also describes the character that God wants to instill in each of us. We should see ourselves reflected in the biblical description of love.

In this book we present ten different sin families. But there is a virtue family too, and its parent is the virtue of love. Just as you will seek the Holy Spirit's help to implant moderation or purity or other virtues into your life, so you should seek His help to make you more loving. Your life will not be fully healed until you exhibit Christlike love for all.

Friend, we know that you want to become more loving and, therefore, more like Jesus. But at the moment you are feeling less like Jesus than like a sufferer from chronic sin sickness—that's why you are reading this book. It is time to turn to God's prescription for healing.

THE SOUL PRESCRIPTION

Today the smallpox virus is believed to exist only in a small number of lab samples which are guarded more carefully than a nuclear bomb. At one time, though, the "speckled monster" was as deadly a disease as cancer or heart disease is today. Smallpox cases were characterized by fever, headache, backache, and vomiting, followed by a skin rash and blisters. In severe cases, patients died of blood poisoning, secondary infections, or internal bleeding. Smallpox killed as many as 20 percent of the population of some towns and cities and in some years was responsible for one in three deaths of children.

The beginning of the end of smallpox occurred in the late eighteenth century when British physician Edward Jenner used the milder cowpox virus to inoculate patients against smallpox. (Jenner coined the term *vaccine*, using the Latin word for cow, *vaca*.) Improved vaccines were developed over time, and in 1967 the World Health Organization (WHO) started a worldwide campaign to eradicate smallpox. The last person on earth to contract smallpox was a Somali hospital worker in 1977. WHO officials literally sat on his doorstep, letting no one go in or out until the patient had fully recovered. On May 8, 1980, the WHO officially declared that smallpox was dead, having become the first major infectious disease to be wiped from the planet.

Like the World Health Organization, we need a plan for healing—that is, a plan of healing from the destructive sin choices that plague our lives. We need to wipe out the lust or gluttony or conceit or other sin that has gotten a hold on our life.

FIVE STEPS TO BREAKING A SINFUL HABIT

Step 1: Adopt a correct view of God. *Make sure you have biblical convictions about God's character and how He acts toward you.*

Step 2: Revise your false beliefs. *Use the Bible to identify your mistaken convictions about yourself, other people, and how life works.*

Step 3: Repent of your sin. *Pray the five prayers of repentance: (1) "I am wrong"; (2) "I am sorry"; (3) "Forgive me"; (4) "Cleanse me"; (5) "Empower me."* [6]

Step 4: Defend against spiritual attacks. *Depending on the Holy Spirit, choose to overcome the world's values, consider the flesh's desires to be dead, and resist the Devil's schemes.*

Step 5: Flee temptation. *Flee from sin by focusing on God, latching on to God's promises, establishing safeguards, and expecting victory.*

God, in His Word, has provided principles for defeating the sins that trouble us. What we have done in this book is to organize these principles into a five-step process which can help put an end to your sin habit. Here are the five steps in an overview:

Step 1. Adopt a correct view of God.
Step 2. Revise your false beliefs.
Step 3. Repent of your sin.
Step 4. Defend against spiritual attacks.
Step 5. Flee temptation.

God, in His Word, has provided principles for defeating the sins that trouble us.

Underlying all of these steps is a prayerful relationship with God through Christ. Prayer starts the healing process, keeps it going, and ensures its lasting effect. Prayer is the means by which we gain God's perspective on our life, and it opens us to His influence on us.

Along with generous doses of prayer, then, the five steps constitute our prescription for your life. It is a proven treatment plan, and many ex-sufferers can testify of its ability to cure the sickness of sin. We urge you to try it if you want to be healed from the soul weakness that a sin habit has given you and to be transformed.

Of course, there is much more to each of these five steps and their implementation than the overview reveals. In the following five chapters we will take each of the steps in turn and explain it in depth so that you will understand thoroughly what it means. This will provide the complete prescription for your healing.

We begin with a step in the process that many people overlook but that is nevertheless foundational to a lasting liberation from sin—and a lasting establishment of holiness. We must see God for who He really is.

LIFE REFLECTION

1. Have you reached a point in your life where you are willing to give up your sin and pursue holiness? Why or why not?
2. How would you describe what it means to be filled with the Holy Spirit? What appeals to you about that, especially as it applies to your struggle against sin?

3. How would you describe spiritual breathing? How can it help you overcome sin?

Visit www.SoulPrescription.com for more insights and resources, and to download a free leader's guide for small group Bible studies.

chapter 3

KNOWING GOD

(Step 1: Adopt a correct view of God)

If we want to deal with our sin problems and be transformed, we should first look at what we are doing and then develop strategies for changing our behavior, right? Wrong. The first step should be to start at the other end—not with ourselves but with God. That is why step one in breaking a sinful habit is to *adopt a correct view of God*. The more fully we understand the nature of God, the better we will understand how we should live in this world.

In general, we make our decisions on a rational basis. We try to understand the facts and then make a reasonable choice based on what we know (or what we think we know) as well as on what we feel. This is true in all areas of life. For example:

- If we believe that hard work leads to success, then we are more likely to be diligent on the job.
- If we believe that for a democracy to work best it requires the participation of all its citizens, then we will probably vote.
- If we believe that rich relationships are among the greatest blessings of life, then we will be more inclined to invest time in our friendships.

In short, our *convictions* influence our *behavior*. For this reason, it is important that we have the right convictions in the first place. And since our convictions about God are above our convictions in all other categories, it is supremely important that we have the right convictions about Him.

We may get our ideas about God from many sources—pop culture, religious teaching in our childhood, the example of human authority figures, conversations with our friends, the latest "spiritual" book on the bestseller list, and so on. Sadly, these sources often provide flawed concepts of God and skewed attitudes about Him. The result is that we act upon mistaken notions of who God is and how He behaves toward us.

One of the most tragic trends in our churches today is the faulty way believers view God. It accounts in large measure for the fact that so many Christians are living with sin in their lives. A. W. Tozer wrote in his book, *The Knowledge of the Holy*:

> The low view of God entertained almost universally among Christians is the cause of a hundred lesser evils everywhere among us....
>
> It is impossible to keep our moral practices sound and our inward attitudes right while our idea of God is erroneous or inadequate. If we would bring back spiritual power to our lives, we must begin to think of God more nearly as He is.[1]

It is impossible to keep our moral practices sound and our inward attitudes right while our idea of God is erroneous or inadequate.

In fact, everything about our lives—our attitudes, motives, desires, actions, and even our words—may be influenced, at least indirectly, by our view of God. An improving view of God, then, means we may be energized to recognize our sin and to deal with it in a godly way. Consider these examples:

- Someone who is learning that God is a Father who promises to provide for His children (Matthew 6:32–33) may worry less about getting enough of this world's goods.

- Someone who has discovered that "God is not a God of disorder but of peace" (1 Corinthians 14:33) might reconsider her irresponsible, disorderly way of life.

- Someone who is beginning to sense that God is not distant but always near to him (Psalm 139:7) might hesitate before indulging in his "hidden" sin of sexually fantasizing about women.

Such examples show that theology (literally, "the study of God") is a most practical exercise. We do not all have to be experts in doctrine, but we do have to have a sound idea of who God is if we are going to act as we should. So, how do we go about knowing God?

GOD'S SELF-PORTRAIT

As we begin our attempts to know God better, we should admit one fact: God is beyond our ability to fully comprehend Him. "My thoughts are nothing like your thoughts, says the LORD. And My ways are far beyond anything you could imagine" (Isaiah 55:8). In the end, God remains a marvelous mystery. Praise God for His incomprehensible greatness!

Yet at the same time this God is a God who wants to be known. He reveals to us everything about Himself that we really need to know. And He bids us to come looking for Him. An honest search for Him is one that He readily rewards with a disclosure of Himself. He promises, "If you look for Me wholeheartedly, you will find Me" (Jeremiah 29:13).

The apostle Paul, in establishing the guilt of sinful people who did not have the advantages of being a part of the Jewish community, explained that God has placed clues about Himself both inside each person and all around us.

> The wrath of God is being revealed from heaven against all the godlessness and wickedness of men who suppress the truth by their wickedness, since what may be known about God is plain to them, because God has made it plain to them. For since the creation of the world

> God's invisible qualities—His eternal power and divine
> nature—have been clearly seen, being understood from
> what has been made, so that men are without excuse.
> —Romans 1:18–20 NIV

Instinctive knowledge of God placed in our hearts: that is the witness of our conscience. God's invisible qualities displayed in the earth and sky and all He has made: that is the witness of nature.

But conscience and nature can only tell us so much about God. They reveal generalities and not specifics. To live life in a fully God-pleasing manner, we need more detailed information about who God is and what He wants of us.

The Bible is our most comprehensive guide to the nature of God. It was "inspired by God" (2 Timothy 3:16), and so it preserves God's own witness to who He is. It is His self-portrait. Above any other source, then, we need to find out what God says about Himself in the Bible. If we will take the time to study what Scripture says, we can arrive at a picture of God that certainly is not complete but that is more than adequate for our needs.

Moreover, we can trust that the God who appears in the pages of Scripture is the same God we are seeking to know better today. "I am the LORD, and I do not change," He testifies (Malachi 3:6). What He says specifically about Himself in Scripture, and what He demonstrates about Himself through His actions recorded in Bible stories, reveals the real God.

We need to be willing to open up our minds to the biblical picture of God. If we ask the Holy Spirit to reveal truth to us from the Bible, He will do so. And as we study Scripture, its picture of God will crowd out our old, mistaken view of God and establish a truer picture in its place.

THE PURIFICATION PROCESS

The ways in which people have gone wrong in their opinions about their Creator are almost as numerous as the human race itself. The diversity of religious beliefs in the world bears witness to how we can be misled about God.

First of all, it is important to believe that God exists. "Anyone who wants to come to him must believe that God exists" (Hebrews 11:6). Certainly atheism has been responsible for some of the most dreadful abuses in history. People have gone astray through the rejection of God. The psalmist was right:

> Only fools say in their hearts,
>   "There is no God."
>
> —Psalm 14:1

But of course, most people in our land *do* believe in God. In fact, only 8 percent of Americans describe themselves as atheists or agnostics.[2] Naturally, though, this does not mean that 92 percent of us have an accurate or adequate view of who God is. Misunderstanding about God's nature, even when it comes to the basics, is widespread, despite the prevalent belief in the existence of God.

One key reason why so many misunderstand God today is the current do-it-yourself approach to religion. At one time, Christianity was the starting point for the theology of most Americans (whether or not they actually had a saving faith in Christ). Today, though, many put together pieces of Christianity, New Age spirituality, and whatever else appeals to them, then endorse the resulting hodgepodge as their theological doctrine. Consequently, while they may be enthusiastic about "God," the God they have in mind bears little resemblance to the God of the Bible.

If you are reading this book, most likely you are not an atheist. However, there is a good chance that your image of God has been distorted in some significant ways with additions from worldly sources. So prepare to go through a purification process as you filter out mistaken notions about God that you have acquired.

There is a good chance that your image of God has been distorted in some significant ways with additions from worldly sources.

Having flawed convictions about God is not necessarily a sin in itself—your education in this area may have been at fault. But do not let yourself become comfortable with unexamined convictions. Get to know God better in His self-portrait, the Bible, and start erasing those parts of your image of Him that do not fit what He says about Himself. Then fill in the picture with true ideas about God's nature. You will benefit from knowing more about both who God is and how He acts toward you. Transformation of your heart, soul, and will occurs as you choose to discover and believe the truth about God.

GOD IS ONE GOD— THREE PERSONS

Father, Son, and Holy Spirit

ATTRIBUTES OF GOD

Sovereign
All-Powerful
Ever-Present
All-Knowing
Loving
Merciful
Faithful
Unchanging
Holy
Truthful
Righteous
Just

WHO GOD IS

Some years ago I (Bill) wrote a book about the attributes of God, called *God: Discover His Character*.[3] I got the idea for the book as a result of being interviewed by Dr. James Montgomery Boice on the *Bible Hour* radio program. One of the first questions Dr. Boice asked was "What is the most important truth to teach any follower of Christ?"

No one had ever asked that question of me before, so for a moment I was speechless. Finally I answered, "The attributes of God." Later I thought about my answer (prompted, I believe, by the Holy Spirit) and realized that it really was true. Human problems are commonly due, at least in part, to a faulty or inadequate understanding about God.

This is why I would urge you to learn more about the attributes of God. These attributes are primary qualities or characteristics belonging to God.

1. *God is all-powerful.* "LORD, there is no one like You! For You are great, and Your name is full of power."
   —Jeremiah 10:6

2. *God is ever-present.* "I can never escape from Your Spirit! I can never get away from Your presence!"
   —Psalm 139:7

3. *God is all-knowing.* "How great is our Lord! His understanding is beyond comprehension!"
   —Psalm 147:5

4. *God is sovereign.* "Yours, O LORD, is the greatness, the power, the glory, the victory, and the majesty. Everything in the heavens and on earth is Yours, O LORD, and this is Your kingdom."
   —1 Chronicles 29:11

5. *God is holy.* "Holy, holy, holy is the LORD of Heaven's Armies! The whole earth is filled with His glory!"
—Isaiah 6:3

6. *God is truthful.* "It is impossible for God to lie."
—Hebrews 6:18

7. *God is righteous.* "He is the Rock; His deeds are perfect. Everything He does is just and fair."
—Deuteronomy 32:4

8. *God is just.* "Mighty king, lover of justice, You have established fairness."
—Psalm 99:4

9. *God is loving.* "See how very much our Father loves us, for He calls us His children, and that is what we are!
—1 John 3:1

10. *God is merciful.* "But God is so rich in mercy, and He loved us so much, that even though we were dead because of our sins, He gave us life when He raised Christ from the dead."
—Ephesians 2:4–5

11. *God is faithful.* "Your faithfulness extends to every generation, as enduring as the earth You created."
—Psalm 119:90

12. *God is unchanging.* "He never changes or casts a shifting shadow."
—James 1:17

For you, as someone who is seeking to overcome a sin problem, these attributes of God all relate to the issue of trust. Can you trust God to help you with your sin problem? In what ways is He trustworthy? Only when you know God will you be able to trust Him with all your heart.

"How do I know I can trust God?" you might ask. Well, how do you determine if you can trust people when you have a need?

For example, if you needed a ride home from a party late at night and someone said, "I'll take you," you would quickly assess whether you could or could not trust that person. First, you might consider that person's ability. *Does he have a car and a driver's license?* Next, you might look at that person's integrity. *Does he keep his promises?* And finally you might think about his commitment to you. *Does he care enough to want to help?*

God is able. God has integrity. And God is committed to you.

God is able (He is all-powerful, ever-present, all-knowing, and sovereign). God has integrity (He is holy, truthful, righteous, and just). And God is committed to you (He is loving, merciful, faithful, and unchanging). You can trust Him as you make choices day by day.

HOW GOD ACTS TOWARD US

Learning about the nature and attributes of God, as revealed by the Bible, is far from being a mere academic exercise. We discover in the process a God who cares about us, who is intimately involved in our lives, and who wants to help us heal from our sin habits.

Let's consider the twelve attributes of God listed above in terms of how they relate to our problems with personal sins. Each attribute should be an encouragement to us.

1. Because God is all-powerful, He is stronger than the hold that sin has over us.
2. Because God is ever-present, He is always with us in our struggles against temptation.
3. Because God all-knowing, we can go to Him with all our questions and concerns about becoming holy.
4. Because God is sovereign, we can submit to His will for our ethical actions.
5. Because God is holy, He offers the model of morality we strive to copy.
6. Because God is truthful, we can believe what He says about sin and holiness and live accordingly.
7. Because God is righteous, He provides the standards we seek to live up to.

8. Because God is just, He always treats us fairly, even when we disappoint Him.

9. Because God is loving, He is unconditionally committed to our spiritual well-being.

10. Because God is merciful, He forgives us of our sins when we sincerely confess them.

11. Because God is faithful, we can trust Him to always keep His promises to help and to forgive.

12. Because God is unchanging, His commitment to our spiritual health is fixed and dependable.

What a God we serve! His every quality is suited to drawing us nearer to Him and to helping us become the kind of people He wants us to be.

Furthermore, the fact that God is a Trinity—Father, Son, and Holy Spirit together—teaches us that God values fellowship. God enjoys fellowship among the three persons that make up the unity of the Godhead, and He enjoys fellowship with us, His most beloved creatures. And so the three divine persons work together to solve our sin problem: the Father established the standards of justice; the Son sacrificed Himself to earn our forgiveness; and the Spirit comes alongside us to aid us in our attempts at living holy lives.

Isn't this a God you want to know better? We promise that as you get to know Him more fully, He will begin to change your thoughts and feelings in ways that will make you more ready to part with your habitual sin and to embrace holiness. One person who is starting that journey is a former military officer named Eldon.

God's every quality is suited to drawing us nearer to Him and to helping us become the kind of people He wants us to be.

GOD AND HOLINESS

A retired lieutenant colonel in the Air Force, Eldon prided himself on his strength of will and self-reliance. That is why it hit him so hard when he could not beat the habit of taking painkillers.

It all started innocently enough when his doctor prescribed pain medication following back surgery. Later, even though the back pain was gone, Eldon felt out of sorts once the pill bottle was empty. His thoughts kept returning to the pills and the way they had made him feel. So he found a black-market supplier and bought the pills illegally.

For a while, Eldon told himself that he needed the pills for medicinal reasons. But before long, his natural honesty kicked in, and he woke up to what he was really doing. He realized that he was taking the pills simply because he *wanted* to and not because he *had* to.

Eldon defined his problem as an addiction. But at the same time, he realized that what he was doing was a crime and a sin. As a longtime Christian, Eldon knew he was to blame before God. He felt a shame unlike any he had known before.

True to his character, Eldon tried to break the habit by going cold turkey. And more than once he thought he had succeeded just by "gutting it out," as he described it. But then—somehow—he always found himself calling his supplier once again.

Then one time, unbeknownst to Eldon, his supplier was under surveillance by a plainclothes police officer when Eldon drove up for a buy. The humiliated colonel was arrested with a bag of pills in his automobile's glove box.

As part of his sentencing, Eldon was ordered to see a counselor. He chose a Christian counselor who, among other things, delved into Eldon's attitudes toward God.

It turned out that Eldon viewed God as distant, rather like his father had been. God judged, but God did not help. This was not so bad when Eldon was behaving properly, but such a conception of God plunged Eldon into guilt and fear when his considerable willpower was not enough, as with the pills.

"Has it ever occurred to you that God aches when He sees you returning to your drug habit?" asked the counselor one time.

"Oh, no," replied Eldon without hesitation. "He must be angry with me. How could He be otherwise? I was doing something wrong."

On another occasion, the counselor inquired, "How do you seek God's help with your problem?"

"I don't. It's not His place to reach down and get involved in my petty problems. That's my job."

The counselor urged Eldon to work with one of the pastors at his church to learn more about God as He is portrayed in the Bible. The counselor said good-bye to Eldon at the end of that session in the hope that he would learn that God is merciful as well as righteous, involved in our lives as well as reigning above us.

How good it is to know God as He really is! A revolution in our view of God can start a revolution in our behavior, making us more holy like the holy God. However, adopting a correct view of God is only the beginning. We move from there to evaluating other ideas and feelings that may underlie our sinful behavior.

A revolution in our view of God can start a revolution in our behavior.

LIFE REFLECTION

1. What words would you use to describe the qualities you see in God? What do you think may be the connection between your view of God and your sin?
2. Do you trust God to help you with your sin problem? Why or why not?
3. What do you need to do to learn more about what God is really like?

Visit www.SoulPrescription.com for more insights and resources, and to download a free leader's guide for small group Bible studies.

chapter 4

EMBRACING TRUTH

(Step 2: Revise your false beliefs)

One time a man named George came to me (Henry) for counseling. Actually, I was the second counselor this man had gone to. George wanted me to interpret what the first counselor had said.

George's perceived problems included feeling bored with church, dissatisfied with his wife, and annoyed with his colleagues at work. He had a gnawing sense of anxiety and unhappiness that he hoped to clear up. But he did not know what lay at the bottom of it all.

The first counselor pressed George to say what he was angry about. George kept insisting that he had no antagonism—until suddenly he blew his top about some things that had been bothering him. The counselor told George he was filled with hate and anger.

George came to me and explained the situation. He said, "Ever since this counselor forced me to blow up, I've been nasty to a lot of people. What did he do to me?"

I pointed out to George that the other counselor had forced him to face the facts about himself. George had been pretending to be a happy man and had even believed he was. He had acted like a kind, loving person, when, in reality, he was annoyed, bitter, and even hateful. What George was dealing with now was the truth.

As much as we may like to think that we are smart people who have got life all figured out, we actually get off base in our thinking or our feelings in many ways.

The truth. It is sometimes hard to discover and even harder to accept. As much as we may like to think that we are smart people who have got life all figured out, we actually get off base in our thinking or our feelings in many ways. As we have already seen (chapter 3), we may have a distorted image of God. However, it goes beyond that. We may also have false convictions about ourselves, about others, and about life in general. These false convictions can contribute in a major way to our sin problem, as they did for George.

We might say that wrongdoing starts with wrong thinking. Step two in the process of breaking a sinful habit, therefore, is to *revise your false beliefs*. We need to start believing what is true. Being mistaken is not necessarily a sin itself (we might have just had an honest misunderstanding), but it can lead to sin. That's why having convictions based on truth is so important.

But someone may jump in here to ask, "Can we really know what is 'true'? I mean, is *your* truth necessarily the same as *my* truth?" Let's consider that.

HOW TRUE IS TRUTH?

If we had written this book fifty years ago, we would not have needed to defend the concept of truth. Back then, if anyone had been asked, "Do you believe there is such a thing as absolute truth?" he or she would almost certainly have replied, "Well, sure there is."

Today that is not the case. It is far more common nowadays for people to think of truth as an unstable quality, varying from situation to situation and from person to person. Ideas about truth develop differently within different cultures, relativists insist, and therefore, what anyone believes to be true is just that person's opinion. Truth is a human "construct," not an objective reality.

Is this perspective—dare we say it—true?

First let's make some admissions. To some extent, one's upbringing and culture do color how one looks at the world. Also, there are areas where the issue can be one of preference rather than rightness. (You may like spinach, while I do not—neither one of us is "right" about this.) Sometimes people are too dogmatic, close-mindedly promoting a certain viewpoint even though what they are talking about lies in a genuine gray area. We do not know all the facts, and in any case facts always require interpretation. Even when we know the truth for certain, our attitude in defending it can turn others off because it contains none of the love and respect that we ought to have for those who disagree with us.

Nevertheless, we have to accept that there is such a thing as absolute truth, or what the twentieth-century theologian Francis Schaeffer called "true truth." This is truth that is true for all people at all times and in all places. As a matter of fact, we cannot go forward in addressing our sin problems unless we believe in this kind of truth. And we have good reason for such a belief.

When relativists declare, "There is no absolute truth," they are making an absolute statement. Theirs is a self-refuting claim. If everything is relative, then the idea that everything is relative is itself relative.

Furthermore, no one can consistently live according to the belief that truth is relative. Law, society, and relationships are impossible to sustain in an environment of thorough relativism. We cannot invent reality for ourselves at every turn.

We cannot go forward in addressing our sin problems unless we believe in truth.

The way it usually works is that people trot out relativism when they want the freedom to do something which, deep down, they know is morally wrong. For example, someone who lusts after his wife's best friend may suddenly be converted to the idea that the inviolability of marriage vows is a relative concept. In fact, there is a close connection between a relativism of truth and a relativism of morality—this is a valuable warning for those of us who want the wickedness rooted out of our lives.

There really is such a thing as absolute truth. If there were no God, then perhaps human beings would have to make up their own "reality." But since there *is* a God, He is the determiner of truth and reality. Truth is rooted in His unchanging nature. "I am the truth," said Jesus (John 14:6). It is no wonder, then, that "the word of our God stands forever" (Isaiah 40:8).

Furthermore, because God's nature is truthful, people who have entered into a relationship with Him through His Son can know truth. "Jesus said *to the people who believed in Him, 'You are truly*

My disciples if you remain faithful to My teachings. And you will know the truth, and the truth will set you free'" (John 8:31–32, emphasis added). Faith enables us to have convictions based on truth.

More specifically, we believers have God's personal guidance in knowing what is true. Before departing this world, Jesus said He would send the Counselor, the Holy Spirit, to dwell in the hearts of His followers. Jesus added, "When He, the Spirit of truth, is come, He will guide you into all truth" (John 16:13).[1]

The primary way the Holy Spirit guides us into truth is by opening our minds and hearts to the truth that God has inscribed in His Word, the Bible.

A STRATEGY THAT WORKS

In this life "we see things imperfectly as in a poor mirror," admitted Paul the apostle. Mirrors, at the time Paul wrote, were mere polished pieces of metal, and so their imperfect reflection, especially in the worst of them, well represented how the truths about life are often murky or incomplete to us. At death or when Christ returns, whichever comes first, we will "see everything with perfect clarity" (1 Corinthians 13:12). But how about until then?

On one of his missionary journeys, Paul and his companion Silas preached to a community of Jews living in a town called Berea in Greece. These people listened eagerly to the preaching, then "searched the scriptures daily, whether those things were so." (Acts 17:11). They saw that the two men were in fact teaching the truth, and these Bereans believed in Christ.

This gives us our procedure. We can search the Word, not only to test what others are saying, but also to check up on what we ourselves think and feel about things. After all, we pick up ideas from many sources, and these may or may not be accurate. Some older translations of the Bible describe the Bereans as "noble."[2] It is a noble thing to test all our convictions by biblical revelation.

The Bible lets us see into the areas where we have blind spots, just as I (Henry) helped George see the anger that lay in his blind spot. The Bible "is useful to teach us what is true and to make us realize what is wrong in our lives. It corrects us when we are wrong and teaches us to do what is right" (2 Timothy 3:16). In fact, we will not know that we are mistaken in our convictions until the Scriptures reveal our error. The Bible is a great gift that God has given us for our betterment.

The word *canon*—often used for the body of biblical writings— means "measuring stick." Of course, each one of us has his or her own measuring stick for what is right, but our own measuring stick is never as reliable as that of Scripture. Let's measure our beliefs by the Bible, identifying our false convictions and correcting them according to biblical truth. As our thinking and feeling become more godly, so will our acting. By correcting our convictions about ourselves, others, and life in general, we will be well on our way to beating the sin habit.

We will not know that we are mistaken in our convictions until the Scriptures reveal our error.

WHAT DO YOU BELIEVE ABOUT YOURSELF?

There are many false ways of seeing ourselves. These perspectives are fueled by guilt, insecurity, selfishness, pride, hate, and numerous other negative emotions. The input of others can serve to establish and reinforce these beliefs. Events in our lives may also seem to validate what we believe and have been told about who we are.

For example, a single person who looks at life from a fatalistic or "destined to fail" perspective might reason, *I'm unattractive and I'll never get married. I might as well get all the loving I can while I can, because this is as good as it's going to get.* This person's projection of a lonely future might lead him to indulge his sexual drives in improper ways.

Another person who has risen in the ranks of her profession might come to think of herself as superior to others. She might think, *I have accomplished all this by my own brains and hard work. If others were as capable as me, they could have done as much. But, they have not.* So she tyrannizes her employees and makes others around her feel small.

A third person might feel it is not his fault that he gets into fights. *My father was a violent person. My grandfather was a violent person. And my grandmother was even worse!* he thinks. *It's in my blood.* So he excuses himself when he resorts to using his fists at the slightest provocation.

The list of possible convictions about ourselves is almost endless. But are these convictions biblical?

We need to develop a scripturally-based view of who human beings are. On the one hand, God loves us and has fashioned us in His own image. So we have great worth. On the other hand, we are finite, created beings who have been twisted by sin. Thus we have every reason for humility.

In the case of believers in Jesus, we have been made over anew. "Therefore if any man be in Christ, he is a new creature: old things are passed away; behold, all things are become new" (2 Corinthians 5:17 KJV). The following verse reveals what is new about us: "And all things are of God, who hath reconciled us to Himself by Jesus Christ" (2 Corinthians 5:18 KJV). Due to our salvation, we have access to a whole new source of life. We are not depending on our willpower, our education, or any other personal resource to live a good life; we are depending on God. And that dependence is rewarded.

The image of what it means to be human, as revealed by Scripture, gives us a real basis for triumphing over the sin in our lives.

There are many reasons why we do not always live like the new creations we are. These reasons include tendencies in our personality, spiritual warfare, and the conviction that these two verses in 2 Corinthians are not really true. Nevertheless, we *are* new creations—we know this because God said it. And we *can* live as such, by God's grace.

God said to the Israelites, "You must consecrate yourselves and be holy, because I am holy" (Leviticus 11:44). Jesus echoed this sentiment when He said, "You are to be perfect, even as Your Father in heaven is perfect" (Matthew 5:48). God makes it possible for us to be holy through the power of His Spirit.

This image of what it means to be human, as revealed by Scripture, is more realistic than any of our false and distorted opinions of ourselves. Furthermore, it gives us a real basis for triumphing over the sin in our lives.

Other opinions about who we are may have their allure, but the *truth* about ourselves is what we must seek. "Not to think of himself more highly than he ought to think" (Romans 12:3).

WHAT DO YOU BELIEVE ABOUT OTHERS?

It stands to reason that if we cannot see ourselves as we are, there is no way that our perceptions of others can be accurate either. We look at others through lenses that have been distorted by our own mistaken beliefs. We do not see them as God sees them.

One of the worst ways to view others is through the lens of prejudice.

An employer may pay his Latino workers less than their Anglo counterparts and never give them a chance to rise into management positions. Why? Because he has an unacknowledged belief that immigrants from south of the border are not quite as good as whites like himself. He thinks he is treating his employees as they deserve, but he is sinning against them.

Similarly, a woman might believe that men are clods who have only two emotions—anger and arousal. She sees this stereotype on television and hears it in popular music. She even sees examples of it (or at least what she *thinks* are examples) in the men around her. And so she is suspicious of every man she meets. If she marries and has children, she disciplines her male children excessively for their aggressive behavior.

If we look upon other people as mattering less than ourselves, we will use them for our own selfish purposes. This view will encourage sin habits such as stealing, dishonesty, betrayal, sexual immorality, and violence. After all, if our neighbor is not even worthy to live on the same street as we, then he deserves to have his property trashed, right? And why stop there? If women are inferior to men and are only good for "one thing," then lustful advances are exactly what women desire and deserve.

Just as bad is putting others above us, seeing them as somehow more worthy or better than ourselves. This places us in the position of a victim and reduces our existence to a less than human level. Our behavior can become antisocial because we do not believe we are worthy or capable of relating to others. This belief will also justify personally destructive habits (such as drug abuse) as we think, *It's not important that I'm hurting myself, because I don't matter anyway.*

Jeremy was a young man who thought little of himself. He saw other people achieving greater success than he did, so he assumed the fault was in his circumstances. Other people went to college, but they had wealthier parents than he did. Other people got good jobs, but they had more skill and intelligence than he had. What was the result of such thinking? Jeremy concluded that he would just go along in life, not working hard at anything, not dreaming, not accomplishing more than the minimum.

The same truths about humanity that apply to us apply equally to others: we are made in the image of God (that's good); we have been damaged by sin (that's bad); we are enabled by God to overcome our sin (that's really good). And so we should look at people neither as objects we can use for our own desires nor as superior beings who have a right to dominate us. Perhaps that is in part why Jesus said, "Love your neighbor as yourself" (Matthew 22:39) and "Do to others as you would like them to do to you" (Luke 6:31).

We should look at people neither as objects we can use for our own desires nor as superior beings who have a right to dominate us.

We are equal with others in terms of our humanity and how much God loves us. This is the truth that can help us relate to others more wholesomely.

WHAT DO YOU BELIEVE ABOUT HOW LIFE WORKS?

Beyond our mistaken convictions about ourselves and other people, we may not understand how the world really works. And so our choices about how to act may be equally as faulty.

One commonly held false conviction has to do with the purpose of human life. Are we here on earth for our own pleasure, or are we here to honor God? Let's face it: hedonism makes for a workable philosophy of life. However, those who follow the "eat, drink, and be merry" approach to life discover at the last that they are spiritually bankrupt and that what they had pursued all their lives adds up to a heap of ash. Serving God is the harder road to take. Still, Jesus said, "If you cling to your life, you will lose it; but if you give up your life for Me, you will find it" (Matthew 10:39). In the upside-down economy of God's kingdom, the counterintuitive idea is often proved correct.

Another common falsehood about life is that we can get away with our wrongdoing. Of course, in human justice, this belief is often true. Many a criminal has escaped being caught, and many a guilty defendant has manipulated the court system to escape judgment. As a result, perhaps we have come to believe that we will find a loophole to slip through God's justice, too. But, there is no such loophole. God knows all that we do, and He will call us to account in the last judgment. We ought to admit with David,

> I could ask the darkness to hide me
> and the light around me to become night—
> but even in darkness I cannot hide from You.
> —Psalm 139:11–12

True, Christ takes the punishment for our sins upon Himself when we trust in Him, but this does not mean that our sins are not known and will not be revealed (as pardoned sins) on Judgment Day.

A third type of false conviction about life has to do with God's commands. To many, the biblical refrain "Thou shalt not" speaks only of restriction. They want to shout, "Hey, I can do anything I want." But when they violate God's commands, they find that it brings hardship along with whatever fleeting enjoyment the sin may offer. God's commands are actually designed to keep us safe and give us a life of peace. Our suffering due to sin is a measure of how wrong we are when we behave in ways that are not consistent with the sort of people God created us to be.

Someone who lies, for example, may get out of a tight spot in that way. But then he has to remember what he said so he does not contradict it later. And quite likely, he will have to compound his dishonesty with a second and a third lie to buttress the first one. All the time he is sweating over whether he will be found out. One who tells the truth, on the other hand, knows the serenity of being in an unassailable position.

God's commands are given for our good by our heavenly Father, just as a human parent instructs a small child in what the child may or may not do.

As you endure this divine discipline, remember that God is treating you as His own children. Who ever heard of a child who is never disciplined by its father? If God doesn't discipline you as He does all of His children, it means that you are illegitimate and are not really His children at all. Since we respected our earthly fathers who disciplined us, shouldn't we submit even more to the discipline of the Father of our spirits, and live forever?

For our earthly fathers disciplined us for a few years, doing the best they knew how. But God's discipline is always good for us, so that we might share in His holiness. No discipline is enjoyable while it is happening—it's painful! But afterward there will be a peaceful harvest of right living for those who are trained in this way.
—Hebrews 12:7–11

We have to make a choice: will we believe the messages we receive from worldly sources, or will we believe that what the Bible says is true?

When it comes to our convictions about life, just as with our convictions about ourselves and others, we have to make a choice: will we believe the messages we receive from worldly sources, or will we believe that what the Bible says is true? If we will let the Bible form our ideas and feelings, we will find it easier to abandon our sinful ways.

A woman named Mrs. Washington learned the importance of seeing things the way they are.

FREE TO SEE THE TRUTH

One day in the summer of 1998 I (Henry) got a call from the Christian ministry *Prison Fellowship* requesting that I evaluate a woman who wanted to visit a prisoner in a penitentiary in Houston, Texas. I agreed and was on a plane headed to Texas the next day, ready for my meeting with Mrs. Washington.

When I was introduced to her, I discovered that Mrs. Washington was a stately, well-dressed woman in late middle age. She had been a schoolteacher for more than thirty years and was a pillar of her church. The reason *Prison Fellowship* wanted a recommendation on whether such a fine woman should be allowed to visit a prisoner was that this particular prisoner had murdered Mrs. Washington's daughter.

She told me the story.

Fourteen years earlier, when Mrs. Washington's daughter, Dedra, was twenty-seven years old, the daughter went out on a date. Unfortunately, she had chosen her boyfriend poorly, and he stopped at a crack house to buy some drugs. Three men were in the process of holding up the crack house when Dedra and her boyfriend arrived. In the mix-up, one of the thieves, a man named Ron, fired shots at the new arrivals. Soon Dedra was lying dead.

Ron was arrested, tried, and convicted of the murder of Mrs. Washington's daughter. However, that was not the end of the tragedies. Mrs. Washington's husband was grief-stricken at the death of their daughter, became bedridden, and died within months. Some years later, Mrs. Washington's son died of AIDS acquired through taking intravenous drugs.

Mrs. Washington felt that drugs had deprived her of her entire family, and she focused her hatred upon Ron, the killer of her daughter. Whenever a parole hearing came up, Mrs. Washington sent a letter of protest to the parole board. Ron remained behind bars for fourteen years, although he denied any guilt in Dedra's death. Meanwhile, Mrs. Washington remained inside the prison of her own hate.

Then in June of 1998 Mrs. Washington learned that Ron had been transferred to a penitentiary near her home in Houston and that he was coming up for parole again. Deciding that she had carried her hatred long enough, she repented and turned the problem over to God. Then, she wrote to the parole board telling them that she had forgiven Ron and that she recommended his parole.

Word of Mrs. Washington's change of heart reached Ron. He was deeply moved by her forgiveness as well as by the grief he had caused her. As a result, he finally admitted that he was the one who had pulled the trigger, killing Dedra.

I was convinced of both Mrs. Washington's repentance and of Ron's (I met with him, too), and so I gave approval for their meeting. Mrs. Washington told me later that she locked eyes with Ron as she was coming down the hallway and knew exactly who he was, even though she had never seen him in person up to that point. With tears, she repeated her forgiveness of Ron in his presence.

Now, I have told this story in some detail, not only because it is a good reminder that people can turn from their sins under even the most difficult conditions, but also because it illustrates the way we need to clear away false convictions before we can repent.

For fourteen years, Mrs. Washington believed that she was entitled to nurse her grudge for the terrible crime of her daughter's murder. That was false. With God's help, she *was* able to forgive.

Mrs. Washington also believed that Ron was the personal embodiment of all the evil that had beset her family. That was false too. He bore only partial responsibility for the death of her husband and no responsibility at all for the death of her son.

We need to give up our false but cherished ideas and feelings about reality if we are ever to see our sin habit broken.

Seeing the truth for what it was, Mrs. Washington could turn from her sin of hatred. In the same way, we need to give up our false but cherished ideas and feelings about reality if we are ever to see our sin habit broken. But that means humbling ourselves. It means admitting we have been wrong.

This takes us to the next step in the process of breaking a sinful habit: repentance.

LIFE REFLECTION

1. Do you accept that God's truth is *the* truth? Why or why not?
2. What falsehoods in your convictions about yourself, others, or life have you uncovered so far?
3. What topics might you need to study in the Bible to uncover more truth that will help you?

Visit www.SoulPrescription.com for more insights and resources, and to download a free leader's guide for small group Bible studies.

Chapter 5

TURNING AROUND
(Step 3: Repent of your sin)

One time my wife and I (Henry) were driving to Detroit where I was engaged to speak. At one point in the trip my wife said, "Henry, you are going the wrong way."

I felt defensive and replied, "Don't you think I know where Detroit is? Look, do you want to drive this car, or do you want me to drive this car?"

We both sat in silence, staring straight ahead. After a while, we came to an exit. A huge sign with an arrow pointed in the direction we were going. Above the arrow was the word Chicago. That was the opposite direction from Detroit.

In my pride, I chose to ignore the sign.

We came to the next exit, some distance from the last one. Again the sign had a big arrow pointing toward Chicago.

I began to feel that I might be wrong. But I did not want to appear mistaken in front of my wife after what I had said. So I decided to try one more exit.

The next exit was the same. There was that arrow pointing toward Chicago. Now I was sure that I was going the wrong way, but hoping to save face, I started trying to figure out some way to get to Detroit without turning around.

I finally gave up and turned the car around. If I had been willing to humble myself earlier, we would not have gone so many miles out of our way and had to backtrack.

That's the way it is with repentance. The New Testament word for "repent" means to turn around—we turn 180 degrees away from sin and toward God. The longer we delay in making the U-turn of repentance, the harder we make it on ourselves.

After adopting a correct view of God and revising false beliefs, step three in the process we are outlining is to *repent of your sinful habit*.

Over the years, I (Henry) have defined a five-part process of repentance that we can use when we are dealing with a habitual sin we are prepared to turn away from. Each of the parts of the process can be summarized in a particular prayer offered to God. The five prayers are progressively more difficult to say and to mean, but each is a vital part of repentance.[1] (This five-part process dovetails neatly with Bill's concept of "spiritual breathing."[2])

Bill and I have prayed these prayers many times when we have sinned. If you have sinned, do the same. Breathe spiritually and pray these five prayers of repentance.

PRAYER 1: "GOD, I AM WRONG."

Repentance begins with acknowledging before God that we have willfully violated His holy standards. We must understand what we have done, and we must admit it to God.

The little word *I* which begins this prayer is more important than its size might lead one to expect.

Some of us might be too quick to feel guilty or to feel more guilt than we deserve. Many others of us, however, have a tendency to look around for someone else to shift our blame onto: "It's my brother's fault I'm immoral; he introduced me to pornography"; "Yeah, I'm angry, but I have every right to be angry after the way I've been treated at work"; "I may have passed on that piece of gossip, but someone else passed it to me in the first place."

This sort of blame shifting will never do. Others may be at fault too, but we have to admit our own part in the wrongdoing. We pray, "*I* am wrong."

FIVE PRAYERS OF REPENTANCE

1. "God, I am wrong."
2. "God, I am sorry."
3. "God, forgive me."
4. "God, cleanse me."
5. "God, empower me."

SPIRITUAL BREATHING

Exhaling: Releasing guilt through confession
Inhaling: Receiving grace from the Holy Spirit

The word *wrong* is important too. What we are talking about is sin. If we have broken the law of God, it is not an "error in judgment," a "peccadillo," or a "misdemeanor." We stand in the position of a wrongdoer before God.

"Self-knowledge is the first condition of repentance," declared Oswald Chambers. Without knowing ourselves as sinners, we either will not see a need to repent or else any supposed "repentance" of ours will be a selfish attempt to manipulate God. It is not enough to say, "I messed up" or "I lost my head"; we have to say, "I am wrong."

The apostle John implied the importance of acknowledging our wrongdoing when he wrote, "If we claim we have not sinned, we are calling God a liar and showing that His word has no place in our hearts" (1 John 1:10).

Without knowing ourselves as sinners, we either will not see a need to repent or else any supposed "repentance" of ours will be a selfish attempt to manipulate God.

PRAYER 2: "GOD, I AM SORRY."

Admitting wrongdoing (the first prayer) is no easy thing. However, there is any number of reasons why someone might admit to doing wrong without really being sorry for it—they might plan to go back to wrongdoing as soon as it is convenient—that is not being sorry. Or, a person might be sorry for getting caught but not be sorry for the sin itself. Or someone might be sorry about hurting other people but have no sense of having grieved God.

A lack of sorrow over one's sin is revealed when we quickly begin to make excuses. "Yeah, I was wrong, but _____ [fill in the blank]." "Someone else drove me to it." "That's just the way I am; I can't help it." "This was nothing compared to what's been done to me." Contrary to such excuses, repentance requires us to feel truly sorry for what we have done and to say so to God.

We live in a society that places a high value on feeling good as much as possible. But when we have sinned, it is appropriate to meditate on how we have hurt ourselves, other people, and God by what we have done. In other words, that is the time to let ourselves feel the bad feelings for a while. As the apostle James urged his readers, "Let there be tears for what you have done. Let there be sorrow and deep grief. Let there be sadness instead of laughter, and gloom instead of joy" (James 4:9).

Did you know that feeling remorse for sin is a lot like grieving a loved one's death? We see this, for instance, in one of Jesus' parables when a repentant tax collector "beat his chest in sorrow, saying, 'O God, be merciful to me, for I am a sinner'" (Luke 18:13). Beating one's chest was an extraordinary sign of mourning in Hebrew culture. The only other time it is mentioned in the New Testament is when Jesus' friends "beat their breasts" at His death (Luke 23:48 NIV). Our grief over the way we have let down God with our sin should be this deep.

When we sense the true gravity of what we have done, we are ready to admit our sin and tell God we are sorry—and mean it. Experiencing remorse is an important stage to pass through and allow God to use in our transforming and healing. This sort of sorrow over our sin is what Paul was referring to when he said, "The kind of sorrow God wants us to experience leads us away from sin and results in salvation. There's no regret for that kind of sorrow" (2 Corinthians 7:10).

PRAYER 3: "GOD, FORGIVE ME."

Once people feel the full weight of what they have done by their sin, they often move into fix-it mode.

Once people feel the full weight of what they have done by their sin, they often move into fix-it mode. They want to do a greater amount of good than the harm they have done. They may even want to penalize themselves in some way, as if they could pay for their wrongdoing. In my counseling experience, I (Henry) have often heard people say things like "I'll be good from now on," or "Can't you see I'm crying?" and "I hate myself."

Some people would like the third prayer of repentance to be "God, watch me make up for what I have done." But no, that will not do. All such efforts must be futile. We can only go to God in faith and plead, "Forgive me."

God's forgiveness is an extraordinary thing. Because of His unmatched love, it comes as a free gift to those who are prepared to humble themselves before Him. One person, indeed, did have to pay for sin (other people's sin)—that person was Christ dying on the cross. Now He has the power to forgive our sins when we turn to Him in repentance. Freely He grants this forgiveness.

The sacrificial system of the Old Testament era offered a set of rituals by which one could seek forgiveness. But as the book of Hebrews says, in Christ we have a better way. "Once for all time, He has appeared at the end of the age to remove sin by His own death as a sacrifice" (Hebrews 9:26). The work has been done. All we have to do is ask for forgiveness, and it will be given to us. Our guilt is gone!

The prayer for forgiveness is so important that Jesus made it a part of the model prayer He gave us: "Forgive us our sins" (Matthew 6:12). As often as we need to pray this, we can pray it. And as often as we do pray it in sincerity, God will grant our request for the sake of Christ.

John expressed the free nature of Christ's forgiveness of sin when he wrote, "If we confess our sins to Him, He is faithful and just to forgive us our sins and to cleanse us from all wickedness" (1 John 1:9).

PRAYER 4: "GOD, CLEANSE ME."

Sinners often feel dirty. Habitual sinners may feel covered by layer upon layer of dirt. We do, in fact, stain our spirits when we sin. Christ gives us clothes, "Made them white in the blood of the Lamb" (Revelation 7:14), and we blemish them with roadside mud. How sad!

A wise teacher asked, "Who can say, 'I have cleansed my heart; I am pure and free from sin'?" (Proverbs 20:9). Answer: no one. We are all sinners and none of us can remove the spiritually staining effects of our sin. We need the supernatural operation of the Holy Spirit to spiritually wash us clean, when we repent. "God, cleanse me," we ask. And He says, "I will!" Yet some do not want to proceed to this stage of repentance.

I (Henry) spoke with a man who for ten years had held a grudge against a former friend of his who had failed to repay a loan. This man went through stages one through three of repentance with little trouble, but he balked at the idea of being cleansed from his sin. He said, "I'd rather keep on hurting than give up this grudge."

Here is the Lord's promise to all who sense themselves blemished by their sinful wrongs and desire to be cleansed: "Though your sins are like scarlet, I will make them as white as snow. Though they are red like crimson, I will make them as white as wool." (Isaiah 1:18).

King David understood the need for cleansing from sin. After his sin of adultery with Bathsheba, he composed Psalm 51 as a hymn pleading for purification on the basis of his "broken and repentant heart" (verse 17). He invited God to purify him with hyssop and wash him "whiter than snow" (verse 7). He asked God to create in him "a clean heart" and renew in him "a loyal spirit" (verse 10). The opening of the psalm runs like this:

> Have mercy on me, O God,
> > because of Your unfailing love.
> Because of Your great compassion,
> > blot out the stain of my sins.
> Wash me clean from my guilt.
> > Purify me from my sin.
>
> —Psalm 51:1–2

There is no better feeling than to know you are purified and are now able to stand before a pure and holy God.

PRAYER 5: "GOD, EMPOWER ME."

To say "Empower me" is to admit that we need God's help if we are to remain clean.

When we pray for cleansing, we are asking for the spiritual effects of our past sin to be wiped away. When we pray for empowerment, on the other hand, we are asking for God's help to avoid a repetition of our sin in the future. This is the fifth and last prayer in the process of repentance.

As we have said, the five prayers of repentance are progressively more difficult to really mean what we say. So if we successfully make it through the fifth prayer, with a sincere heart, we can know that our repentance is complete. To say "Empower me" is to admit that we need God's help if we are to remain clean after our repentance.

One time a student came up to me (Bill) and said, "I have given up. I can't live the Christian life. There is no hope for me."

I replied, "Good. At last you have recognized that you cannot live the Christian life. Now there is hope for you, for the Christian life is a supernatural life and the only one who can live it is Jesus Christ Himself."

Particularly for the self-reliant type of person, the temptation is strong to attempt to remain pure through self-control alone. And of course, an exertion of our will is important in avoiding sin; we have our part to play. However, in the end, it is Christ's power, through the Spirit, who enables us to walk away from sin. The power of sin, no matter how great it may seem to us, is no match for the power of God.

The apostle Paul, suffering from a "thorn in the flesh," prayed for deliverance.[3] God responded by assuring the apostle, "My gracious favor is all you need. My power works best in your weakness." Paul was then able to declare, "Now I am glad to boast about my weaknesses.... For when I am weak, then I am strong" (2 Corinthians 12:9–10). Paul declared that we believers have available to us "the same mighty power that raised Christ from the dead" (Ephesians 1:19–20). This resurrection power is the mighty power that we have experienced many times—and that you can experience too.

"The power of the life-giving Spirit has freed you from the power of sin that leads to death" (Romans 8:2). Believe it!

DOING BUSINESS WITH GOD

Having identified the five prayers, we want to make sure we have not left a false impression with you.

While each of the five prayers represents a crucial part of repentance, we have to remember that repentance is not a mechanical process but rather a personal process and a spiritual process. In practice, the different aspects of repentance blend into a single spiritual turnaround. Thus each of us needs to approach repentance within the context of an honest, ongoing relationship with God.

Since this process takes place within a relationship, it is not one-sided; God has a role in our repentance too. We can be certain that if we are sorry for our sin and want to embrace God, He will embrace us in return. "For the LORD your God is gracious and merciful. If you return to him, he will not continue to turn his face from you" (2 Chronicles 30:9).

Isn't repentance a marvelous gift of God? He knows we will do wrong, and our sin hurts Him, but He loves us so much that He provides the means to repair the relationship between us. Repentance becomes a decisive step in enabling us to resist the temptations that trouble us.

It has been said that the problem with living sacrifices is that they keep crawling off the altar. But as we remain ready to repent of our sin, spiritual breathing (out with guilt, in with grace) can become almost as automatic as physical breathing. We can learn to repent quickly and move on. How wonderful!

Still, there is one more aspect to turning from our sin that we must consider. It is the companion to repentance and the result of spiritual breathing: apologizing to others.

SAYING WE ARE SORRY

Just as we need to make things right with God, so we need to try to make things right with those whom we have hurt by our sin.

Just as we need to make things right with God, so we need to try to make things right with those whom we have hurt by our sin. In fact, Jesus said that reconciliation is so important that it is worth interrupting worship for. "If you are presenting a sacrifice at the altar in the Temple and you suddenly remember that someone has something against you, leave your sacrifice there at the altar. Go and be reconciled to that person. Then come and offer your sacrifice to God" (Matthew 5:23–24).

Unlike our relationship with God, we do not *repent* to other people when we have wronged them by our sin—but we do *apologize* to them. The same humble attitude is required whether we are healing our relationship with God or healing our relationships with other people.

We can take the first three prayers of repentance ("I am wrong," "I am sorry," "Forgive me") and turn them into statements of contrition to use with other people. Someone who has gossiped about a friend, for example, can go to the friend and say, "I have wronged you by telling stories about you behind your back. I am sorry for that. Please forgive me."

Of course, when we apologize like this, we do not have control over how the other person will react. For our part, we open the door to reconciliation. Perhaps the other person will slam it in our face, or perhaps he or she will step through. All we can do is to be ready to embrace the other if we get permission.

And then, along with reconciliation, another part of making things right is restitution.

When a crooked tax collector named Zacchaeus put his faith in Jesus, he volunteered, "Half of my goods I give to the poor; and if I have taken anything from any man by false accusation, I restore him fourfold" (Luke 19:8). Perhaps Zacchaeus was inspired by provisions of the Old Testament law stipulating that thieves were to pay back two or more times what they stole. (See Exodus 22:1–4.)

Stealing provides a clear-cut measurement for restitution: if I have stolen a thousand dollars, I need to return the thousand dollars—if not more. With other kinds of sin, the restitution may not be so easy to measure. But that does not mean we cannot find ways to make amends.

Did you react in a burst of anger toward an erring child? Make up for it with kindness that is equally as extreme.

Were you insubordinate to your boss? Be a more dutiful employee than ever before.

Did you fail on your promise to keep the apartment clean? Amaze your roommate by how neat you become.

In these ways we can set the stage for the Holy Spirit to heal the damage our sin has done to other people and to our relationships with them. Along the way, we will also be completing our duty toward God, who cares not only about how our sin has affected Him but also about how it has affected others. In this way, making things right with others can be considered a part of our repentance to God.

Repentance is essential when we have been caught in a web of sin. It takes us one long step toward healing of the soul. But it is not the last step. Some of the fiercest fighting may lie directly ahead.

LIFE REFLECTION

1. In your own words, what is repentance?
2. Of the five prayers of repentance, which is hardest for you to pray sincerely right now, and why?
3. To whom do you need to apologize? How can you reconcile with, and make amends to, this person?

Visit www.SoulPrescription.com for more insights and resources, and to download a free leader's guide for small group Bible studies.

chapter 6

DEFENDING YOUR GROUND

(Step 4: Defend against spiritual attacks)

I (Bill) became a Christian in my early twenties through the influence of a group of young adults at Hollywood Presbyterian Church in California. I immediately began ministering in a number of ways and saw God quickly blessing my efforts. Around the same time, though, I accepted a member of my church as a partner into my specialty-foods business, and this partner falsely accused me of dishonesty. I was distressed about the situation and talked it over with my pastor, Dr. Evans.

The problem came to a head when my name was put up for election as a deacon at Hollywood Presbyterian. A member of the family who had invested in my business stood up and said, "We know him, and he's not worthy of such a responsible trust." I was humiliated. I had not expected to be nominated in the first place—and I certainly had not expected to have my reputation challenged in public.

During a recess in the proceedings, I pleaded with Dr. Evans to withdraw my name from nomination. Although I was not guilty of the charge, I did not want to involve the church in any conflict; I preferred to let the whole matter fade away.

Dr. Evans turned to the committee for the election and said, "I know all the issues in this situation; I have studied them carefully, and the accusations against this man are not true. I insist that you leave this man's name on this list."

When the business meeting resumed, a spokesperson told the congregation that the committee had considered the accusations against me and that they believed my name should continue to stand for election. At that, the congregation rose to its feet in applause. As for me, I was set free from feeling that no one trusted me.

I believe that the doubt cast upon my character was in part a spiritual attack designed to cut short my effectiveness for Christ. Thankfully, it was resolved in a positive way. Others, though, struggle mightily against spiritual attacks of many kinds—and not always with such a good result.

The fact is, our enemy, Satan, does not like it when we repent of sin. He wants to pull us back into sin as soon as he can, and he will use every weapon in his arsenal to that end. That is why we can never relax our vigilance once we have repented. Life happens day by day, and we have to be prepared for what comes our way.

The great reformer Martin Luther famously categorized our spiritual enemies as "the world, the flesh, and the devil."[1] These words may sound old-fashioned in the twenty-first century, but they represent spiritual realities that are just as active and dangerous as they have ever been. The "world" represents values that contradict the values of God. The "flesh" represents our sinful desires that continue to trouble us as Christians. And the Devil is our personal spiritual enemy who employs schemes to entice us into doing wrong.

As we seek to break a sinful habit, we must use the resources of God to *defend against spiritual attacks*—the fourth of the five steps. We do this by overcoming the world, putting our flesh to death, and resisting the Devil's schemes.

OVERCOMING THE WORLD

God made the world and declared it "that it was very good" (Genesis 1:31). And even though our planetary home has been damaged by sin, we should not think of it as inherently evil. But

Our Spiritual Enemies
- The world—*values that contradict the values of God*
- The flesh—*sinful desires that trouble us as Christians*
- The Devil—*a spiritual enemy who employs schemes to entice us into doing wrong*

the Bible uses the term "world" in another way, that is, to represent a system of values that is opposed to God.

We see this perspective, for example, in Jesus' words to His disciples: "I chose you to come out of the world, so it hates you" (John 15:19). Similarly, the apostle John warned, "Do not love this world nor the things it offers you, for when you love the world, you do not have the love of the Father in you. For the world offers only a craving for physical pleasure, a craving for everything we see, and pride in our achievements and possessions. These are not from the Father, but are from this world " (1 John 2:15–16). The "world," in this sense, is the enemy of Christians.

We are constantly exposed to worldly messages about what is important, and these can make it hard to live in a way that is consistent with our repentance.

We are constantly exposed to worldly messages about what is important, and these messages can make it hard to live in a way that is consistent with our repentance. Someone who is struggling to break the habit of greed, for example, will have to oppose the materialism that surrounds us. We are told in subtle and not so subtle ways every day that the point of life is to accumulate cash and belongings, that those who have the most matter the most. The person seeking to give up greed, then, must see this value for the lie that it is and strive to achieve a godly perspective on wealth.

Another message the world system gives us is that we have to look out for ourselves. So we do whatever we think it will take to get ahead. This can result in many kinds of sin, including backstabbing fellow employees, cheating on taxes, and lying on résumés. All this even though God has clearly told us in His Word that He will provide for us and give us what we need. "Your heavenly Father already knows all your needs. Seek the Kingdom of God above all else, and live righteously, and he will give you everything you need" (Matthew 6:32–33).

If we do not guard our affections, we will begin to place them on unworthy objects. The world is full of tangible things that can attract us. One person may place great importance on one thing— while another is interested in something else entirely. However, if whatever appeals to us gets in the way of spiritual matters, as measured by our obedience (or disobedience) to biblical commands, it is a danger to us.

An exchange of value systems *is* possible. We are promised, "Every child of God defeats this evil world, and we achieve this victory through our faith" (1 John 5:4). This means we go to Christ again and again for help to understand what He wants us to do, and then we are to obey Him. We build our lives on the solid rock of His teaching, not the shifting sands of worldly wants. In prayer, we ask the help of His Holy Spirit to purify our value system so that over time we come to desire what God desires.

The apostle Paul told the Romans, "Don't copy the behavior and customs of this world, but let God transform you into a new person by changing the way you think" (Romans 12:2). If we have bought into the values of the world system, God can override worldly influences and supplant our unworthy values with His values. And as He does so, we become holy nonconformists.

CONSIDERING THE FLESH TO BE DEAD

When we speak of "flesh," it is important to understand that we are *not* talking about the human body.[2] Rather, the "flesh" is the part of us that is opposed to the Spirit of God—our ungodly desires and selfish motives. Thus, while the "world" is an outward spiritual enemy, the "flesh" is the spiritual enemy inside us. Our sinful nature, though dead, has a residual effect upon us in our Christian life.

Our sinful nature, though dead, has a residual effect upon us in our Christian life.

Just as a smoker who gives up cigarettes has to struggle against the effects of a nicotine addiction which pushes him from the inside, so we have to struggle against our inner compulsion to sin. We can adopt a correct view of God, revise our false beliefs, and repent of our sinful habit, but a part of us may want to commit that sin again. We all have been disappointed in ourselves when we have thought we had left a sin behind, only to sense that deep inside we *really* want to go back to that sin. That's our flesh calling us.

A person may repent of gluttony, but does that mean she will always automatically stop eating when she has had enough? Not likely. Her sinful desire for the pleasuring of her taste buds and the comforting sense of being overfull will tempt her to keep putting her fork to her mouth long after she has consumed all the calories she needs.

Someone else might have asked God to help him quit criticizing his wife and kids. Will every word out of his mouth from then on be full of kindness? Only if he overcomes the pattern he has developed to spit out comments with an edge to them.

So, does all this mean we are doomed to do what our flesh wants? By no means! The apostle Paul assured us, "you have no obligation to do what your sinful nature urges you to do" (Romans 8:12). That's good news indeed. But, how do we avoid the effects of our flesh? Paul continued: "If through the power of the Spirit you put to death the deeds of your sinful nature, you will live" (verse 13). The phrase "turn from it," in the Greek, more literally means "put it to death." Through the power of the Holy Spirit, we can consider the flesh, or our sinful desires, to be dead.[3]

In another place, Paul described it this way: "Those who belong to Christ Jesus have nailed the passions and desires of their sinful nature to His cross and crucified them there" (Galatians 5:24). We can crucify our flesh (sinful desires) spiritually because Christ's flesh (His body) was crucified physically for our sake. We no longer need to obey our flesh as it seeks to govern our words, thoughts, and actions.

Of course, just because we have the power to refuse temptation, does not mean we will necessarily use the power. We might choose to do what is comfortable and familiar. That is, we might follow the preferences of our old sin nature, even though it is dead.

It is like getting a new computer with an upgraded operating system. We might be inclined to continue using the old computer, just because the software on it is familiar to us. But, if we take the time to learn the new operating system, we will see how superior it really is. We do not need the old computer; it is obsolete.

In the same way, we have to stop thinking of the "old man" (King James terminology for our sinful nature) as still being who we are. He is dead. We are "a new person" through faith in Christ (2 Corinthians 5:17). We are spiritually alive.

Remember, the Spirit is opposed to the flesh. As we pray, following the Holy Spirit, and refuse to sin, gradually the sinful desires lose their power over us. Their influence will diminish like a nicotine addiction that fades away.

RESISTING THE DEVIL'S SCHEMES

Along with the world and the flesh, another spiritual enemy is the Devil. This is the being known as Satan, or the Adversary. We do not know everything about him, but we know clearly from the Bible that he is both God's enemy and ours. Along with his fellow evil spirits, he seeks to orchestrate events to harm us, spiritually, and otherwise. "Watch out for attacks from the Devil, your great enemy," warned the apostle Peter. "He prowls around like a roaring lion, looking for someone to devour" (1 Peter 5:8). "He is the spirit at work in the hearts of those who refuse to obey God" (Ephesians 2:2).

While too much human wrongdoing has been attributed to the influence of Satan (the Devil does not always make us do it), certainly evil spirits will do what they can to put us in situations where it is easy to do wrong. They do not have ultimate control over our experiences—God does. But they may seek God's permission to tempt us. In the early chapters of the book of Job, we are given a glimpse into how this worked for one Old Testament believer.

Is it a coincidence that a person who has a problem with stealing is presented with an opportunity to steal someone's wallet? Perhaps not. Is it chance that someone who is trying to quit gossiping hears a juicy tidbit about an enemy? Possibly not. In such situations, Satan may be setting out bait for us.

The Devil whispers temptations, suggests evil courses of action, and tries to implant doubt. These temptations make us susceptible to sin. Sometimes our susceptibilities may surprise us.

A number of years ago, I (Bill) began having obsessive thoughts about a female staff member at Campus Crusade. I became focused on her beauty and charm and even began to wonder, *Is she the one for me?* I knew such thoughts were wrong, and I never stopped loving my wife, but I could not stop thinking about this other woman and what a life with her might be like.

My thoughts of this woman never descended to the level of impurity, and I never told her what I was thinking about her. Nor did I do anything inappropriate with her. Looking back, I am glad I took the right approach: I just kept praying to God for help.

Finally, one day while I was in my car at an intersection, I was praying, and suddenly I felt the obsession lifted from me. I do not know why God chose to remove the temptation at that particular moment, but it was a true deliverance. Never, again, would I struggle with such thoughts about this staff member or any other woman. Healing had finally come after I had long sought it.

Satan sets out the bait, but it is up to us to decide whether we will nibble at it.

I realized later that what I had been feeling was not a true romantic attraction. The staff worker was not really the woman God intended for me—He had already given me the right woman. What I had been experiencing was satanic oppression, and I was so glad that God had delivered me from the temptation before any real harm had been done.

Satan sets out the bait—but, it is up to us to decide whether we will nibble at it. For His part, God always leaves us an escape route from temptation.

> The temptations in your life are no different from what others experience. And God is faithful. He will not allow the temptation to be more than you can stand. When you are tempted, He will show you a way out so that you can endure.
> —1 Corinthians 10:13

God wants us to succeed in resisting temptation, and He gives us help to do what is right. "The Lord is faithful; He will strengthen you and guard you from the evil one" (2 Thessalonians 3:3). We are capable in the Lord's power of defeating the Devil, even though he be ferocious. "Resist the Devil, and he will flee from you," we are assured (James 4:7).

Furthermore, God equips us for our contest with the Devil in specific ways. Paul wrote,

> Put on every piece of God's armor so you will be able to resist the enemy in the time of evil. Then after the

battle you will still be standing firm. Stand your ground, putting on the belt of truth and the body armor of God's righteousness. For shoes, put on the peace that comes from the Good News so that you will be fully prepared. In addition to all of these, hold up the shield of faith to stop the fiery arrows of the devil. Put on salvation as your helmet, and take the sword of the Spirit, which is the word of God. Pray in the Spirit at all times and on every occasion.

—Ephesians 6:13–18

With such armor, we "will be able to stand firm against all strategies of the devil" (verse 11).

Let's look at how the pieces of the armor help us in our struggle against the Devil.

- *The belt of truth:* The Devil likes to interfere in our perceptions of reality. God's truth shows us the way things really are.
- *The body armor of God's righteousness:* Satan accuses us concerning our shortcomings. God's righteousness, given to us through faith in Christ, protects our spiritual self-image.
- *The shoes of peace:* Satan tries to interrupt harmonious relationships with God and unity among believers. Peace protects the well-being and effectiveness of the body of Christ.
- *The shield of faith:* The tempter suggests that we will experience greater satisfaction, fulfillment, and happiness if we do something forbidden by God. Faith in God and His ways protects us against these flaming arrows of temptation.
- *The helmet of salvation:* Satan tries to darken our minds with godless thoughts and human-centered illusions. The helmet of salvation protects us against Satan's efforts to fill our minds with poisonous thoughts.
- *The sword of the Spirit:* This is the only offensive weapon Paul listed as part of our spiritual armor. If we know and understand the Bible, the Holy Spirit can guide us to use specific passages against Satan in each tempting situation that arises.

- *Prayer:* As we humbly kneel before the Lord and pour out our concerns and struggles to Him, we submit our will to our glorious Savior.

The Devil will try to attack you through a chink in your armor. Make sure you are wearing all the protection God gives for spiritual safety—never fear. "The Spirit who lives in you is greater than the spirit who lives in the world" (1 John 4:4).

GOD ON THE THRONE

It is important that we see the world, the flesh, and the Devil as acting together in opposition to us. Sometime ago I (Bill) tried to explain how it all works to a young woman who came to see me.

This young woman was unattractive and overweight and her face was covered with acne. Suffering from low self-esteem because of her appearance, she was miserable and wished she had never been born. As we talked together, I explained that God loved her as much as He loved the most beautiful woman in Hollywood. It did not seem to give her much comfort.

Suddenly, I had an inspiration. As we continued to talk, I drew a diagram that helped her understand why she was suffering from such low self-esteem. On a piece of paper, I drew a large circle representing the Christian life. Within the large circle, I drew two smaller circles, one representing the flesh, the other representing the Holy Spirit. "The flesh is influenced by Satan, and the Spirit is directed by God," I told the young woman.

"Now, there is a control center or throne in every life," I continued. "If self is on the throne, the flesh is in control, and Satan influences one's life through the flesh. However, if Christ be on the throne, God is directing our lives through His Spirit."

Galatians 5:16–17 tells us that the flesh wars against the Spirit, and the Spirit against the flesh. As long as we live, there will be this warfare. Whenever you allow your mind to think upon anything that is contrary to the Word and will of God, you know that it is all being orchestrated by Satan through the flesh, because self is in control. On the other hand, good thoughts about yourself, things that are godly, and things that draw you to Christ come from God through His Spirit."

Then I asked her, "Who do you think is making you feel so negative about yourself and trying to destroy your self-esteem?"

Her face brightened as she exclaimed, "It would have to be Satan, wouldn't it?"

I continued to explain this principle to her. "Now, let's picture a dial like that on a radio. If you don't like a particular program, what do you do?"

She replied, "Well, I turn the dial."

I explained that she was getting a message from Satan telling her that she was unattractive and that nobody cared for her. Then I asked, "What do you want to do about it?"

She replied, "I want to turn the dial and listen to God." Immediately, I sensed that she was relieved. Her attitude had changed and her face was aglow with this new discovery.

Even though Satan comes against us through the world, the flesh, and his demons, we can stand against his schemes. By faith we can reject the world's value system, put our flesh to death, and resist demonic influence. In order to do these things, however, we must be consistent in praying, walking in the fullness of the Spirit, practicing spiritual breathing, and tuning out the Enemy's lies.

Defending against spiritual attacks successfully, is a vital part in our quest for transformation and freedom from bondage.

LIFE REFLECTION

1. What values of the world system have led you toward sin?
2. How have you been giving in to the desires of your sinful nature, even though it is dead?
3. How has the Devil been attacking you with temptation?

Visit www.SoulPrescription.com for more insights and resources, and to download a free leader's guide for small group Bible studies.

chapter 7

PREVENTING SETBACKS

(Step 5: Flee temptation)

Since the beginning of Campus Crusade for Christ, I (Bill) have made it my policy never to be alone with any woman other than my wife, Vonette. I have seen the way other Christian leaders have failed in the area of sexual purity and have brought disaster on their ministries as a result. Even the *appearance* of wrongdoing can be harmful. So although I love Vonette dearly, and although I do not fear women, I have made a choice not to be alone with other women. I take sin seriously and want to make matters easier for myself by cutting off this potential for temptation.

That sort of definite action in avoiding temptation is in keeping with Jesus' shocking words when He said, "If your eye—even your good eye—causes you to lust, gouge it out and throw it away. It is better for you to lose one part of your body than for your whole body to be thrown into hell. And if your hand—even your stronger hand—causes you to sin, cut it off and throw it away. It is better for you to lose one part of your body than for your whole body to be thrown into hell" (Matthew 5:29–30). The Lord was clearly using exaggeration to make a point. And, it is equally apparent that, according to Jesus, we should be willing to take radical action to keep from sinning. To do that, we need to follow the fifth and last step of breaking a sinful habit: *flee from temptation.*

The apostle Paul instructed the Corinthians, "Flee from sexual immorality" (1 Corinthians 6:18 NIV) and "Flee from the worship of idols" (1 Corinthians 10:14). He told Timothy, "Flee the evil desires of youth" (2 Timothy 2:22 NIV). In other words, get away from temptation as fast as you can.

As a tool to help us in avoiding temptation and preventing relapses in our spiritual healing, we can remember the acrostic FLEE. The four aspects of FLEE are capable of leading us away from the danger of temptation and toward the holiness we seek.

Aspects of Fleeing Sin

Focus on your relationship with God—*Concentrate on what God is doing in your life instead of on your sin habit.*

Latch on to God's promises—*Claim God's promises that you can be free of your habitual sin.*

Establish safeguards—*Make choices that will help you avoid tempting situations.*

Expect victory—*Anticipate being delivered from your sin habit and having virtue established in its place.*

FOCUSING ON YOUR RELATIONSHIP WITH GOD

People who are struggling with sin often get fixated on their most troublesome temptation. Such a reaction may be natural enough. But is it any wonder that they go back to the sin?

Imagine you are on a diet and someone sets a freshly baked chocolate cake on the kitchen table. If you hang out in the kitchen and keep eyeing the cake, how long will it be before you cut off a piece and take your first bite? Probably not long. The more you look at the cake, the more you want it. But if you leave the kitchen and get involved with something else, you will most likely be able to resist the temptation to break your diet.

In the same way, someone who has a problem with alcohol might keep thinking about taking a drink—or someone who is bearing a grudge might spend time crafting the next cutting comment with which he will wound his enemy. Sometimes our thoughts can get caught in harmful loops like this. We need to break out of these loops and establish more constructive, healing pathways for our thoughts.

"Fix your thought more on the God you desire than on the sin you abhor," advised the fourteenth-century writer Walter Hilton. It is still good advice today.

If you have been a Christian for any time at all, you have a history with the Lord. Think about what you have learned of God. Think about all He has done for you and the victories He has given you. Spend time cultivating your relationship with God through such spiritual disciplines as worship, prayer, and devotional reading.

With your mind on higher things like these, you will be far less susceptible to the pull of sin. Not only will you have distracted yourself from temptation, you also will have garnered greater confidence in your ability to be healed of your habitual sin.

The writer of the book of Hebrews compared the life of faith to a footrace. He encouraged his readers to strip off every weight that would slow them down, "especially the sin that so easily hinders our progress." Then he said, "Let us run with endurance the race God has set before us." How? "We do this by keeping our eyes on Jesus, the champion who initiates and perfects our faith" (Hebrews 12:1–2).

With your mind on higher things, you will be far less susceptible to the pull of sin.

While fixing our eyes on temptation makes us more liable to give in to it, fixing our eyes on Jesus gives us strength to use against temptation. He is standing at the finish line of life, beckoning us on. We have His help in our struggles against sin day by day.

LATCHING ON TO GOD'S PROMISES

Shortly before His death, Jesus pleaded with His Father on behalf of His followers, "Make them holy by Your truth; teach them Your word, which is truth" (John 17:17). Our loving God has given us a tool for our spiritual well-being: His written Word, which is "alive and powerful" (Hebrews 4:12).

This was a tool used by Jesus Himself when He was tempted in the wilderness. For forty days Jesus fasted, and during this time Satan tempted Him to turn stones into bread, to jump off a high point of the temple, and to receive the whole world in exchange for bowing to Satan. Each time, Jesus countered the Devil's temptation with a scriptural quotation. The Devil was silenced by Jesus' last statement. (See Matthew 4:1–11).

The Bible is a multipurpose tool. It "is inspired by God and is useful to teach us what is true and to make us realize what is wrong in our lives. It corrects us when we are wrong and teaches us to do what is right. God uses it to prepare and equip His people to do every good work" (2 Timothy 3:16–17).

The Word of God, or the Bible, is called a "sword" in Ephesians 6:17. We would be foolish not to take up this weapon in our battle against sin. We can use the truths of Scripture against sin when we read them or recall them from memory to remind ourselves that, through Christ, we *can* have victory over sin. God's healing does not wipe out our sinful nature. It empowers us to choose obedience to God's truth.

These are just a few of the Bible's powerful messages about freedom from sin:

> The power of the life–giving Spirit has freed you from the power of sin that leads to death.
>
> —Romans 8:2

> You were cleansed; you were made holy; you were made right with God.
>
> —1 Corinthians 6:11

> Put on your new nature, created to be like God—truly righteous and holy.
>
> —Ephesians 4:24

Does one of these verses give you courage for your struggle against sin? Or can you think of an encouraging verse related to your particular sin problem?[1] Commit one or more verses to memory and then recall them when you need a reminder that you need not give in to temptation. Let them permeate your thought life and your prayer life.

Bible promises are not mantras. They are not magic spells. But they *are* powerful, Holy Spirit–inspired truths that God can use to change us inside as we allow their meaning to permeate our being. He has promised to make us holy—and He fulfills His promises!

ESTABLISHING SAFEGUARDS

Solomon urged, "Don't do as the wicked do, and don't follow the path of evildoers. Don't even think about it; don't go that way. Turn away and keep moving" (Proverbs 4:14–15). He was saying we need to take steps to keep away from temptation to do wrong, just like I (Bill) have refused to be alone with any woman besides Vonette.

Why not make avoiding sin as easy as possible? If you sometimes overindulge in alcohol, get rid of the liquor bottles in your house. If you are tempted to click your way to immoral websites, install filtering software on your computer. If you keep thinking about embezzling from the accounting department where you work, request a job transfer. If another person seems to always get you started gossiping, tell that person you will have to stop talking to him or her. If you dabble in the occult, throw out your tarot cards.

It is a matter of being practical. John F. MacArthur Jr. said, "If you do not want to fall, do not walk where it is slippery." Whatever the temptation is for you, be aggressive in cutting yourself off from its influence as much as possible. Be bold! Act now!

If you do not want to fall, do not walk where it is slippery.

One way that all of us can safeguard ourselves from sin, regardless of our moral weak spots, is by seeking help from our fellow believers. The Christian life is not something we were meant to do on our own. Let other trusted Christians into your life through participating in a small group or finding an accountability partner who will check up on your progress toward holiness. Bring the power of other people's prayers and wisdom to bear on your sin problem.

Of course, even if you establish every possible safeguard, you will still sometimes be tempted. That's because temptation is essentially a crisis of the spirit, and you can never entirely hedge your spirit from wicked influences. But having temptation tap you on the shoulder to try to get you to turn around is a lot different from what happens when you are already facing in the direction of the sin that most tempts you. Prayerfully consider how to establish every possible safeguard against temptation.

EXPECTING VICTORY

Golfing legend Arnold Palmer said, "I've always made a total effort, even when the odds seemed entirely against me. I never quit trying; I never felt that I didn't have a chance to win."[2]

What Palmer and other successful athletes have in common is a winner's attitude. They know that if you go into a game believing you are going to win, you will play very differently than if you think you are going to lose. It is the same with sin habits. We must expect victory over the sins that beset us and expect victory in establishing new habits of holiness.

Of course, the contest with sin is no game—it is deadly serious. And our confidence about replacing sin with godliness is no mere exercise in positive thinking. Rather, it has a solid basis, because our confidence is not in our own powers of self-control but in the power of God to change us as we cooperate with Him.

This is what I (Bill) have long called "supernatural thinking." By that term, I refer to hope that may seem like bold ambition but that is actually a reasonable and faithful response to what God has revealed in His Word.[3] Thinking that we are capable of defeating a serious sin problem on our own is foolish—down deep we know how weak we are. However, if the Scriptures are correct in saying that God is all-powerful (He is), and if they are correct that He has promised to help us if we will ask (He will), then we have every reason for a bold faith that sees victory where others would expect defeat.

We have every reason for a bold faith that sees victory where others would expect defeat.

When the teenage David went down to the field of battle to face the giant Goliath, David said that his victory would come from the Lord. "This is the LORD's battle, and He will give you to us!" (1 Samuel 17:47). Moments later Goliath was lying dead in the dust, no doubt looking much smaller than before. One plus God is a majority against any foe.

Tired of fighting against sin? Remember, the battle is the Lord's. With His help, you will prevail. He will help you eliminate the troublesome sin from your life. And as you continue to pray and surrender your will to Him, He will fill the empty place in your life (the one formerly occupied by the sin habit) with a new virtue habit. This kind of complete victory can be yours.

"Overwhelming victory is ours through Christ, who loved us" (Romans 8:37).

APPLYING THE FIVE STEPS

Healing from sin is the goal we are after, and the five-step process we have outlined is how to get there. To review:

> *Step 1. Adopt a correct view of God.* Make sure you have biblical convictions about God's character and how He acts toward you.

Step 2. Revise your false beliefs. Use the Bible to identify your mistaken convictions about yourself, other people, and how life works.

Step 3. Repent of your sin. Pray the five prayers of repentance: (1) "I am wrong"; (2) "I am sorry"; (3) "Forgive me"; (4) "Cleanse me"; (5) "Empower me."

Step 4. Defend against spiritual attacks. Depending on the Holy Spirit, choose to overcome the world's values, consider the flesh's desires to be dead, and resist the Devil's schemes.

Step 5. Flee temptation. Escape from sin by focusing on your relationship with God, latching on to God's promises, establishing safeguards, and expecting victory.

If you have read chapters 3 through 7 carefully, you know the process that enables us to achieve greater holiness, no matter how much we have struggled with a particular sin in the past. But theory is always one thing and application another, isn't it? For all of this to really matter to you, you need to apply it to your own sins.

Next we will consider how each of us needs to diagnose our own sin sickness and apply the soul prescription to it.

LIFE REFLECTION

1. How can you strengthen your devotional life to help you in your battle against sin?
2. What biblical promises apply to your sin concerns?
3. What practical safeguards would help you in avoiding a repeat of sin?
4. How could you grow in your confidence in God's ability to heal your sin problem?

Visit www.SoulPrescription.com for more insights and resources, and to download a free leader's guide for small group Bible studies.

Chapter 8

YOUR SIN DIAGNOSIS

Both of your authors know what it is like to be ill. I (Bill) have been diagnosed with a progressive lung disease, while I (Henry) have suffered from Parkinson's disease for years. For each of us, it was crucial to get an accurate diagnosis in order to begin the appropriate form of treatment for our ailment.

Equally, we both know what it is like to suffer from sin sickness—a more serious matter. And we know how important it is to get an accurate diagnosis for this kind of sickness as well. Sometimes the symptoms can be misleading. For example, when it comes to sinning, we often have to keep probing beyond the obvious explanation, because it may turn out that we have multiple cases of habitual sin at one time.

If you are reading this book, chances are that you have one particular sin in mind that you want to deal with. Maybe you have a problem with lust. Or maybe it is anger. Or perhaps it is a critical spirit. Typically, a person focuses on the one sin to which he or she has become most sensitized.

Before you start trying to treat your troublesome sin, do a careful self-diagnosis. Consider whether there may be other sins in your life that you are overlooking or downplaying. Ask God to show you all that is wrong with your behavior. While we may have one dominant sin, rarely if ever do we have just one sin acting in our life at a time. We have many.

You may be worried about your tendency to be envious. But if you think about it, you may realize that you also have problems with vanity and flattery.

Or you may feel guilty about your tendency to take things that do not belong to you. Keeping company with the sin of thievery, though, may be laziness, greed, and complaining.

Sins like these interact and feed on each other. Without Divine healing, one symptom may improve and others will likely grow more grave.

Biblical Sin Catalog

Matthew 15:18–19	Mark 7:21–22	Romans 1:29–31	1 Corinthians 6:9–10	Galatians 5:19–21, 26	Ephesians 4:31
Evil thoughts	Evil thoughts	Wickedness	Those who indulge in sexual sin	Sexual immorality	Bitterness
Murder	Sexual immorality	Sin	Idol worshippers	Impure thoughts	Rage
Adultery	Theft	Greed	Adulterers	Eagerness for lustful pleasure	Anger
Sexual immorality	Murder	Hate	Male prostitutes	Idolatry	Harsh words
Theft	Adultery	Envy	Homosexuals	Participation in demonic activities	Slander
Lying	Greed	Murder	Thieves	Hostility	Malicious behavior
Slander	Wickedness	Fighting	Greedy people	Quarreling	
	Deceit	Deception	Drunkards	Jealousy	
	Eagerness for lustful pleasure	Malicious behavior	Abusers	Outbursts of anger	
	Envy	Gossip	Swindlers	Selfish ambition	
	Slander	Backstabbers		Divisions	
	Pride	Haters of God		The feeling that everyone is wrong except those in your own little group	
	Foolishness	Insolent		Envy	
		Proud		Drunkenness	
		Boastful		Wild parties	
		Inventing new ways of sinning		Conceited	
		Disobedient to their parents		Irritate one another	
		Refuse to understand		Jealous of one another	
		Break their promises			
		Heartless			
		Unforgiving			

We cannot afford to take a simplistic view of our sin problem. "The human heart is the most deceitful of all things, and desperately wicked. Who really knows how bad it is?" (Jeremiah 17:9). Only God knows. With His help, we can keep testing and examining our lives to expose ever more thoroughly the wickedness that is lodged there.

THE BIBLE AS A MIRROR

The sins in our lives are not like the stars in a constellation, with the number never varying and their positions remaining fixed. Instead, our sins are more like a flock of birds on a fence rail, with some birds joining their fellows, others flapping away, and the whole flock milling about. In other words, sins may disappear from our lives and then reappear, perhaps joined by others, recombining in a somewhat different form every time. There is, in fact, an infinite number of formations that sin may assume.

Because our sin diagnosis keeps changing, we need to constantly remain on the alert. First we need to be alert to what we are doing and thinking. Then we need to be alert to how our actions and thoughts line up with the Bible's teaching.

We glance at ourselves in a mirror several times a day to see how we look. In the same way, Scripture is like a mirror that shows us who we really are. And we need to keep turning back to it to remind ourselves of how human beings are capable of going wrong.

The laws and commands of Scripture tell us what kinds of behaviors make God frown. The stories contained in Scripture show us the ways that real (that is, sinful) people like us have interacted with a holy God. In other words, both the Bible's "prescriptions" and its "descriptions" help us understand our condition better.

Not only do we need to listen to what Scripture tells us; we also have to obey it. That was the apostle James' point:

> If you listen to the word and don't obey, it is like glancing at your face in a mirror. You see yourself, walk away, and forget what you look like. But if you look carefully into the perfect law that sets you free, and if you do

what it says and don't forget what you heard, then God
will bless you for doing it.

—James 1:23–25

*Identifying all our
sins in a biblical way
is a prerequisite to
successful healing of
the soul.*

The broad diversity of human sin appears in Scripture. These
include sins of action, thought, and feeling. They also include
sins of commission and sins of omission—that is, doing things
that we should not and not doing things that we should do.
"Remember, it is sin to know what you ought to do and then not
do it" (James 4:17).

Identifying all our sins in a biblical way, then, is a prerequisite
to successful healing of the soul. We have to know what sins to go
after in our lives if we want to defeat them. What symptoms of a
sin-sick soul have cropped up in your spiritual system?

One tool that may help you identify your sins is reflection on
your own personality and how that predisposes you more to some
sins than to others.

THE PERSONALITY OF SIN

Have you ever wondered why you are more vulnerable to certain
types of temptation than to others? Have you ever wondered why
your sin diagnosis looks different from that of a friend or a family
member? Why does your problem happen to be with *this* sin and
not *that?*

Each of us has a unique personality, and our personality type
predisposes us more to certain kinds of sin than to other kinds. By
understanding our personality type, then, we can better predict what
kinds of temptation most easily waylay us. We all are born with a
sin nature, but the way in which our innate sinfulness is manifested
will vary based on at least three areas affecting our personality.

The first factor is our *family environment*—what kind of home we
grew up in. For example, a woman who received little love from
her father when she was a girl might be more susceptible to the
seductions of men. A man who was frequently criticized and made
fun of by his parents in youth might be cruel to others in turn.

It may seem that our childhood was a long time ago. But because
childhood experiences happen at a formative time in our lives,

they can exert an influence on us for the rest of our lives, whether for good or for ill. They help to determine our sin diagnosis.

A second factor helping to determine our particular tendencies to sin is our individual *temperament*. Someone who is an introvert, for instance, might gravitate toward a particular group of sins, while a strong extrovert might struggle more with others.

Are you a highly visual person? If so, you might have more of a problem with pornography than someone else does. Are you pessimistic? If you are, then maybe you have a problem with worry. The many factors of temperament can influence how our sin nature expresses itself.

A third factor that affects our sin diagnosis is the impact of *external events*. A boy who is sexually molested by a man may have greater trouble with homosexual temptations as an adult. Someone who undergoes a trauma may struggle with fear in later years. In ways such as these, our experiences sometimes make us more liable to certain sins.

You have been through a unique series of experiences in the course of your years, and these have contributed to make you who you are. How have these experiences affected your spiritual health? External events build on the foundation of family environment and temperament to set the pattern for sin susceptibility.

"Know thyself" is an ancient maxim of philosophy. It is good advice in many areas of life, not least in applying the soul prescription to your sin problem. Take some time to ask God for insight into yourself, to think through your personality history, and to get the opinions of those who know you best so that you can use your personality as a clue to your sin diagnosis.

As we continue in our investigation of sin sickness, we will learn that if we do not deal with our sins early on in their development, they have a way of gathering *more* sins and *worse* sins. They snowball. Or maybe it is more like an avalanche!

THE PROBLEM WITH "LITTLE" SINS

One day, back when I (Henry) was conducting a prison ministry, I found myself in a jail sitting across the table from a confessed murderer. This young man had killed his own mother. *What an unimaginable crime!* I thought. *To kill the woman who bore you, the woman who loved you and raised you. How could such a thing be?* As he told me his story, though, I realized that his sin had not begun with the enormity of murder; it had begun much smaller than that.

As a youth, this young man had begun to rebel against his mother, not wanting to follow the rules she laid down. This was nothing unusual for a teen, but in his case it was more than a youthful phase. He became bitter and began to hate the sight of his mother. He stole money from her purse. He argued with her and even struck her with his fists. Then it turned really serious. In the midst of a heated exchange of recriminations, he reached for a gun and shot her.

Do you see the accumulation and the escalation of sin in this man's life? From rebellion to bitterness to hatred to stealing to arguing to fighting to murder. That is the sort of pattern we see repeated over and over in people's lives. For instance, we see such a pattern in the life of King David.

When we think of David and sin, our minds often jump immediately to Bathsheba. Perhaps David's first sin in that period of his life was *irresponsibility*, since he chose not to go to war with his troops. Then, he entertained *lust* as he ogled the bathing Bathsheba. This led swiftly to *adultery* when he had sex with the neighbor woman. Then he practiced *deception* in trying to get Bathsheba's husband, Uriah, to sleep with her to account for her pregnancy. Finally, he arranged for Uriah's *murder*. (See 2 Samuel 11:1–15, for the whole story.)

That's how little sins grow into big ones. For David, the sequence of events led to a dramatic change for the worse in his fortunes. His family life and kingship were never the same again.

Many of us are like David, thinking we can safely dabble in little sins. That is foolish thinking! For one thing, what we consider "little" may not be so little to God. In the Sermon on the Mount, for example, Jesus seemed to suggest that anger can be the moral equivalent of murder, and lust can be the moral equivalent of adultery.

> You have heard that our ancestors were told, 'You must not murder. If you commit murder, you are subject to

judgment.' But I say, if you are even angry with someone, you are subject to judgment!...

You have heard the commandment that says, 'You must not commit adultery.' But I say, anyone who even looks at a woman with lust has already committed adultery with her in his heart.

—Matthew 5:21–22, 27–28

Sin is sin. It is always serious. It always erects a barrier between us and God. Any sin can become a beachhead for others, affecting not only ourselves but also others in a myriad of harmful ways. The ripples of sin spread and grow.

Dabbling soon becomes outright indulgence. Invariably, if a Christian has seemed to take a sudden fall into sin, a closer inspection will show that the person had for some time been flirting with sin before openly courting it. Adultery may trace back to pornography and sexual fantasy. Fist-fighting may have come from lying and name-calling.

One time I (Henry) was talking to a woman friend of mine about a time when she was playing golf with a female friend. The women were moving through the course rather slowly, so the two men coming up behind them asked to play through. The women agreed. It was the polite thing to do.

As the men played the hole, they chatted pleasantly with the women. Then, they suggested making their game a foursome. This seemed innocent enough—and maybe the golfing would be more fun this way. The women agreed to the proposition.

Later, after playing the eighteenth hole, the men asked the women to have a drink with them at the clubhouse. Suddenly, the situation was not looking so innocent; it was looking more like a date. All four people were married, none of them to each other. My friend wisely said no. What might it have led to if she had agreed to the *date*?

"That was the day I realized how easy it is to get yourself into trouble," my friend commented.

If you want to keep your sins from multiplying like cancer cells and growing like monsters in a nightmare, you need to do what my

Invariably, if a Christian has seemed to take a sudden fall into sin, a closer inspection will show that the person had for some time been flirting with sin before openly courting it.

friend did: act soon and act decisively. The earlier in the process of sin you act, the easier spiritual healing will be. However well-developed the sin in your life has become, whether your sins are small or large, it is best to act today rather than tomorrow. Never forget the way sins have of getting worse and more numerous.

Since we never get past the danger of temptation, we never get past the need for vigilance and prevention of those sins to which we are prone.

Since we never get past the danger of temptation, we never get past the need for vigilance and prevention of those sins to which we are prone.

BECOMING A RECOVERING SINNER

Trying to live a holy life is a complex proposition. It is not as simple as deciding to obey a few rules and then doing it.

It has been said that life is like swimming in a dirty swimming pool. We pick up filth that has been deposited in the pool by others, and we add our own filth to the mix. Keeping clean in such an environment is no easy task. There is plenty of blame to go around.

While temptation may change its aspect or approach us from a different angle, it never goes away. It is like driving a car. Whenever you drive a car, you are continually subjecting yourself to the risk of an accident. In the same way, just by going through life, you are continually subject to temptation.

Bathsheba was plainly visible from David's rooftop while she was taking her bath. She must have known this. Could it be that she was hoping for attention from the king? Maybe, maybe not. But if so, it is an example of how we have to deal with temptation from others.

Every day, we are an invitation for temptation. The temptations we give in to reveal our peculiar weaknesses and then they produce the sin symptoms that comprise our particular diagnosis at a particular time.

It would be easier to resist temptation if sin were not so attractive. With most sins, we are not talking about something that seems awful; we are talking about something that could potentially feel wonderful. Many times, to do the wrong thing is more agreeable than to do the right thing. So even though we know that the right thing is best for us in the long run, we choose the fleeting pleasures of sin anyway. It is only when we realize the true destructiveness of sin that we are willing to seek change.

A complete cure for sin will come only at our glorification after death. In this life, we will never stop struggling with sin—we will never entirely settle the matter.

However, there is cause for hope. Salvation opens the doors to God's resources, and so the Spirit can substantially defeat sin for us in this life as we obey God's commands.

Remember this: we can get to a point where we never again re-peat a sin that was once a regular habit for us. It really is possible to win over a sin. We may never be free from the temptation again, and we likely will fail God again in another way later on. But as we deal with our sins one after another, we can experience victories over each of them and over time raise our level of holiness.

Alcoholics who have not taken a drink for a long time call them-selves "recovering alcoholics," not "recovered alcoholics." Their wording indicates they know they could slip back into drinking at any time, given the right circumstances. "One day at a time" is one of their slogans.

You can be a "recovering worrier" or a "recovering gossiper" or a "recovering glutton." You can get past your sin, even if the possibility of slipping back into it never quite goes away.

It is a mystery why some people struggle with certain sins. Equally, it is a mystery why some people have an easier time than others in leaving sins behind. Sometimes God immediately takes a sinful desire away, while at other times He lets us struggle against the desire because we have not truly repented. In every case we can be confident that it is His will for us to resist temptation, and that He is present with us to help us remain pure.

Be not proud of yourself. Neither be hopeless, since God is at hand.

Do not be proud of yourself. Neither be hopeless, since God is at hand. Prayerfully, develop a list of your sin symptoms in your mind through prayer and self-reflection; then plan to treat them all through the power of the Spirit. Perhaps you will add to your list later as you learn more about yourself, but for now the list gives you a place to start.

To help you in your struggle against sin, we would like to give you a way of mentally organizing the universe of sins.

INTRODUCING THE SIN FAMILIES

Sins tend to gather in what we call "families"—groups of related sins. If you have a problem with drinking, for example, it is a part of the overindulgence family, which includes such sins as gluttony, drunkenness, drug abuse, shopaholism, and the overuse of media. All such sins relate to indulging too much in some kind of substance or experience.

But overindulgence is just one example. We have come up with ten sin families, each with its own parent sin. The "parents" include such foundational sins as pride, anger, and immorality. In the families headed by these parent sins, there may be found several, other related sins.

Of course, describing sins in families this way is somewhat artificial. It would be possible to come up with a different list of sins and to arrange them in a different way. Furthermore, there is overlapping among the families. Violence, for example, might be considered to partake of both anger and divisiveness (two different "parents" in our scheme). Real life is not as cut and dried as our list of sins may appear. Nevertheless, we believe our sin families represent a helpful way of looking at the universe of sins and figuring out where our particular sins fit in.

Each of the ten chapters in part 2 is focused upon a particular family of sins. The beginning of each chapter presents some material that will help you understand one set of sins from a biblical perspective. Then, at the end of each chapter, comes a special section called "Soul Prescription." Here you will be guided through a process of applying the five steps of spiritual healing to your particular sin problem. This is where it all gets practical.

The sidebar on these 2 pages (88 and 89) includes all of the sin families. Think of this as a visual table of contents to help you determine which chapters in part 2 you want to read. Of course, you may want to read them all. But then again, you might prefer to focus on just the chapters that address your own problem areas or those of a loved one.

By the way, you may be surprised at some of the chapters you wind up reading. For example, you may not have thought of yourself as having a dissatisfaction problem, but if you have a problem with envy, chapter 13 will show you how dissatisfaction is at the root of your problem.

To determine which chapters to read, think about *all* the sins that are troubling you now. These make up your own hit list of tenacious sins. Plan to deal with them all, if not at the same time, then one right after the other. The five steps in the soul prescription will show you how to do that.

When you are done reading the chapters of your choice in part 2, be sure to turn to the conclusion at the back of the book. It will give you some further encouragement about the potential for spiritual wholeness and holiness in your life.

We recommend that you hang on to this book for a long time, even after you have completed the spiritual healing process with all the sins that you care to. Why should you hang on to it? Because later on you may find yourself facing a sin that had not been a problem for you previously. You can then turn to the chapter that deals with that sin and start healing your life all over again.

Regardless of the areas that concern you, your success in finding freedom from sin habits depends on how honest you are prepared to be with God and yourself. It is true that in this life you will never cease struggling with temptation. Nevertheless, as you approach the chapters in part 2, tell yourself, *I will face my problems head-on. With all my strength, I will seek out God and His will for my life. I will settle for nothing less than ever-advancing progress toward becoming more like Christ.* God will honor your authentic attempts to draw near to Him, and as you do, you will find that He is already there.

LIFE REFLECTION

1. What sins are in your sin diagnosis right now?
2. Which chapters in part 2 do you want to read, and in which order?
3. What gives you the most hope as you head into a process of healing from your sin?

Visit www.SoulPrescription.com for more insights and resources, and to download a free leader's guide for small group Bible studies.

Immorality

See chapter 14.
Lust
Premarital sex
Adultery
Pornography
Homosexuality
Immodesty

Deceit

See chapter 15.
Lying
Fraud
Hypocrisy
Flattery
Cheating

Divisiveness

See chapter 16.
Gossip
Slander
Arguing
Criticism
Judgmentalism

Rebellion

See chapter 17.
Disobedience
Insubordination
Insolence
Betrayal
Disrespect

Irresponsibility

See chapter 18.
Laziness
Apathy
Procrastination
Negligence
Disorderliness

Part II

THE SIN FAMILIES

chapter 9

PRIDE: IT'S ALL ABOUT ME

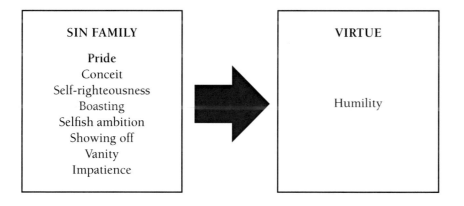

SIN FAMILY		VIRTUE
Pride Conceit Self-righteousness Boasting Selfish ambition Showing off Vanity Impatience	→	Humility

It is no accident that we start our tour of the sin families with the sin of pride. In some sense, pride is the foundational sin. As Bible commentator William Barclay declared, "Pride is the ground in which all the other sins grow, and the parent from which all the other sins come." With pride, we can justify any other form of rebellion against God's commands.

Pride may also have literally been the first sin to pollute God's creation. Many a theologian has speculated that what caused the angel Lucifer to rebel against God was pride—he would rather reign in hell than serve in heaven.[1] We thus follow the Devil's well-worn path into sin when we put our thoughts, feelings, and desires ahead of serving God.

And how easy it is to slip into pride!

As a young man in college and later in business, I (Bill) used to be proud of what I could do on my own. I believed that a man could do just about anything he wanted to do through his own effort, if he were willing to pay the price in hard work and sacrifice.

Then, when I became a Christian, the Bible introduced me to a different philosophy of life—a life of trusting God. It took me a while to see the inadequacy of trying to serve God in my own strength and ability, but that new life of faith in God finally replaced my old life of pride.

Others who are struggling with pride have the same opportunity to overcome this sin that I had and replace it with its opposing virtue, humility. We will shortly learn more about how to do just that. However, first we must find out how to distinguish between sinful pride and justifiable pride.

WHAT NUMBER IS YOUR PRIDE?

If a woman is pleased with herself because she received a promotion at work, is that kind of pride wrong?

And what about a father who is proud of his son when the boy makes the varsity football team? Is there anything ungodly about that?

While calling pride "the great sin," C.S. Lewis, nevertheless, assured his readers that pleasure in being praised is not pride. Nor, he said, is there anything wrong in being proud of the accomplishments of someone dear to you (as long as you do not give yourself airs as a result).[2] Even the apostle Paul said to some of his spiritual children, "I have the highest confidence in you" (2 Corinthians 7:4). Thus not everything that goes by the name of pride is wrong.

But a pridefulness that causes someone to think more highly of himself or herself than is justified by the facts crosses the line—it becomes sinful. Certainly, any pride that ignores God, taking credit for His gifts, is to be condemned. The same goes for any pride that elevates one person by pressing another down.

Along these same lines, Frederica Mathewes-Green has distinguished between what she calls "Pride One" and "Pride Two." According to her, Pride One is a narcissism that constantly compares itself with others. She says, "Pride One is always asking anxiously, Am I smarter than they are? Richer? Better-looking?"

Pride Two, meanwhile, is "more akin to confidence." It is "a quiet, centered pride that is compatible with modesty because it doesn't have a fretful need to show off." It grows out of a realistic appraisal of one's God-given gifts and cultivated abilities.

We should seek and encourage Pride Two, but at the same time we must remember that we are susceptible to Pride One. "This is why we need a Savior," concludes Mathewes-Green. "We look so nice on the outside, but in the caverns of the heart vicious Pride is always brooding, ready to spring."[3]

This sort of "vicious" or sinful pride is what we are concerned with in this chapter. And as with other parent sins, we have to recognize that pride does not stand alone. It is at the head of a family of sins related to a puffed-up ego. Together, they make up a dark rainbow of character qualities that are devilish rather than godly.

These sins of the ego fall into two larger categories: those involved when we think too highly of ourselves and those involved when we choose to act on our unrealistic self-evaluation.

ME, MARVELOUS ME

At least three key terms define the tendency of a person to think he or she is more wonderful than the next person. They are the terms *conceit*, *vanity*, and *self-righteousness*. Can you recognize your own attitude in any of these terms?

Conceit is an excessive appreciation of one's own value or significance. Another word for it is *arrogance*. Ashleigh Brilliant once said, "All I ask of life is a constant and exaggerated sense of my own importance." That expresses the essence of conceit.

Is human conceit acceptable in God's eyes?

On one occasion Paul wrote, "Don't be too proud to enjoy the company of ordinary people. And don't think you know it all!" (Romans 12:16). On another occasion he wrote, "Let us

---

Are You Proud?

The following self-evaluation quiz will help you determine whether you have a tendency toward pride.

- Do you spend more time thinking about yourself than about God or about other people?
- Do you make yourself the center of most conversations?
- Do you compare yourself with others often, judging yourself favorably?
- Do you take credit for your own looks, intelligence, or ability?
- Do you try to make sure that others are aware of your personal gifts or possessions?
- Do you think you deserve more of this world's good things than other people do?
- Are you willing to pursue your selfish goals even if it means others are hurt in the process?
- Do you think God must be pleased with you because of how ethical or religious you are?
- Do you ever think you do not really need God or other people?

not become conceited" (Galalations 5:26). God's view of conceit could hardly come through any clearer than that.

Such conceit may take many different forms. One of these forms is vanity, or thinking highly of one's appearance.

The foolishness of this type of pride should become apparent as soon as we really think about it. After all, who among us can take credit for how we look? God gives us our appearance through our genes. At most, we can maximize our appearance through diet, exercise, clothing, makeup, and the like. Even then, in time, our looks are destined to fade.

The apostle Peter told women of his day, "Don't be concerned about the outward beauty of fancy hairstyles, expensive jewelry, or beautiful clothes" (1 Peter 3:3).[4] Women—and men—in our day could use the same advice. If we are good-looking, we can be thankful to God for it. But, we should never take our looks as grounds for pride.

While vanity is pride about one's outward appearance, self-righteousness is pride about one's inner being, that is, thinking highly of one's own goodness or spiritual standing. This is a sin that religious people are particularly prone to—and it is a serious one. C. S. Lewis said,

> There are two things inside me, competing with the human self which I must try to become. They are the Animal self, and the Diabolical self. The Diabolical self is the worst of the two. That is why a cold, self-righteous prig who goes regularly to church may be far nearer to hell than a prostitute. But, of course, it is better to be neither.[5]

Self-righteousness was exemplified by the Pharisees of Jesus' day, who thought they made themselves acceptable to God through their pious deeds. Jesus once told a story about a Pharisee to a group who "had great confidence in their own righteousness and scorned everyone else." The Pharisee stood by himself and prayed this prayer: "I thank you, God, that I am not a sinner like everyone else. For I don't cheat, I don't sin, and I don't commit adultery. I'm certainly not like that tax collector! I fast twice a week, and I give You a tenth of my income" (Luke 18:9, 11–12).

This attitude of self-righteousness is alive and well in the twenty-first century. When we are self-righteous, we are both the judge and the accused—and we declare ourselves not guilty. We think God must love us because of all the ways we appear religious or moral on the outside.

When we are self-righteous, we are both the judge and the accused—and we declare ourselves not guilty.

Sadly, the self-righteous ignore the truth that none of us possesses any righteousness apart from the grace of God. For this reason, it was not the Pharisee in Jesus' story but rather a repentant tax collector who found favor with God. "I tell you, this sinner, not the Pharisee, returned home justified before God. For those who exalt themselves will be humbled, and those who humble themselves will be exalted" (Luke 18:14).

None of us has justification for conceit, "spiritual" or otherwise. As the great preacher of the nineteenth century Charles Spurgeon said, "Be not proud of race, face, place, or grace."

LOOK HERE

If you are conceited, vain, or self-righteous, you probably want others to know how great you are. There are different ways you can do that. Three key terms for these strategies are *boasting*, *showing off*, and *selfish ambition*.

Boasting may come in an obvious form, or it may be more subtle. If someone openly proclaims to you how much money he is making, there is no mistaking what is going on. The more sly boasters have perfected the art of dropping names and letting slip what they have accomplished or purchased or experienced. But this artfulness is really no different from more transparent forms of boasting; it is all meant to impress. Scripture takes a realistic view of boasting. "When people commend themselves, it doesn't count for much" (2 Corinthians 10:18).

We are told in God's Word that if we want to boast, we should learn to boast about the right thing. "This is what the LORD says: 'Don't let the wise boast in their wisdom, or the powerful boast in their power, or the rich boast in their riches. But those who wish to boast should boast in this alone: that they truly know me and understand that I am the LORD'" (Jeremiah 9:23–24).

But in addition to attracting attention to oneself with words, a person can do the same through actions. That's showing off.

Showing off may be pardonable in children. Every parent has heard a child cry, "Look at me!" and has indulged her by watching as she performs a cartwheel or him as he rides by on his two-wheeler. However with grown-ups, showing off is not so cute.

What is displaying one's intellect except showing off? What is clowning around so that the attention stays riveted on you? What is making sure others see your new car or fancy clothes? All this is the equivalent of calling out to the world, "Look at me!"

Is this acceptable behavior in God's eyes? Hardly. "Don't try to impress others," He instructs us (Philippians 2:3).

Also, we are not to let selfish ambition determine how we live our lives. Certain types of ambition might be good, such as striving to do well at work in order to be able to provide for your family better. But *selfish* ambition is the single-minded pursuit of what you think you deserve, regardless of what it might cost others.

The man who becomes a workaholic because he wants others to see him as a success, even though the overwork makes him a stranger to his family, is selfishly ambitious.

The church member who pursues a leadership position on a church committee because of the prestige it carries, not out of a desire to serve, is selfishly ambitious.

Our society applauds hard-charging, "self-made" men and women. But if that go-getter quality is actually an expression of selfish ambition, it is foolish and ungodly.

> If...you are bitterly jealous and there is selfish ambition in your heart, don't cover up the truth with boasting and lying. For jealousy and selfishness are not God's kind of wisdom. Such things are earthly, unspiritual, and demonic. For wherever there is jealousy and selfish ambition, there you will find disorder and evil of every kind.
>
> —James 3:14–16

Those who are selfishly ambitious often display another quality of pride: impatience.

CLOCK CONTROL

One time your two authors were running late for a joint speaking engagement at a church. I (Bill) was driving, and I was exceeding the speed limit by several miles per hour in an attempt to get to the event location on time. It was wrong and I knew better, but I did it anyway.

Sure enough, I soon saw flashing lights in my rearview mirror and heard a siren approaching from behind. The process of pulling over and receiving a ticket took up more time than I would have saved by speeding all the way to the church. (The good news is that I got a chance to speak about Christ to the officer—though I would not recommend breaking the law to gain an opportunity to witness!)

When we are feeling prideful, we think we have the right to control our schedule, even if it means breaking the rules or making life harder for others. That is what I was doing when I was speeding, and it is what many of us do when we are concerned about our efficient use of time to the exclusion of all other concerns.

Working hard and trying to be a good steward of our time is one thing. After all, we are to "make the most of our time" (Psalm 90:12) and "make the most of every opportunity" (Ephesians 5:16; Colossians 4:5). But rushing and pushing as if our scheduling preference is what matters most is another thing altogether.

The Old Testament patriarch Abraham got impatient when God seemed lax in fulfilling His promise to give Abraham a son. When Abraham's wife, Sarah, suggested that he have a child with her maid, Hagar, Abraham agreed. (See Genesis 16.) He and Hagar indeed did have a son, Ishmael, but this boy was not the fulfillment of God's promise. Years later, God had to tell Abraham, "As for Ishmael, I will bless him… But my covenant will be confirmed with Isaac, who will be born to you and Sarah about this time next year" (Genesis 17:20–21).

We cannot rush God. We cannot control all the events in our lives. We must not forget that others might be trampled in our pursuit of our own timing for events. Therefore, we should not get restless and impatient. Of course, we need to be faithful and diligent, but at the same time we can be resting in the fact that God is in charge of the times and seasons of our lives.

If our pride is expressed in impatience or in any other way, we need to face up to what we are really doing and why and what it will cost us.

THE PRICE OF PRIDE

Just as pride's expressions are diverse, so are its causes.

Some people are born into privilege or were blessed by God with great physical beauty or other outstanding attributes. The flattery they receive can easily go to their heads.

Other people buy in to cultural messages saying that pride is good. When singers or pop psychologists or others urge them to put themselves first, they take it literally.

Still other people have a poor self-image that—paradoxically—expresses itself as pride. They are trying to make themselves feel better by getting strokes for their ego. (Believe it or not, it is possible to be arrogant and insecure at the same time.)

Given all this, we do not want to oversimplify our conception of pride. But at the same time we want to be firm in saying that wrong types of pride are all alike in being sinful. In the words of the sixth-century desert ascetic John Climacus, "Pride is utter poverty of soul disguised as riches, imaginary light where in fact there is darkness. This abominable vice not only stops our progress but even tosses us down from the heights we have reached." The sin of pride is disgraceful to the proud person, harmful to others, and dishonoring to God.

Through pride, we disgrace ourselves. In an often quoted (or misquoted) proverb, Scripture says, "Pride goes before destruction, and haughtiness before a fall" (Proverbs 16:18). If we present ourselves as greater than we are, we run the risk of looking foolish when our real nature begins to show itself. In fact, it is only a matter of time before we "fall" in this way.

In 1963 the writer John Steinbeck was in Russia and, feeling confident of his Russian language skills, preceded to order breakfast at his hotel. He wrote shortly afterward, "So in our pride, we ordered for breakfast an omelet, toast and coffee and what has just arrived is a tomato salad with onions, a dish of pickles, a big slice of watermelon and two bottles of cream soda."

In addition to the way pride bounces back and embarrasses the proud, so also pride injures those all around like a grenade that sends shrapnel flying. One person's pride makes another person feel small, squelching that person's self-respect. That's why Paul urged us not to become "puffed up" with knowledge but instead to "build up" other people. (See 1 Corinthians 8:1 NIV.) In a reverse of pride, we are to think of others "as better than yourselves" (Philippians 2:3).

Pride injures those all around like a grenade that sends shrapnel flying.

Worst of all, pride is a snub toward God. It indicates we have forgotten that we are mere created beings, finite and flawed. It takes credit for what God has done for us. Ultimately, then, pride is a faith issue because it causes us to focus on ourselves, ignoring what God has done and disobeying what He has commanded.

One time Jesus called a small child over to Him and put the child among the people He was speaking to. Then He said, "I tell you the truth, unless you turn from your sins and become like little children, you will never get into the Kingdom of Heaven" (Matthew 18:2–3). To become as a little child means to become humble. If we want to be right with God, we have to ask God to replace our pride with humility.

Humility is a quality every Christian should possess. As Puritan pastor Richard Baxter said, "Humility is not a mere ornament of a Christian, but an essential part of the new creature. It is a contradiction in terms, to be a Christian, and not be humble."

But what, exactly, is humility?

THINKING LESS OF ONESELF AND THINKING OF ONESELF LESS

Is humility thinking that you have no value or that you are the worst person who ever lived? Is it abasing yourself and cutting yourself down every chance you get?

No, of course not. Humility is being realistic about the human condition. This means we recognize that whatever advantages we possess were given to us by God. It means we recognize that as sinners we are not so different from other people. And most importantly it means we recognize that, compared to God Himself, we are not marvelous at all.

Esther de Waal put it well when she said, "Humility is facing the truth."

Humility is being realistic about the human condition.

> It is useful to remind myself that the word itself comes from *humus*, earth, and in the end simply means that I allow myself to be earthed in the truth that lets God be God, and myself his creature. If I hold on to this it helps prevent me from putting myself at the centre, and instead allows me to put God and other people at the centre. For if I want to return to God I must reverse the destructive journey of Adam and Eve which began with that subtle temptation to be as gods.[6]

When we are realistic about who we are, we stop trying to magnify ourselves and start magnifying God instead. It is no wonder that the apostle Paul told us, "Be honest in your evaluation of yourselves, measuring yourselves by the faith God has given us" (Romans 12:3).

It has been said that humility is not only about thinking less of yourself but also about thinking of yourself less. Of course, thinking of yourself less is no easy task. So insidious is pride that one can even become proud of being humble. (At that point, though, you are not really humble anymore!)

Benjamin Franklin recorded in his autobiography, "There is, perhaps, no one of our national passions so hard to subdue as *pride*. Disguise it, struggle with it, beat it down, stifle it, mortify it as much as one pleases, it is still alive, and will every now and then peep out and show itself.... Even if I could conceive that I had compleatly [sic] overcome it, I should probably be proud of my humility."[7]

Still, humility is possible for us to achieve. It is possible when we surrender our pride to the Holy Spirit's ministrations. He will make us humble. And as He does so, He will make us more like Christ.

Beginning at His birth in a manger, and throughout His life as a carpenter and itinerant rabbi, Jesus dwelt among humankind humbly. "Though He was God, He did not think of equality with God as something to cling to. Instead, He gave up His divine privileges; He took the humble position of a slave and was born as a human being. When He appeared in human form, He humbled himself in obedience to God and died a criminal's death on a cross" (Philippians 2:6–8). Along the way, He taught His disciples about servant leadership (see Matthew 20:25–28), and demonstrated it visibly by washing the dust from their feet (see John 13:1–17).

As followers of Christ, we are to model ourselves after our humble Lord. As Paul taught, "You must have the same attitude that Christ Jesus had" (Philippians 2:5).

And then, God elevated Him "to the place of highest honor" and "gave Him the name above all other names" (Philippians 2:9), so also we will be raised up in honor by God if we will first voluntarily lower ourselves in humility. "Those who humble themselves will be exalted" (Matthew 23:12). "Take the lowest place at the foot of the table. Then when your host sees you, he will come and say, 'Friend, we have a "better place" for you!'" (Luke 14:10). "Whoever wants to be first must take last place and be the servant of everyone else" (Mark 9:35).

We should not pursue humility for the sake of its rewards; rather, we should pursue it because it is right. But if we are humble, we can expect God to bless us for it. As Jack Miller put it, "Grace runs downhill to the humble."

If you need to think less of yourself and think of yourself less, begin the spiritual healing process now. The Holy Spirit will help you identify ungodly pride in your life and replace it with Christlike humility.

SOUL PRESCRIPTION FOR PRIDE

Are you struggling with a form of sinful pride? We have outlined a five-step process to help you work through the repair of that area of your life. Take all the time you need with each of the steps below.

Step 1: Adopt a Correct View of God

When you have a distorted view of who God is, you will not give Him the reverence and respect which are due to Him. As a result, your arrogance will be free to develop until you suffer the consequences of your pride.

Consider some truths about God that will help you with your pride problem.

- God is infinitely superior to us. He is absolutely perfect and we are not.

> How can a mortal be innocent before God? Can anyone born of a woman be pure? God is more glorious than the moon; He shines brighter than the stars. In comparison, people are maggots; we mortals are mere worms.
> —Job 25:4–6

- God has supreme authority over us. He determines our eternal future.

> How foolish can you be? He is the Potter, and He is certainly greater than you, the clay! Should the created thing say of the one who made it, "He didn't make me"? Does a jar ever say, "The potter who made me is stupid"?
> —Isaiah 29:16

If you tend to think too highly of yourself, focus more on the greatness of God. Undertake a Bible study on the nature of God, especially His majesty and power. Ask God to reveal Himself more clearly to you.

Step 2: Revise Your False Beliefs

God wants His people to be living examples of His love to others. Yet pride is the single greatest obstacle to loving people. Reflect on your attitudes with the help of the questions that follow.

- Do you think you are better than others?

    What gives you the right to make such a judgment?
    What do you have that God hasn't given you? And if
    everything you have is from God, why boast as though
    it were not a gift?
    —1 Corinthians 4:7

- Do you think that you are indispensable?

    By the grace given me I say to every one of you: Do not
    think of yourself more highly than you ought, but rather
    think of yourself with sober judgment, in accordance
    with the measure of faith God has given you.
    —Romans 12:3 NIV

- Do you think that your accomplishments and position en-
  title you to special favor?

    It's not good to eat too much honey, and it's not good to
    seek honors for yourself.
    —Proverbs 25:27

Such beliefs are all self-centered, self-appreciating, and degrading to others. Even so, your identity in Christ is not to be one of
selfish ambition and pride but rather one of self-denial and grace-
filled humility. Allow Scripture to inform your views of yourself,
other people, and life in general so that you will not be proud in
a sinful way.

Step 3: Repent of Your Sin

The hardest thing for a proud person to do is admit that he or
she is wrong. Are you prepared to do that? If so, give your type of
pride a specific name (conceit, vanity, or whatever).

Then pray the following prayer (or a similar one of your own
making) in faith that God will forgive your sin and empower your
obedience. Insert the name of your particular type of pride in the
blanks.

> God, I know I have sinned by _____. I am sorry
> for the pain I have given to You and to the people around
> me. Please forgive me for my sin. Wash away all of the
> _____ from me. And by Your Spirit, give me the
> strength to sin no more in this area but instead to live in
> humility. In Christ's name, amen.

If you have harmed others with your sin, apologize to them. Seek reconciliation and offer restitution where appropriate.

Step 4: Defend against Spiritual Attacks

Pride is easy to slip back into after you have repented. You can even become proud of your humility! Be certain that the world, the flesh, and the Devil will do all they can to pull you back into your sin of pride.

- The values of the world system are topsy-turvy, including promoting pride as a positive thing. The world system gives us messages like "You should think highly of yourself" and "Try to keep yourself in the spotlight." Overcome the world by inviting God to transform your thinking so that you come to agree with Him about the importance He places on humility.
- Your flesh (sinful nature) craves the good feeling it gets when you inflate your ego and selfishly seek attention from others. So remind yourself that your sinful nature is actually already dead. Cooperate with the Holy Spirit, who seeks to magnify God, not God's creatures.
- Satan will lay opportunities in your path that will make it easy for you to exercise your pride. Resist his schemes by putting on the whole armor of God. Especially use the "belt of truth" (Ephesians 6:14) by reminding yourself that God is the one who deserves honor, not you.

Spiritual attacks will never cease. So remain alert. The power of God is more than enough to defend you against spiritual attacks so that you may continue to live in a way that is consistent with your repentance.

Step 5: Flee Temptation

You will never fully be able to escape temptations to be proud. But you can significantly reduce these temptations—and thus improve your chances of remaining free of pride—if you will just take specific steps to avoid temptation.

- Focus on your relationship with God.
  Strengthen your devotional life. In particular, focus on giving God glory and humbling yourself before Him.

- Latch on to God's promises.
  Search the Scriptures for truths about pride and humility, then memorize the verses that you think can best help you to resist pride. Recall these verses whenever temptation arises. The following are a couple of verses you might want to memorize.

  Anyone who becomes as humble as this little child is the greatest in the Kingdom of Heaven.
  —Matthew 18:4

  Humble yourselves under the mighty power of God, and at the right time He will lift you up in honor.
  —1 Peter 5:6

- Establish safeguards.
  Make changes in your lifestyle that will reduce your temptation to be prideful. Be bold here! Be creative! These are a few possibilities to get your thinking going:

  - If you tend to look down on people of a lower social class than your own, volunteer to serve some of society's down-and-outers.
  - If you are proud of your looks, get rid of the clothes or makeup which you think flatter your looks the most.
  - If you like to show off by driving up in a flashy car, trade it in for a vehicle that is more modest and practical.
  - Ask a trusted Christian friend to hold you accountable in your commitment to not be prideful.

- Expect victory.

  Do not focus on your failures of the past but rather on God's ability to give you lasting victory over pride. Believe that He will implant a more humble attitude in your heart—for good. And give Him the praise in advance!

Visit www.SoulPrescription.com for more insights and resources, and to download a free leader's guide for small group Bible studies.

Chapter 10

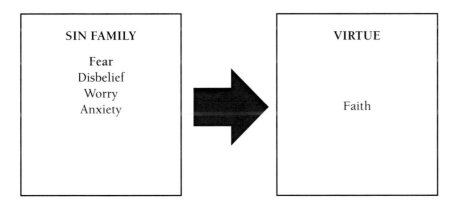

FEAR: FROM DOUBT TO DREAD

SIN FAMILY	VIRTUE
Fear Disbelief Worry Anxiety	Faith

"Fuss and feverishness, anxiety, intensity, intolerance, instability, pessimism and wobble, and every kind of hurry and worry—these, even on the highest levels," declared spiritual writer Evelyn Underhill, "are signs of the self-made and self-acting soul; the spiritual parvenu."[1]

A parvenu is someone who has been raised to a new position but has not yet acquired the manner of it. Becoming a child of God certainly qualifies as being given a high position. Are you acting like a parvenu child of God (whether or not you really are new to the faith) because you cannot warm the cold region of fear in your soul?

Certain Christians circle back again and again to the same place of fear or anxiety, whether it relates to their health, their family, their finances, or whatever else may be troubling them. Some fear may be natural and acceptable. But *living in* fear because you refuse to move on is another matter: it is sin. A person can have a sinful fear habit just as surely as an immorality habit or a drunkenness habit.

The problem, to use Underhill's terminology, is our "self-made and self-acting soul." If we are not trusting in God's care for us, we naturally react to our circumstances by trying to figure out how we can meet our own needs. It is a kind of homegrown providence, and it will never do. We know inside that we will never be capable of anticipating all the situations we may face. If we attempt to cut our way out of all the problems that may entangle us, we get stuck in a round of anxiety and dread.

We (Bill and Henry) have had our own times of fear and worry, and so we are empathetic to others who are fearful. However, we are not content merely to make people feel better by helping them cope with their worry. We would rather help them get past the anxiety or the fear altogether. And that means dealing with the sin that lies at the root. Where circumstances might naturally inspire worry, we want Christ's followers to renew their trust in God and move on in confidence of His care.

We want Christ's followers to renew their trust in God and move on in confidence of His care.

If you have a fear habit, letting go of your fear and trusting God completely might seem like an impossibility. So let us assure you with Scripture that it *is* possible to substitute faith for the anxiety and the worry you are presently feeling.

FEAR AND GOD

Susie outwardly seemed to be a well-poised young wife and mother with everything under control. She was active in her church and attended other Christian gatherings during the week. But secretly she was filled with fears from which psychologists and psychiatrists were unable to free her.

"What can I do?" she asked me (Bill) through her tears. "I have everything to live for and no real reason to be afraid, but I am consumed with worry and dread. I anticipate all kinds of evil things happening to me, my husband, and my children."

"Do you believe that God in heaven has the power to remove your fears, Susie?" I asked.

"Yes, I believe that," she replied.

To reinforce her belief, I read Psalm 34:4 to her.

> I prayed to the LORD, and He answered me,
> He freed me from all my fears.

Then I asked her if she wanted to join with me in a prayer of faith to ask God to deliver her from her fears as He had delivered the psalmist. She agreed. So together we prayed. Though she experienced no immediate deliverance, with the passing of days, God set Susie free from fear.

Can you relate to Susie? What are your fears about? Be assured that others have had them before you.

Do you fear other people? So did ten of the twelve spies whom Moses sent into the Promised Land to scout out the opposition. This was their report to Moses: "The people living there are powerful, and their towns are large and fortified…. We can't go up against them! They are stronger than we are!" (Numbers 13:28, 31).

Are you afraid of something bad coming at you from what appears a cold and impersonal nature? The disciples felt the same way when a storm came up as they were sailing in a boat. They woke Jesus and cried out, "Lord, save us! We're going to drown!" (Matthew 8:25).

The timid spies and the frightened disciples both received criticism from God for their faithlessness. God complained to Moses, "How long will these people treat Me with contempt? Will they never believe Me, even after all the miraculous signs I have done among them?" (Numbers 14:11). Jesus said to His disciples, "Why are you afraid? You have so little faith!" (Matthew 8:26).

Disbelief of God is a sin, and non-Christians are not the only ones who have a problem with this sin. Though we are saved, we Christians, too, may doubt God's promises to care for us. Such disbelief lies at the root of our ungodly instances of fear.

Are You Fearful?

The following self-evaluation quiz will help you determine whether you have a tendency toward fear and worry.

- Are you scared of losing your health or wealth or of something bad happening to one you love?
- Do you have trouble sleeping because you are up at night imagining all the things that could go wrong?
- Do you tend to have anxious thoughts about the same thing over and over?
- Do others ever kid you about being a worrywart?
- Do you have a nervous habit like tapping your foot or drumming your fingers?
- Have you ever sought treatment for stress-related symptoms?
- Do you hesitate to make plans because you are worried that things will not turn out well?
- Are your thoughts of the future filled with fear instead of hope?

It is a truism that most of what we fear never comes to pass. And even when bad things do happen (certainly people do face some serious problems sometimes), *God is still in control*. This is when we need the faith to believe that God is in control. There is no cause to give in to fear.

Well, that's not quite right. There is one kind of fear we *should* cultivate: the fear of God. Jesus warned, "Don't be afraid of those who want to kill your body; they cannot touch your soul. Fear only God, who can destroy both soul and body in hell" (Matthew 10:28). This sort of fear is a compound of awe and reverence.

The remarkable thing about fearing God is that when you fear God you fear nothing else, whereas if you do not fear God you fear everything else.

Oswald Chambers said, "The remarkable thing about fearing God is that when you fear God you fear nothing else, whereas if you do not fear God you fear everything else." If you have too many of the wrong kinds of fear, maybe you need to get more of the right kind: fear of God. This godly fear comes from recognizing who God really is and deciding to trust in Him.

COURAGE TO WALK ON WATER

The Bible is full of encouragement for the fearful. These are just a few examples:

- The Lord said to Abram in a vision, "Do not be afraid, Abram, for I will protect you, and your reward will be great" (Genesis 15:1).
- "Don't be afraid," he said, "for you are very precious to God. Peace! Be encouraged! Be strong!" (Daniel 10:19).
- The angel who came to Mary to preview the birth of the Lord said, "Don't be afraid, Mary," the angel told her, "for you have found favor with God!" (Luke 1:30).[2]

Does it seem reasonable to trust God because of who He is? Or does it seem crazy? George MacDonald wrote, "This is a wise, sane Christian faith: that a man commit himself, his life, and his hopes to God; that God undertakes the special protection of that man; that therefore that man ought not to be afraid of anything."

The apostle Peter had a chance to exhibit what MacDonald assures us is a "sane" faith. The disciples were in a boat, struggling against a headwind to bring their boat to shore when the following happened:

> About three o'clock in the morning Jesus came toward them, walking on the water. When the disciples saw Him walking on the water, they were terrified. In their fear, they cried out, "It's a ghost!" But Jesus spoke to them at once. "Don't be afraid," He said. "Take courage. I am here!"
>
> Then Peter called to him, "Lord, if it's really you, tell me to come to you, walking on the water."
>
> "Yes, come," Jesus said.
>
> So Peter went over the side of the boat and walked on the water toward Jesus. But when he saw the strong wind and the waves, he was terrified and began to sink. "Save me, Lord!" he shouted.
>
> Jesus immediately reached out and grabbed him. "You have so little faith," Jesus said. "Why did you doubt Me?" When they climbed back into the boat, the wind stopped.
>
> —Matthew 14:25–32

Peter represents any follower of Christ who has a problem with fear. We know we should trust God, and we even make efforts at acting courageously, but, then our faith falters, and we fear again. Are you ready to put one foot in front of the other and walk across the water to Jesus?

Neil Anderson wrote, "Fear is like a mirage in the desert. It seems so real until you move toward it, then it disappears into thin air. But as long as we back away from fear, it will haunt us and grow in size like a giant."[3] Whatever your fear may be, move toward it—and toward Christ—in faith.

"God has not given us a spirit of fear and timidity, but of power, love, and self–discipline" (2 Timothy 1:7 NASB). We need not live with fear, nor must we give in to worry or anxiety.

AN ANXIOUS HEART

You might not describe your problem as fear. You might think *worry* or *anxiety* describes it better. Sometimes you might not even be sure what you are anxious about. Or, you might have feelings of apprehension that do not rise to the level of fear, though they are troublesome enough. Persistent worry or anxiety is another condition that Christians need not and should not live with.

Meredith tended to worry about what other people thought of her. Her anxiety was particularly intense at work as she constantly wondered how to present herself at meetings or second-guessed what she had said in a conversation. The problem got so intense that Meredith turned to counseling.

After doing a little probing, the counselor was surprised to learn that in fact Meredith was doing well at work and was one of the most popular employees in the office. She was in particular known for her tactfulness. So the truth was that Meredith had no good reason for her worries about her reputation. She was anxious for no good reason, and it stole from the peace God wanted her to have.

C. S. Lewis wrote, "Anxiety is not only a pain which we must ask God to assuage but also a weakness we must ask him to pardon—for he's told us to take no care for the morrow." Lewis was referring to a famous passage on worry from Jesus' Sermon on the Mount. Let's take a look at it.

> That is why I tell you not to worry about everyday life—whether you have enough food and drink, or enough clothes to wear. Isn't life more than food, and your body more than clothing? Look at the birds. They don't plant or harvest or store food in barns, for your heavenly Father feeds them. And aren't you far more valuable to him than they are? Can all your worries add a single moment to your life?
>
> "And why worry about your clothing? Look at the lilies of the field and how they grow. They don't work or make their clothing, yet Solomon in all his glory was not dressed as beautifully as they are. And if God cares

so wonderfully for wildflowers that are here today and thrown into the fire tomorrow, he will certainly care for you. Why do you have so little faith?

"So don't worry about these things, saying, 'What will we eat? What will we drink? What will we wear?' These things dominate the thoughts of unbelievers, but your heavenly Father already knows all your needs. Seek the Kingdom of God above all else, and live righteously, and he will give you everything you need.

"So don't worry about tomorrow, for tomorrow will bring its own worries. Today's trouble is enough for today.
                                        —Matthew 6:25–34

Bible teacher Joyce Meyer says this passage means "we need to concentrate our full attention on today and stop being so intense and wrought up."

Calm down and lighten up! Laugh more and worry less. Stop ruining today worrying about yesterday or tomorrow—neither of which we can do anything about. We need to stop wasting our precious "now," because it will never come again.[4]

If you have a worry problem, we recommend you read Matthew 6:25–34 every day for a month and make it a springboard for prayer.

Life is a day-by-day affair. We do not know all that will happen in the future—*but we do not need to*. God will be with us in the future just as surely as He is with us in the present. Our part is to develop our trust in Him, leaving fear and anxiety behind in the process.

A SINGLE-MINDED APPROACH TO ENDING ANXIETY

The New Testament word for anxiety means "doubled-minded." That's the problem with people who have an anxiety habit. With part of their mind, they are looking to God; but with another part of their mind, they are fretting about what might happen to them. God desires for them to have their mind wholly fixed on Him, for then they could know peace. As the prophet Isaiah confessed to God,

> You will keep in perfect peace all who trust in You, all whose thoughts are fixed on You!
> —Isaiah 26:3

How do we get rid of our anxiety? Not by trying through an act of will to make our worries go away. Rather, by handing them over to God.

But how do we become single-minded, fixing our thoughts entirely on God? How do we get rid of our anxiety? Not by trying through an act of will to make our worries go away. Rather, by handing them over to God. One psalmist wrote,

> Please listen and answer me, for I am overwhelmed by my troubles.
> —Psalm 55:22

Late in life, the apostle Peter (evidently having learned his lesson when his feet slipped into the waves!) echoed the psalmist in saying, "Give all your worries and cares to God, for He cares about you" (1 Peter 5:7).

We give our cares to God through the miracle of prayer. That is why Paul advised, "Don't worry about anything; instead, pray about everything."

> Tell God what you need, and thank Him for all He has done. Then you will experience God's peace, which exceeds anything we can understand. His peace will guard your hearts and minds as you live in Christ Jesus.
> —Philippians 4:6–7

Instead of trying the useless self-talk of worry, assuring ourselves that things will go wrong, we need to be talking to God about our concerns.

TRUST IN GOD

An old scenario goes this way: fear knocked at the door; faith answered; no one was there. In truth, the answer to worry and fear in all their forms is faith in God.

George Müller, director of a network of orphanages in nineteenth-century England, could have wasted much energy worrying about how he would provide for the two thousand orphaned children under his care. But instead he operated on the faith principle. He refused a salary and trusted that his material needs and those of his orphanages would be met entirely by seeking God in prayer. And do you know what? That is just what happened. Müller once said, "The beginning of anxiety is the end of faith; and the beginning of true faith is the end of anxiety."

Fear knocked at the door; faith answered; no one was there.

Similarly, Neil Anderson defined courage as "making the choice to walk by faith and do what's right even in the face of fear." He added, "Being alive and free in Christ doesn't mean that we will never feel fear. It means that such fears no longer have any power over us if we exercise our faith in God."[5]

The Scriptures teach us that "perfect love expels all fear" (1 John 4:18). We acquire such love "as we live in God" (verse 17). This means exercising faith and growing in faith over time. In this way, we can even cease to be "slaves to the fear of dying" (Hebrews 2:15). Imagine that—no fear of death!

Faith is not the risk it seems. Our faith has a solid basis because the One whom we trust is all-powerful and cares about us. We can be free from anxiety and full of joy because, as Philippians 4:5 (NIV) says, "The Lord is near."

John Edmund Haggai, author of *How to Win over Worry*, commented on that verse.

> A literal translation of Philippians 4:5b shows that the verb is missing—"the Lord near." No verb was needed. It is abrupt, staccato. It is a bolt of light. The awareness of His nearness gives great calm in the storm and stress of life.

Living in the awareness of that fact brings about a behavioral change that cannot be explained in human terms. It's often the only major difference between a defeated Christian and a victorious Christian. Fortune may have eluded you. Professional success, which you have sought so laboriously, may have slipped through your fingers. Love may have betrayed you. All these may be true. But the Lord is near! There is no mockery in that statement.[6]

Do you want more faith that the Lord is near to you for help? If so, you are not alone in that desire. A father who sought Jesus' healing power for his son said to Jesus, "I do believe, but help me overcome my unbelief!" (Mark 9:24). The disciples likewise one time appealed to Jesus, "Show us how to increase our faith" (Luke 17:5).

The apostle John wrote, "We are confident that He hears us whenever we ask for anything that pleases Him. And since we know He hears us when we make our requests, we also know that He will give us what we ask for" (1 John 5:14–15). Surely having faith is in line with God's will. So if we ask Him for it, He will give it. We've got His Word on that.

With the Spirit's supernatural enabling, you can be a person of greater faith and you can shed your fear habit for good. Let the healing in this area of your life begin now.

SOUL PRESCRIPTION FOR FEAR

Are you struggling with fear, worry, or a related sin habit? We have outlined a five-step process to help you repent and heal in this area of your life. Take all the time you need with each of the steps below.

Step 1: Adopt a Correct View of God

If you are worried, fearful, or despairing, chances are that you are failing to see just how capable and willing God is to keep all His promises to you. Consider these truths:

- God is faithful; He will always be there for you.

  > The faithful love of the LORD never ends! His mercies
  > never cease. Great is His faithfulness; His mercies begin
  > afresh each morning.
  >   —Lamentations 3:22–23

- God is all-powerful, and He uses that power for your good.

  > He gives power to the weak and strength to the
  > powerless.
  >   —Isaiah 40:29

Make sure your ideas about God our protector match what He
says about Himself in the Bible. Why worry about anything when
the Creator of the universe is watching over you?

Step 2: Revise Your False Beliefs

How do ideas about people or life influence your worry-related
habit? Your ideas may have gotten off track in a number of different ways, but think about these possibilities:

- Do you believe that you must pull yourself up by your own
  bootstraps?

  > It is not that we think we are qualified to do anything on
  > our own. Our qualification comes from God.
  >   —2 Corinthians 3:5

- Do you think of yourself as a born loser in the game of life?

  > I can do everything through Christ, who gives me
  > strength.
  >   —Philippians 4:13

- Do you believe that your circumstances are beyond God's
  power to help?

> Don't worry about anything; instead, pray about every-
> thing. Tell God what you need, and thank Him for all
> He has done.
>
> —Philippians 4:6

Scan the Bible for its messages about how unnecessary worry really is. Make a conscious decision to identify and abandon any concepts about yourself, others, or life in general that contribute to your worry. Believe God, and trust in His power to meet your every need.

Step 3: Repent of Your Sin

What type of worry-related habit do you have? Is it fear? Is it anxiety? Are you discouraged or nervous or impatient? Make sure you are clear about your specific problem.

If you are prepared to leave your sin behind, pray a prayer of confession and commitment. You may use the prayer below, or you may pray in your own words.

> God, I have a problem in the area of _____, and I
> know it is sin. I know also that my failure to trust You
> has grieved You. I am sorry for that. Please forgive me
> for my sin. Cleanse me of it completely now—wash it
> away as if it had never existed. Give me now the ability
> to live my life in Your strength and not in mine. Lord,
> I believe; help me in my unbelief. In the name of Jesus
> Christ, amen.

If you have harmed others with your sin, apologize to them. Seek reconciliation and offer restitution where appropriate.

Step 4: Defend against Spiritual Attacks

The last place the enemies of your soul want to see you is at rest in the Lord's grace. You have put your trust in God; now you must keep it there.

- Watch out for the false values that the world system entices you to adopt. The world will say you have to take care of yourself, and this will naturally lead to worry. In God's value system, trust in Him takes the place of self-effort.
- Watch out for the way your flesh (that is, your sinful nature) attempts to have you return to that paradoxical feeling of control that comes from worrying about the unknown. When the feeling comes upon you, tell the flesh, "You're already dead! I don't have to do what you want." Rely on the Spirit's help to remain strong in your faith.
- Watch out for Satan's schemes to persuade you to worry about your circumstances again. You can resist him with the "shield of faith" that God gives as a part of our spiritual armor (see Ephesians 6:10–18).

Do not expect the temptation to be anxious, fearful, or discouraged to disappear any time soon. Remember that God is bigger than the world, the flesh, and the Devil. With Him on your side, you are a winner!

Step 5: Flee Temptation

In practical terms, certain situations can "give you an excuse" to worry. So take active steps to prevent returning to your bad habits of the past.

- Focus on your relationship with God.
  In your personal devotional time, focus on God as your provider and sanctuary. Use the power of praise and thankfulness to bolster your faith in Him.

- Latch on to God's promises.
  Many passages in Scripture speak of God's care for us. Search out ones that give you the most comfort and confidence, then commit them to memory. Here is one to memorize:

For God has not given us a spirit of fear and timidity,
but of power, love and self-discipline.

—2 Timothy 1:7

- Establish safeguards.

  Take practical steps to cut off common sources of temptation. These should be strategies tailor-made for you, but
  here are some examples to get you started thinking:

  - If you begin to feel discouraged, rehearse in your mind
    the victories that God has given you in the past.
  - If you are feeling fearful about tasks you need to accom-
    plish, break it down into small steps and take them one
    at a time.
  - If you are prone to nervousness, learn to meditate on
    God.
  - Ask a trusted Christian friend to hold you accountable
    for not worrying nor fearing so much.

- Expect victory.

  God has promised to always take care of you, and He will.
  Believe that He will enable you to beat the worry habit and
  build a stronger faith.

Visit www.SoulPrescription.com for more insights and resources,
and to download a free leader's guide for small group Bible
studies.

Chapter 11

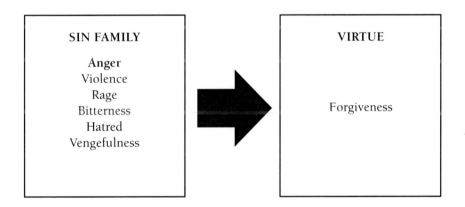

ANGER: WHEN MAD IS BAD

SIN FAMILY		VIRTUE
Anger Violence Rage Bitterness Hatred Vengefulness	→	Forgiveness

Some years ago, I (Henry) traveled to Zimbabwe for a conference and spoke about forgiveness. Afterward, a couple asked to speak with me in private. They were from Uganda, and they told me their story.

During the brutal reign of Uganda's Idi Amin, the couple received a note telling them that their twenty-six-year-old son had been kidnapped and was being held for ransom. Before the couple had met with Ugandan authorities how best they should respond, they received another note informing them that their son was dead.

The following self-evaluation quiz will help you determine whether you have a tendency toward anger.

- Do the people who know you well worry that you will blow up at them?
- Do you have a lot of enemies?
- Do you ever scheme to get back at people?
- Do you try to control situations by "powering up" on others?
- Have you ever been in trouble with authorities for fighting?
- Does the thought of certain people cause you to tense up or grow cold?
- Are there people whom you try to avoid because you are holding something against them?
- Have you had anger-related physical symptoms, such as stomach pains, high blood pressure, or sleeplessness?
- Do you keep reliving in your mind the wrongs others have done to you?

The father tried to locate his son's body. In doing this, he was seized by soldiers and taken to the same prison cell where his son had been held. There he was whipped with leather strips before being loaded onto a pickup truck and dropped off at a street corner. As a parting shot, the soldiers shouted that if he ever tried to locate his son again, he would be killed.

Two years had passed. I met the couple in Zimbabwe. They wanted to know if I believed they were wrong to keep alive their hatred for the soldiers who had treated their family so cruelly. Might it not even be disloyal to the memory of their son if they were to forgive his murderers?

I have had my own struggles with anger and hatred from time to time, but never with a cause as reasonable as this hurting couple. I did not know what to say to them. "God, help me," I prayed.

We sat in silence for a while. It seemed to me that God was telling me to gently urge this couple to let go of their hostility. So I suggested they needed to pray for a change of heart.

The man said in a trembling voice, "I am ready."

The wife added, "So am I."

The three of us knelt on the floor. I have never heard such moving prayers. We stood up afterward and embraced each other with tears of joy streaming down our cheeks.

The next day the man stood up at the conference and told the entire gathering that he and his wife were leaving a heavy burden behind.[1]

A heavy burden indeed is the anger that many of us carry. Like the Ugandan couple, we may have good reasons for our emotion, but we are weighed down by it all the same.

Anger is a strong feeling of dislike, displeasure, or antagonism. It is connected to a host of other negative feelings and behaviors, including rage, hatred, bitterness, vengefulness, and violence. In this chapter we will look at how to lay down such burdens. Before that, though, we must learn how to separate sinful anger from the rarer, but still possible, forms of acceptable anger.

THE DANGER IN ANGER

Just as there is such a thing as justifiable pride, so also there is such a thing as righteous indignation. When Jesus chased the merchants out of the temple (see John 2:13–17), He was angry at them for defiling God's house and hindering Gentile worship. He had good reasons to have godly anger. Likewise, in some cases, there may be nothing wrong with our anger.

When we see unrighteousness or injustice, getting upset is a reasonable response. But at other times our anger is improper, such as when we misinterpret what is going on or are too quick to take offense or let our anger grow out of proportion to the cause. Our anger is also unrighteous if we hang on to it for too long.

Anger is inherently dangerous. That's why the apostle Paul warned, "Don't sin by letting anger control you. Don't let the sun go down while you are still angry, for anger gives a foothold to the devil" (Ephesians 4:26–27).[2] In other words, even if your anger falls into the category of righteous indignation, get past it quickly before it has a chance to harm you. Anger cherished becomes like rot or gangrene. It opens the door to hatred and other sins.

Archibald Hart wrote, "It is not the anger (as feeling) that is wrong, but...anger has the potential for leading you into sin." If we choose to be angry at the wrong time or for the wrong reason, we are guilty before God. And if we are angry much of the time, we are dealing with a habitual sin—one that has a potential to harm not only those around us but also ourselves.

Rage is one term used to describe an excessive and uncontrolled anger.

LASHING OUT

I (Henry) arrived at my counseling session half an hour late, and I was nervous about making my apologies. The man I was making them to was Jay Carty, former professional basketball player with the Los Angeles Lakers—six feet, seven inches tall, and all of it muscle. With him was his wife, Mary.

My nervousness was due not so much to Jay's size as to what I had learned from a temperament test Jay had taken. It showed that Jay was an extremely dominant, very hostile, and strongly expressive person. As I had expected, he glared at me for showing up late.

- Do you have either a short fuse or a smoldering fire burning within you?
- Do others ever describe you as "cold" or "hard"?

I ignored the look and got the session started by asking, "What's the problem?"

Jay said, "I'm having trouble making a job change and thought you could help us sort out the decision-making process."

"Well," I said, "it's easy to see what the problem is. There's sin in your life."

An uncomfortable pause followed. Finally, with an impatience that was impossible to disguise, Jay said, "Henry, perhaps you could elaborate just a little bit."

Over the next few minutes, I pointed out the web of sin that his temperament test had revealed. I told him his anger was like a pot on boil. I told him that everyone irritated him and that when they failed him, he would blow up at them.

"You hotshot!" Jay shouted. "You don't care about me, or you wouldn't have forgotten about the appointment. Then, you pull this grandstand move by telling me there's sin in my life, pat me on the rear, and send me on my way so I can tell people I talked to the great Dr. Henry Brandt. Well, thank you, but I'm not impressed. I think you're a fraud."

He got up and motioned for his wife to follow him out the door.

I said, "No, no, don't go. Right now, Jay, how do you feel down in the pit of your stomach? Is it the fruit of the Spirit—love, joy, peace, patience, kindness, goodness, faithfulness, gentleness, self-control?"

"That answer's easy," Jay snorted. "None of those qualities typifies the way I feel, at least not right now."

I asked him pointedly, "Do you feel angry most of the time?"

It was so quiet that you could hear the three of us breathing. "Yes."

Jay sat back down and poured out his story. He was someone with great gifts and a powerful personality who had been fixing most of his problems by just trying harder and expecting everyone else to follow his lead.

At last Jay asked, "Henry, how bad am I? What am I going to do? I've spent a lifetime learning to live this way."[3]

Jay Carty is an example of someone whose anger built up over time and produced a lifestyle of rage. Others, though, have what's called a "short fuse." Their anger flares out suddenly and then subsides just as quickly. Is that type of rage any better?

A woman once came to evangelist Billy Sunday and tried to rationalize her angry outbursts. "There's nothing wrong with losing my temper," she said. "I blow up and then it's all over."

"So does a shotgun," Sunday replied, "and look at the damage it leaves behind!"

Wise Solomon said, "Control your temper, for anger labels you a fool" (Ecclesiastes 7:9).[4]

Whether rage is of the slow or the fast variety, it is so common that you might almost think that people *want* to be angry. And maybe some do—to their harm. Frederick Buechner said in *Wishful Thinking*:

> Of the Seven Deadly Sins, anger is possibly the most fun. To lick your wounds, to smack your lips over grievances long past, to roll over your tongue the prospect of bitter confrontations still to come, to savor to the last toothsome morsel both the pain you are given and the pain you are giving back—in many ways it is a feast fit for a king. The chief drawback is that what you are wolfing down is yourself. The skeleton at the feast is you.[5]

Anger produces bodily changes that cannot be ignored. Here are just a few of the symptoms doctors and counselors have noticed in persons with rage:

- increased pulse rate
- faster heartbeat
- high blood pressure
- tight throat
- dry mouth
- hair standing on end
- enlarged pupils
- change in skin color
- tense muscles

- shaking or twitching
- insomnia
- stomach pains or nausea
- nagging body pains
- loss of appetite or difficulty in controlling food cravings[6]

In the saddest cases, such symptoms have contributed to the untimely deaths of many rage-filled men and women.

In *Anger Is a Choice*, one of the coauthors tells about visiting a seventy-two-year-old minister who was on a tirade about the medical treatment he had been receiving. The author said to the minister, "Paul, if you don't stop this, you're going to kill yourself!" Within two days, Paul was dead of a heart attack.

Beyond the physical effects, rage is also spiritually destructive. Jesus declared in no uncertain terms, "If you are even angry with someone, you are subject to judgment!" (Matthew 5:22). Furthermore, He said that anger is akin to murder. If you are a person with a rage problem, regardless of the legitimacy of its cause, you are in the wrong.

Suppressing rage—turning "outrage" into "inrage," so to speak—is not the answer. You need to confess your sin. You need to work through the process of soul healing that appears at the end of this chapter so that your body and spirit may be cleansed of this serious condition.

God Himself is "slow to anger" (Exodus 34:6). With His help, we can be too.

He can also help to free us from the related attitudes of hatred and bitterness.

God is "slow to anger." With His help, we can be too.

THE WOLF OF HATRED

A little boy came to his grandfather in tears and declared that he hated a schoolmate. The grandfather said he understood the feeling, then told this story: "It is as if there are two wolves inside me. One is good and does no harm. He lives in harmony with all around him and does not take offense when no offense was intended.

"But the other wolf...Ah! He is full of anger. The littlest thing will send him into a fit of temper. He fights everyone, all the time, for no reason. He cannot think because his anger and hate are so great.

"It is hard to live with these two wolves inside me, for both of them try to dominate my spirit."

The boy asked, "Which one wins, Grandfather?"

The grandfather replied, "The one I feed."

The wolf of hatred is powerful. Unrighteous anger feeds the hatred and allows it to grow more powerful still, until the wolf stretches out its fangs and claws to tear at those around. Such a beast lies within us when we hate. If we are to become holy people, we must starve this vicious predator.

A beast lies within us when we hate. We must starve this vicious predator.

Bitterness is like hatred in that it results from the harm others have done us, but it stays closer to home. While hatred is a feeling of intense hostility toward another person, bitterness is a rancor we nurse in our hearts to keep our anger alive. Hatred is the hostile emissary that we mentally send out to our enemy; bitterness is a fire that smolders deep inside. Both are sinful.

There are some who think hatred is reasonable and just, even admirable. Jesus acknowledged this attitude when He said, "You have heard the law that says, 'Love your neighbor' and hate your enemy" (Matthew 5:43). In fact, Leviticus 19:18 does say to love your neighbor. The religious teachers called Pharisees interpreted this verse to mean it was okay to hate your enemies.

Jesus, though, had a surprising take on the matter. "But I say, love your enemies!" (Matthew 5:44). And what He had in mind by "love" was not some weak "Oh, all right, I love you" attitude but a love demonstrated in action. The examples He gave of love for enemies included the following commands: "Do good to those who hate you. Bless those who curse you. Pray for those who hurt you" (Luke 6:27–28).

Bitterness, likewise, is out of bounds for Christians. One early Christian leader wrote, "Pursue peace with all people, and holiness, without which no one will see the Lord: looking carefully lest anyone fall short of the grace of God; lest any root of bitterness springing up cause trouble, and by this many become defiled" (Hebrews 12:14–15 NKJV).

Bitterness, then, is not only like a smoldering fire; it is also like a root that puts out weedy growth in our spirit if given half a chance. We cannot just prune it back. We must pull it out, roots and all.

Like its cousin hate, bitterness will eat away at us. If we have an ongoing problem with either hate or bitterness, we need to take aggressive action. If we do not, one error we can be led into is revenge.

GETTING MAD AND GETTING EVEN

No one can say for certain how the infamous Hatfield-McCoy feud got started. One thing for sure is that around the time of the Civil War the Confederate-sympathizing Hatfields of West Virginia conceived a hatred for the Union-sympathizing McCoys across the border in Kentucky, and the McCoys returned the favor.

Provocation quickly led to escalation. In 1878 Randolph McCoy accused one of the Hatfields of stealing a pig. The case went to court and the Hatfields won. Later a Hatfield boy got a McCoy girl pregnant and was rewarded with a severe beating by her relatives. Then in 1882 Ellison Hatfield was killed, starting a run of murders that would reach eleven over the next decade.

How bitter is revenge! How destructive!

We may not aim a rifle at anyone from behind a tree, but in a myriad of ways we get back at people who have hurt us. When others wound us by their words or actions, Revenge whispers in our ears, "Give him the cold shoulder!" or "Say something equally harsh in return!" or "Spread a rumor that will wreck her reputation!" Sometimes people will wait for years, nursing their resentment, until they are in a position to harm the one they hate.

Does any of this sound familiar to you? Is any of it acceptable behavior in the eyes of God? The apostle Peter wrote, "Don't repay evil for evil. Don't retaliate with insults when people insult you" (1 Peter 3:9). His colleague Paul similarly instructed readers,

Dear friends, never take revenge. Leave that to the righteous anger of God. For the Scriptures say,

"I will take revenge; I will pay them back,"
says the Lord.
                                                —Romans 12:19[7]

God reserves judgment for Himself. Only He knows all the facts and is capable of rendering justice fairly and comprehensively. True, He gives properly instituted human leadership the authority to handle matters of earthly justice as best they can. But He does not give us as individuals the right to punish those who have hurt us.

Revenge is reputed to be sweet, but it swiftly turns sour.

Revenge is reputed to be sweet, and in fact for a while it may replace our feelings of hurt with a sense of triumph. But revenge swiftly turns sour because inside we know our revenge has lowered us to the level of our antagonist and has laid destruction upon destruction. God is wise in reserving for Himself the prerogative of avenging wrongs.

Besides trusting Him to handle matters of justice, what should we do?

Instead of helping a relationship head downward in a spiral of attack and counterattack, we are to do our best at reversing the direction the relationship is going in. Peter said that rather than retaliating against others, we should "pay them back with a bless-ing" (1 Peter 3:9). Paul said that instead of avenging ourselves, we should "conquer evil by doing good" (Romans 12:21).

Such seemingly illogical responses really make a great deal of sense. They are not likely to make matters worse, and they might make the situation a great deal better. When Abraham Lincoln was chided for not seeking to destroy his enemies, he replied, "Do I not destroy my enemies when I make them my friends?" Paying back evil with good puts a stop to the cycle of revenge.

But in real life—in our lives—is this possible? Can vengeful people learn to lay down their arms and embrace their enemies?

Certainly, it is not easy or enjoyable—nobody is saying that. But possible? Yes. Just ask the Hatfields and the McCoys.

Both clans are still in existence today. And although violence between them ended with the 1800s, the feud continued in the form of legal disputes over timber rights and cemetery plots for another century. But shortly after the conclusion of the final court case between them, the two families joined together to put a formal end to the feud.

On June 14, 2003, representatives of the two families signed a proclamation that read, "We do hereby and formally declare an official end to all hostilities, implied, inferred, and real, between the families, now and forevermore. We ask by God's grace and love that we be forever remembered as those that bound together the hearts of two families to form a family of freedom in America."[8]

God bless the Hatfields and the McCoys! And God bless you if you will keep from returning evil for evil and will return good instead.

Revenge's counterpart, violence, is another evil practice we must avoid.

VIOLENCE: THE SHORTCUT THAT GOES NOWHERE

If asked, a park ranger in British Columbia will be glad to show off the interlocked antlers of two bull moose. Apparently the moose began fighting, their antlers got stuck together, and they could not pull free. Both moose died because of their fighting.

Sometimes people are a lot like animals.

While in some of us anger goes underground as hatred or bitterness, in others it comes right out in the open as violence. Men especially (though not exclusively) will, on occasion, resort to physical coercion in an attempt to solve their problems. Violence seems like such a direct way to react to a situation—not to mention a quick release for pent-up feelings of anger!

The headlines about violence that grab our attention are ones like these:

- STUDENT OPENS FIRE AT SCHOOL, KILLS FOUR
- MOVIE STAR ACCUSED OF DROWNING WIFE
- FACTORY WORKER KILLS BOSS, GUARD, SELF

What we do not see (or at least pay as much attention to) are news stories about the less extraordinary kind of violence that goes on in homes and public places every day. What would you think if you saw these headlines?

- HUSBAND BEATS WIFE, THIRD TIME THIS MONTH
- FRIENDS DRINK AT BAR, FIGHT IN PARKING LOT, REGRET IT LATER
- MAN WHO ATTEMPTED RAPE SAYS WOMEN HAVE SLIGHTED HIM

This kind of "everyday" violence may be too common to get much notice, but its contribution to the sum of human misery is hard to overestimate.

The consequences of violence go beyond the obvious results of physical pain and wounding. Even if no one is permanently injured by an act of violence, the scars on the inside may take a long time to heal—if ever. And one violent person may be producing another. Few things are as self-perpetuating as violence.

The violent person is also degraded by his own violence. He knows he has sunk to an animalistic level. If he has any conscience left, he is ashamed of causing another human being pain. He has to worry about legal ramifications. He is caught in the consequences of his actions—just like the bull moose.

In part for such reasons, violence is like vengeance in that it is something individuals are not permitted to do. The state has the right to pursue justice through criminal punishment and war, but individuals should never use violence (unless necessary for self-defense). Certainly, we should never instigate violence just because we are angry.

The apostle Paul said, "Don't participate in the darkness of wild parties and drunkenness, or in sexual promiscuity and immoral living, or in quarreling and jealousy" (Romans 13:13). In other words, fighting is just as bad as other types of sin like drunkenness and adultery. Aggressive violence cannot be justified.

When Peter drew a sword to protect Jesus from the men who had come to arrest Him, Jesus ordered the hot-tempered disciple,

"Put your sword back into its sheath" (John 8:11). He would say something like that to any of us who would try to solve our problems with violence. Keep your hands to yourself. Put down the knife. Lock up the gun.

If you are habitually violent, work through the soul-healing process. And if you think you may be on the verge of hurting another person, get professional help—now.

THE FORGIVENESS FACTOR

What do you do if you are filled with rage or hatred or bitterness? What do you do if you are vengeful or violent? By God's grace, you get rid of the sin of anger and replace it with the virtue of forgiveness.

Anger is an emotion that is set off when someone else has done something we do not like. We may be quite right in disliking what the other person has said or done. Sometimes, in fact, the offense is monstrous, as in the case of the Ugandan couple whose son was murdered. But because the offense has a personal origin, the only way to free ourselves of the destructive emotion we feel and move ahead in life is to forgive the person who did wrong.[9]

Of course, when we have been hurt, something inside us screams "No!" to the idea of forgiveness. It seems unjust. And do you know what? It is. When we forgive, we pay a price for a wrong that someone else has done. What does that remind you of?

We follow in Christ's footsteps when we forgive.

Jesus Christ paid the penalty for our sins on the cross. It was not just or fair, but He willingly did it so that mercy would triumph over justice. We follow in His footsteps when we forgive one who has committed an offense against us.

Another reason we might resist forgiving is that we conceive of unforgiveness as a type of revenge. We believe we are hurting the one who has hurt us if we withhold our forgiveness. That is foolish thinking. We are only hurting ourselves by holding on to a grudge. In the words of writer Anne Lamott, "Not forgiving people is like drinking rat poison and then waiting for the rat to die."

For these reasons, forgiveness does not necessarily mean suddenly having a warm feeling toward the one who has hurt us.

"Forgiveness is not a feeling, first and foremost. It is a choice that goes beyond feelings; it is an activity of the *will*."[10] We choose first to forgive, and we pray that the loving feelings will follow. This is loving by faith.

What about "forgiving and forgetting"? Can we forget the offense against us once we have forgiven the offender? Of course not. We will still *recall* the hurt—but we need not *relive* the hurt. As David Augsburger said, "The hornet of memory may fly again, but forgiveness has drawn out the sting."

And what about reconciliation? A restored relationship should be our goal whenever it is a possibility. When the one who has offended us is a fellow Christian, we can follow the guidelines of Matthew 18 to initiate a process of confrontation that starts privately and adds on pressure and publicity if needed. When the offender is a non-Christian, we can still seek restoration of our relationship by humbly approaching the other and discussing what happened.

But reconciliation requires two. The other person may be *unwilling* to admit the wrong he or she has done and seek to restore the relationship. Or maybe you are *unable* to reconcile with the other person. You may not know how to get in touch with the offender anymore, or perhaps that person has died. And if the other person still presents a threat to you, as in the case of an abuser, it might not even be wise to reestablish contact. In such cases, remember that you can still forgive the person. Unlike reconciliation, forgiveness requires only one.

Hard as it is, forgiveness is a blessing to us because it frees us from anger and all the ill effects that anger brings upon us. That is why God both commands and enables forgiveness. "Be kind to each other, tenderhearted, forgiving one another, just as God through Christ has forgiven you" (Ephesians 4:32). "Make allowance for each other's faults, and forgive anyone who offends you. Remember, the Lord forgave you, so you must forgive others" (Colossians 3:13).

The New Testament consistently links our forgiveness of others to God's forgiveness of us. Jesus once told a parable in which a servant was forgiven for a vast sum of money the servant owed a king. The servant turned around and shook down a fellow servant for neglecting to repay a much smaller sum. (See Matthew 18:21–35.) Like the unforgiving servant, our sins against God are immeasurably greater than any offense someone else has committed against us. So let us forgive as we have been forgiven.

As often as someone angers you, just so often can you forgive. That's the way to beat the anger habit.

SOUL PRESCRIPTION FOR ANGER

Are you struggling with anger or an anger-related sin habit? We have outlined a five-step process to help you repent and heal in this area of your life. Take all the time you need with each of the steps below.

Step 1: Adopt a Correct View of God

Almost certainly, a distorted perception of God's nature lies at the core of your problem with anger. We do not know exactly what that is for you. But quite possibly you are overemphasizing the wrath of God while underemphasizing His faithful love. Consider these key truths about God's nature.

- God offers forgiveness, reconciliation, and eternity instead of condemnation.

    The LORD passed in front of Moses, calling out, "Yahweh! The LORD! The God of compassion and mercy! I am slow to anger and filled with unfailing love and faithfulness."

    —Exodus 34:6

- God is merciful and expects us to extend His mercy to others.

    There will be no mercy for those who have not shown mercy to others. But if you have been merciful, God will be merciful when He judges you.

    —James 2:13

Search the Scriptures for everything you can find about God's love, mercy, and forgiveness. Allow what you find out about Him begin to change the way you think about God and about yourself as God's child.

Step 2: Revise Your False Beliefs

You may be an angry person because you have developed some mistaken ideas about yourself and other people as well as how to get along in life. Do you believe that? Well, ask yourself these questions:

- Do you believe you are justified in your anger?

   > Sensible people control their temper; they earn respect by overlooking wrongs.
   > —Proverbs 19:11

- Do you believe that your anger is uncontrollable?

   > Don't sin by letting anger control you. Don't let the sun go down while you are still angry.
   > —Ephesians 4:26

- Do you believe that anger is a useful tool in life?

   > People with understanding control their anger; a hot temper shows great foolishness.
   > —Proverbs 14:29

Along with those suggested here, there are many more false beliefs that can keep you a slave to anger. Seek clues in Scripture for ways that your ideas have gone off track, contributing to your anger problem. Ask the Holy Spirit to use biblical truth to change your conscious and unconscious beliefs so that you are living in truth and not falsehood. He will do it!

Step 3: Repent of Your Sin

Are you ready to admit that you are angry and to give it up? In what particular ways (rage, violence, revenge, and so on) do you express your anger? Identify your anger and "own" it.

When you are ready, ask God to forgive you for your anger. You can pray the following prayer (or another like it in your own words). Insert the word for your particular anger problem in the blank spaces.

> God, I am an angry person, especially in the area of _____. And I know that is sinful. I am sorry for how the flames of my anger have singed others, and especially I am sorry for how I have grieved You. Please forgive me for my anger now. Cleanse me completely from the sin of _____ so that it is gone from my life. Furthermore, give me the power never to return to my angry ways again.
>
> I want to be like Jesus, merciful and kind. In His name I pray, amen.

If you have harmed others with your sin, apologize to them. Seek reconciliation and offer restitution where appropriate.

Step 4: Defend against Spiritual Attacks

The enemies of your soul—the world, the flesh, and the Devil—do not like it when you repent of your anger. They will stir up your anger again if you let them. Get ready to defend yourself against these enemies.

- In the world's value system, anger is considered good. The world would tell us that anger confers power. But you can overcome this false system if you hold fast to God's values, which tell us that those who control their anger have the real spiritual power.
- Anger can feel good. Our flesh, or sinful nature, urges us to get that good feeling back by letting ourselves be filled with

rage again. So when you feel that kind of desire rising within you, remind yourself that the flesh is dead and you do not have to satisfy its desires. Turn to the Spirit to help you want what God wants for you: a forgiving spirit.

- Satan will use your sense of personal rights and your selfishness to goad you into angry outbursts and attitudes. Put on the armor of God to resist the Devil's schemes. Above all, put on the "shoes of peace" (Ephesians 6:15), which enable you to move around in harmony with all your Christian brothers and sisters.

Are you ready to be in control of your anger, instead of its being in control of you? The battle has begun and will not be over soon. So the time is now to stand strong in the strength of Lord and ask the Holy Spirit to supernaturally equip you to defeat the enemies of your soul.

Step 5: Flee Temptation

Many of us find that our anger has certain triggers. Walking through a minefield, you have a much better chance of survival if you know where the danger is and learn to avoid it.

- Focus on your relationship with God.
  Cultivate your relationship with God through the spiritual disciplines of prayer and meditation. Learn to hear God's voice so that His whisper of peace will sound louder in your ears than the cry of temptation to lash out in anger.

- Latch on to God's promises.
  Search Scripture for verses and stories that emphasize the danger of anger and the value of forgiveness. Memorize Scriptures that can help you in times of temptation. One relevant scriptural passage is the parable of the unforgiving servant. Read it in Matthew 18:21–35.

- Establish safeguards.

Take specific steps to avoid whatever triggers your anger. Consider these examples:

- If you want to get revenge against somebody, do something good for that person in secret.
- If you have a tongue that is quick with a harsh retort, learn to quickly ask the Holy Spirit for help before saying anything in a potentially explosive situation.
- Ask a trusted Christian friend to hold you accountable in your commitment to not get angry.

- Expect victory.

  As a believer, you are indwelt by the Holy Spirit. He will help you put a clamp on your anger before it can do any damage. Believe that you can go from being an angry person to being a person of forgiveness.

Visit www.SoulPrescription.com for more insights and resources, and to download a free leader's guide for small group Bible studies.

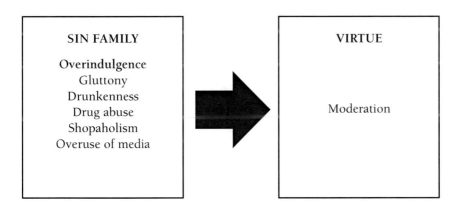

Chapter 12

OVERINDULGENCE: ENOUGH IS NOT ENOUGH

SIN FAMILY	VIRTUE
Overindulgence	
Gluttony	
Drunkenness	Moderation
Drug abuse	
Shopaholism	
Overuse of media	

In my (Henry's) early years, one of my biggest problems was with drinking. Though I grew up in a Christian home where drinking was frowned upon, I rebelled in my teenage years and started drinking in bars, at parties, and in the homes of my friends.

Early signs of the danger in this lifestyle did little good. One of my drinking buddies burned to death in a fiery collision; another committed suicide. I was fired from a job for coming back from lunch drunk. But still I continued drinking.

Then one afternoon I staggered home drunk and dropped off to sleep on the couch. Soon a traveling salesman came to the door, shook me awake, and read me a tract about receiving Christ. I prayed with the salesman, asking God to forgive and save me, then fell back asleep.

I went to a bar as usual that evening, but somehow the lifestyle that had seemed so exciting before now seemed no fun at all. My drunken prayer had made a real difference! My life began to change, and I left drinking behind, completely—though not without some struggles.

As a result of my own experience, I am able to understand those who overindulge in alcohol or other substances and experiences. Both Bill and I have counseled hundreds of persons who have struggled with overindulgence of different sorts. We know the pain it can cause and the difficulty people have in beating these habits.

Of course, everyone overindulges occasionally. For example, just about every American overindulges with food on Thanksgiving. But what we are talking about here is an ongoing overindulgence that interferes with healthy and holy living.

Sinful overindulgence can take many forms. Let us first deal with what is perhaps the most common form: gluttony.

THE LURE OF THE REFRIGERATOR

A pastor had a heart attack and was clinging to life in the ICU of a local church-affiliated hospital. The pastor's adult son came to visit him in the hospital and was praying by his side when a doctor came in. They discussed the father's condition, and the doctor informed the son that being overweight had put a strain on his father's heart.

Then the doctor pointed out that the son seemed to be heading down the same road. And, it was true. Like his father, the son had a sedentary lifestyle and enjoyed large quantities of convenience foods. His belly was already well on its way to matching his father's girth.

"Yeah, I've got an eating problem," admitted the son.

"No, you've got a sin problem," countered the doctor.[1]

Overeating is the more common term these days, but *gluttony* is the time-honored label for the sin of putting more food in your mouth than your body needs for its health and strength. A glutton is the type of person who tells himself or herself, "Eat, drink, and be merry!" (Luke 12:19). In the worst cases, you could say of gluttons that "their god is their stomach" (Philippians 3:19 NIV).

For some gluttons, the appeal of overeating lies in the enjoyment that the taste buds get as the food makes its way to the stomach. For others, the sense of fullness that comes after eating may compensate for emotional absences in their lives. However, while one might understand and sympathize with some causes for overindulgence with food, we must say unequivocally that gluttony is a sin.

Full stomachs and jaded palates take the edge from our hunger and thirst for righteousness. They spoil the appetite for God.

Like any sin, gluttony trails in its wake a host of evil effects. Those who overeat often feel ashamed and guilty. They spend more of their money and time on food than it deserves. As they gain weight, they experience discomfort, reduced physical abilities, and embarrassment over how others view them. And like the pastor who had the heart attack, they may experience significant health problems. Each year, obesity in America accounts for health-care costs of approximately $100 billion as well as contributes to at least three hundred thousand premature deaths.[2]

Gluttony can also damage one's spiritual health. Philosopher Cornelius Plantinga Jr. pointed out, "Full stomachs and jaded palates take the edge from our hunger and thirst for righteousness. They spoil the appetite for God."[3] The person whose body is overfed may have a starving soul.

The same sort of spiritual deprivation may be at work in those with a drinking problem.

BLISS IN A BOTTLE?

For years, Jack Bivans was one of the voices on the popular radio theater program *Unshackled!* Produced by the Pacific Garden Mission in Chicago, *Unshackled!* portrayed the ways that real individuals were freed from alcoholism and other bondages through the power of Christ. What few listeners knew was that Bivans was in shackles himself.

Bivans began drinking while serving in World War II. Over the years, his drinking got worse and contributed to the dissolution of two marriages. "My family life began a downward spiral and my emotional world started crumbling around me," he recalled.

It all came to a head in 1975. Bivans said, "The lives of the people whose true stories I had portrayed on *Unshackled!* began to hit home. One day, following a taping, I was driving home alone and felt the overwhelming presence of the Holy Spirit within me. I changed. I was drinking, and sometimes too much, and so I gave it up."[4]

Of all forms of overindulgence, none is more thoroughly covered in Scripture than drunkenness. Perhaps most notably, Solomon composed a vivid description of the effects of drinking upon the drunkard:

> Who has anguish? Who has sorrow? Who is always fighting? Who is always complaining? Who has unnecessary bruises? Who has bloodshot eyes? It is the one who spends long hours in the taverns, trying out new drinks. Don't gaze at the wine, seeing how red it is, how it sparkles in the cup, how smoothly it goes down. For in the end it bites like a poisonous snake; it stings like a viper. You will see hallucinations, and you will say crazy things. You will stagger like a sailor tossed at sea, clinging to a swaying mast. And you will say, "They hit me, but I didn't feel it. I didn't even know it when they beat me up. When will I wake up so I can look for another drink?"
>
> —Proverbs 23:29–35[5]

Rather than being under the influence of alcohol, we should be under the influence of God's Spirit.

The Romans liked to indulge in drinking parties where matters could get way out of hand. The apostle Peter, therefore, wrote to new believers, "You have had enough in the past of the evil things that godless people enjoy—their immorality and lust, *their feasting and drunkenness and wild parties*, and their terrible worship of idols" (1 Peter 4:3, emphasis added).[6] The message for Christians who have been heavy drinkers is this: Enough! It is time to put away your habit of drunkenness.

Paul made God's viewpoint on drunkenness as clear as it could be: "Don't be drunk with wine, because that will ruin your life." Then Paul went on to say, "Instead, be filled with the Holy Spirit" (Ephesians 5:18). Rather than being under the influence of alcohol, we should be under the influence of God's Spirit.

DRUGS: WHEN ESCAPE BECOMES A TRAP

Unlike alcohol, drugs are not specifically mentioned in Scripture. However, the New Testament word usually translated "witchcraft" or "sorcery" ("participation in demonic activities" in Galatians 5:20) is *pharmakeia,* from which we get our word *pharmaceuticals.* It reflects the fact that mood-altering substances were often used in occult rituals in ancient times.

It is a safe bet that we can take the biblical injunctions against drunkenness as applying to drug abuse as well. We can therefore paraphrase Ephesians 5:18 as saying, "Don't take drugs, because that will ruin your life." The very fact that drug use is illegal puts it out of bounds for Christians, since we are instructed to "submit to governing authorities" (Romans 13:1).

Drug-taking is one sin that many presume Christians will not get involved in. Not so! Singer Johnny Cash is an example. Not long before his death in 2003, Cash told *Relevant* magazine,

> I used drugs to escape, and they worked pretty well when I was younger. But they devastated me physically and emotionally—and spiritually. That last one hurt so much: to put myself in such a low state that I couldn't communicate with God. There's no lonelier place to be. I was separated from God, and I wasn't even trying to call on him. I knew that there was no line of communication. But he came back. And I came back.[7]

As in Cash's case, escape seems to be one motivation of people who take drugs. They think they can leave the difficulty or tedium of their lives behind with the vehicle of drugs. Unfortunately, it does not get them anywhere; they wind up in worse trouble than they started with.

Meanwhile, many drugs have a powerfully addicting effect on those who take them. Drug users still have a choice (that's where the sinfulness comes in), but as the addiction changes their brain chemistry and physiological responses, the choice *not* to take drugs becomes harder and harder. Many find that their temporary "escape" becomes a trap out of which they cannot seem to work their way.

Actor Robert Downey Jr. said, "I'm allergic to alcohol and narcotics. If I use them, I break out in handcuffs." We can laugh at the quip, but the fact is that drug users, while they may not be literally imprisoned as Downey has been, are bound emotionally and spiritually.

SHOPPING AS RECREATION

Some have said that America has been infected with "affluenza." Materialism is a widespread illness, and for many it shows up in the way they buy far more than they really need. They shop just for the fun of it, and for the kick they get from owning new stuff, not because they really need these belongings. A term has been coined to describe these people: *shopaholics*.

While the term is new, the phenomenon it describes is not. Long ago, King Solomon went through a phase in which he deliberately tested what he could gain by spending, spending, spending.

> I...tried to find meaning by building huge homes for myself and by planting beautiful vineyards. I made gardens and parks, filling them with all kinds of fruit trees. I built reservoirs to collect the water to irrigate my many flourishing groves. I bought slaves, both men and women, and others were born into my household. I also owned large herds and flocks, more than any of the kings who had lived in Jerusalem before me. I collected great sums of silver and gold, the treasure of many kings and provinces. I hired wonderful singers, both men and women, and had many beautiful concubines. I had everything a man could desire!
>
> —Ecclesiastes 2:4–8

What was Solomon's conclusion after his spending spree? "This is all so meaningless!" (verse 15).

We do not mean to imply that all buying is bad. God loves to bless His children. It is a good thing when we can meet our own needs and even indulge our moderate and reasonable desires for pleasure. The problem lies in excessive accumulation of "stuff" out of a desire to meet some inner need.

We will let you decide, through seeking the mind of Christ in prayer, what "excessive" means for you. But one thing we know: possessions do not confer meaning upon a person's life. Jesus said plainly, "Beware! Guard against every kind of greed. Life is not measured by how much you own" (Luke 12:15).

Neither do possessions provide real security, though some people may think they do. In His Sermon on the Mount, Jesus taught about this also:

> Don't store up treasures here on earth, where moths eat them and rust destroys them, and where thieves break in and steal. Store your treasures in heaven, where moths and rust cannot destroy, and thieves do not break in and steal. Wherever your treasure is, there the desires of your heart will also be.
>
> —Matthew 6:19–21

As if to illustrate His words in the Sermon on the Mount, at another time Jesus told a story about a farmer who had a string of good harvests. He began to base a hedonistic plan on his wealth. "I'll sit back and say to myself, My friend, you have enough stored away for years to come. Now take it easy! Eat, drink, and be merry!" (Luke 12:19).

But Jesus said this man was a fool, because that very day was marked down in God's calendar as the day when he would be called to account for his life. The lesson Jesus drew from this story is simple: "A person is a fool to store up earthly wealth but not have a rich relationship with God." (See Luke 12:16–21.)

A person is a fool to store up earthly wealth but not have a rich relationship with God.

MEDIA MAD

Our media options are proliferating like never before. Not only do we have television, radio, and movies, but now we also have computerized gaming systems, the Internet, DVDs, MP3s, hand-held computers, and more. Some people spend untold hours with these media, living vicariously through televised sports or reality TV shows or video games, and there are a couple of problems with this.

Are You Overindulgent?

The following self-evaluation quiz will help you determine whether you have a tendency toward overindulgence.

- Do you feel guilty over your use of any substance or other source of pleasure?
- Have family members or close friends warned you that they think something is wrong?
- Do you lie to cover up how much food or drink you obtain?
- Do you use controlled substances in a way not prescribed by a doctor?
- Do you often eat, drink, or engage in an activity more than you had planned?
- Do you obsessively think about a certain substance or behavior?
- Do you vomit after eating or use laxatives to keep your weight down?
- Do you spend more time staring at a cinema, TV, or computer screen than you spend looking into the faces of the important people in your life?

First, excessive use of media can have a mind-numbing effect. A person who spends hours every week playing Xbox games has some fun and develops a certain type of skill, but is he really becoming a wiser, deeper, more godly person? It is not likely.

Second, too much time with entertainment distracts from other activities that are equally or more important. For example, someone who has what is dubbed a "Net addiction" may spend so much time online that she neglects her schoolwork, job, or family.

Perhaps we are in something like the position of the wealthy people of Judah in the prophet Amos's time. Amos warned,

> How terrible for you who sprawl on ivory beds and lounge on your couches, eating the meat of tender lambs from the flock and of choice calves fattened in the stall. *You sing trivial songs to the sound of the harp and fancy yourselves to be great musicians like David.* You drink wine by the bowlful and perfume yourselves with fragrant lotions. You care nothing about the ruin of your nation. Therefore, you will be the first to be led away as captives.
>
> —Amos 6:4–7 emphasis added

Clearly the upper classes of Judah were overindulging in a number of types of luxury, including some we have already covered. As part of their error, they were indulging excessively in the entertainment of music when they should have been attending to more important matters.

Will the consequences for us be "terrible" (as Amos said) if we keep spending our lives with our eyes glued to video screens and with earphones stuffed in our ears? It would be better not to find out.

APPETITES OUT OF CONTROL

Along with more obvious forms of overindulgence, there are many other ways people may let their appetites get out of control like a stallion that leaps a fence. A mother might spend far more time working out at the gym than she needs to keep in shape, neglecting her family responsibilities in the process. A young person might love the adrenaline rush from thrill-seeking activities, such as extreme skiing and class-5 river rafting, to the point that he risks his life. And what about caffeine? Or cigarettes?

As diverse as are the moral weak points of the human race, so diverse are the forms overindulgence may take. Yet all forms of overindulgence have something in common: they are ways of feeding an appetite. "All sins are attempts to fill voids," claimed Simone Weil. That is certainly true of the sins of overindulgence.

As diverse as are the moral weak points of the human race, so diverse are the forms overindulgence may take.

People have a type of hunger, real or perceived, and then try to feed it in a way that is inappropriate. Maybe they are greedy for sensation. Or maybe they have an emotional hurt and are trying to mask it with a high or the yumminess of a dessert or a "fun fix." Either way, they need to understand their real problem and address it in a healthy way. Overindulgence will only make matters worse.

Other motivators may also contribute to an overindulgence problem. For example, someone may abuse drugs as a way of rebelling against his strict upbringing. Rebellion, anger, disobedience—these are just a few of the sins that may complicate our tendencies toward self-indulgence.

"But wait," you might say. "Is overindulgence really our fault? Might the real issue be illness, not sin?" Let's consider that.

THE MEDICAL MODEL

One day I (Bill) received a call from the wife of an alcoholic. The woman said her husband was a wonderful person when he was sober but a demon when he was drinking. Why did he keep drinking?

Another day I talked with a young man who was on drugs. He was deathly afraid that he would be caught, end up in jail, and get a police record. Still, something about drugs wooed him to go on another trip, to smoke another joint.

These people have a compulsion to continue in their particular form of overindulgence—no doubt about it. Many others have the same problem. But how are we to understand such a compulsion?

The preferred approach at present is to use a medical model. In other words, people who cannot seem to stop drinking or taking drugs are deemed to have a disease, called an addiction. A genetic cause is at the root of the addiction, and the addiction needs to be treated with methods commonly used for other physical and emotional diseases.

There is some value in the medical model. Along with such factors as personality or temperament, a person's genes may give him or her some predisposition to addictive behavior. And sometimes medical treatments, such as methadone treatments for heroin addicts, have proven helpful. But even given such advantages, the medical model is woefully incomplete.

By labeling overindulgent behaviors a "disease," the medical model effectively cuts off the spiritual and ethical aspects of the human being involved. A person's behavior may be an addiction, but it is also *sin*. We have a responsibility—and a real potential—to do what is right, even if we have allowed a certain substance to gain a measure of control over us. Ultimately overindulgence is treatable only by the soul surgery of repentance.

That's what a young man named Franklin found out to his great surprise.

A LIAR WHO ENCOUNTERED THE TRUTH

Franklin had it all—all the problems you could imagine, that is. He liked to drink too much, take illegal drugs, and sleep around with both men and women. He was also insecure, unhappy, and riddled with guilt. He knew his life was a time bomb waiting to go off, but he had no idea of how to talk to God about his problems. Finally, he went to a counselor.

"Doc, I need to quit drinking and doing drugs. But I can't stop." Franklin started to sob.

"Well," the counselor replied, "I'm glad you are here. But I already have my doubts that you are ready to change. You've said two things to me, and one of them is not true. We are not going to get anywhere with an attitude like that."

"Lying? What are you talking about? I need help, not word games!"

"You said something irrational, Franklin. You said you couldn't stop drinking and using drugs. Are you drinking and using drugs right now, or are you talking to me?"

Franklin said, "Of course I'm not taking drugs now! I'm talking to a worthless counselor who accuses me of lying the moment I sit down!"

"Then," the counselor replied, "you admit that you can control when you abuse yourself and when you do not?"

Franklin began to think about his level of control. He did not drink until after 5:30 P.M. He did not do illegal drugs except on certain days. He had a favorite drink (gin and tonic) and would not touch domestic beer. He actually began to relax as he described his favorite blend of drugs and alcohol and how, if he timed it right, he could party all night, get an hour's sleep on the bus going to work, and take an "upper" with his first cup of coffee and work all day without a break.

This took up most of Franklin's first session. Before he left, the counselor asked two questions: "Franklin, why do you enjoy talking about the greatest enemies you have—the very things that will kill you if you don't stop using them to alter your thoughts, feelings, and behaviors? Why are you so angry at God that you would keep lashing out at Him in flagrant disobedience?"

Franklin did not have an answer to those questions. But he had started thinking in a new way.

CHOOSE YOUR MASTER

Would Franklin submit to the control of God, or would he give up control to his appetites? All people who overindulge face the same question.

Not being controlled is not an option. We were made to worship and to serve another outside ourselves. And so we will always serve someone or something, and many choose to make their appetite their god, whether that appetite is for Jim Beam whiskey or lines of white powder or a third plateful at Country Buffet. The only worthy master is God. He is the one we were made to serve.

Of course, there is such a thing as Christian freedom. Some would justify indulging their appetites on the basis of that freedom.

We will always serve someone or something, and many choose to make their appetite their god.

But the apostle Paul preempted such an argument: "You say, 'I am allowed to do anything'—but not everything is good for you. And even though 'I am allowed to do anything,' I must not become a slave to anything" (1 Corinthians 6:12).

No, we must not become a slave to anything. Not drink. Not drugs. Not food. Not anything. We must serve God alone. As we do so, He will enable us to make better choices in what we will consume. He will heal us spiritually, enabling us to partake of substances or experiences in moderation (if limited consumption is safe) or keep a distance from whatever substance or experience threatens to destroy us.

EVERYTHING IN MODERATION

Have you had enough of too much? Are you willing to admit that your overindulgence is a sin? If so, we hope you will take action now by emptying your life of the sin and by filling the empty space with something far better. The virtue with which we should replace a sin of overindulgence is *moderation.*

"Do you like honey?" asked Solomon. "Don't eat too much, or it will make you sick!" (Proverbs 25:16). This call to moderation is appropriate to many but not all kinds of overindulgence.

Moderation is the proper response when overindulgence often involves substances or experiences that are good in themselves. In itself, food is good; we need it to survive, and it provides enjoyment. In themselves, a house and the things we put in it are good; they help us to live our lives in safety and satisfaction. In itself, entertainment is good; it gives us both relaxation and mental stimulation. What's bad is when we use these good things to the point of excess. Defining what is "excess" is a challenging, personal struggle.

This perversion of the good for evil is a pattern that has long been understood. Eighteenth-century devotional writer William Law said,

> Our souls may receive an infinite hurt, and be rendered incapable of all virtue, merely by the use of innocent and lawful things....

What is more lawful than eating and drinking? And yet what more destructive of all virtue, what more fruitful of all vice, than sensuality and indulgence?…

Now it is for want of religious exactness in the use of these innocent and lawful things, that religion cannot get possession of our hearts. And it is in the right and prudent management of ourselves, as to these things, that all the art of holy living chiefly consists.[8]

In other cases, however, overindulgence involves substances or experiences that are wrong, period. Shooting heroin, for example, is always illegal and always destructive. The response in a situation like this should be what we might call an extreme form of moderation: abstinence. Here, any indulgence is overindulgence.

Also, there are the gray areas. We can all agree that it is wrong to get drunk, since the Bible is so clear on that point, but should Christians drink only in moderation or should they not drink at all? Both the authors of this book have chosen not to drink at all, so as to avoid any risk associated with drunkenness or dependence on alcohol. We would advise anyone else who has had a problem with overindulgence to likewise avoid the risk of drunkenness by avoiding alcohol altogether. For the rest, we say again: moderation. Through prayer, you can seek God's help to know whether moderation or abstinence is right for you in a given instance—and what "moderation" would mean in your case.

Moderation is what God wants to see in our lives.

Truly, moderation is what God wants to see in our lives. As we overindulge in our favorite ways, God grieves because He knows we are not filling ourselves with what we really need, and that is more of Himself. We can never get too much of God.

SOUL PRESCRIPTION FOR OVERINDULGENCE

Are you struggling with some form of overindulgence? We have outlined a five-step process to help you repent and heal in this area of your life. Take all the time you need with each of the steps below.

Step 1: Adopt a Correct View of God

If you are overindulgent with yourself, it is important that you understand God better as the loving Father. He has promised you that He will always provide for your physical, emotional, and spiritual needs. You do not need to stuff yourself with whatever you can get your hands on.

- God is all-knowing. He designed you and knows what would make you the happiest.

   > "I know the plans I have for you," says the LORD. "They are plans for good and not for disaster, to give you a future and a hope."
   > —Jeremiah 29:11

- God is love. He will always give you only what is good for you.

   > Whatever is good and perfect comes down to us from God our Father, who created all the lights in the heavens.
   > —James 1:17

- God is faithful. He will always provide for your needs.

   > The LORD will withhold no good thing from those who do what is right.
   > —Psalm 84:11

Do not let a warped view of God justify your overindulgent lifestyle any longer. Undertake a search of Scripture for passages that depict God as your provider who satisfies you.

Step 2: Revise Your False Beliefs

God has called you to a life of holiness and moderate living. When you choose a different course for life, it proves that you really do not believe God will hold you accountable for your actions.

The following questions are designed to expose false beliefs of overindulgence.

• Do you believe you have the right to party excessively?

> You have had enough in the past of the evil things that godless people enjoy—their immorality and lust, their feasting and drunkenness and wild parties, and their terrible worship of idols.
>
> —1 Peter 4:3

• Do you believe you have no choice in controlling your appetites?

> Therefore, dear brothers and sisters, you have no obligation to do what your sinful nature urges you to do.
>
> —Romans 8:12

• Do you believe you are not responsible for your sinful overindulgence?

> We are each responsible for our own conduct.
>
> —Galatians 6:5

Try as you may, you just cannot lay the responsibility for your excessive self-indulgence on the shoulders of anyone other than yourself. Learn from Scripture what is really true about self-indulgent behavior versus self-control.

Step 3: Repent of Your Sin

You must make the decision to turn away from your lifestyle of overindulgence and to disconnect your heart, mind, and spirit from that which enslaves you. Give your particular type of over-indulgence a name (drunkenness, gluttony, or whatever else it may be).

Confess your sin to God and ask His forgiveness. If you wish, you can use the following prayer (inserting your own sin in the blank).

> Father, I have sinned against you by _____. I know that this hurts You, and I am sorry for that. Please forgive me for the sake of Christ. Make me clean, Lord, removing from my heart the desires that have enslaved me. Fill me with the Holy Spirit, and through Him give me the strength to walk the path of righteousness one day at a time. In Jesus' name, amen.

If you have harmed others with your sin, apologize to them. Seek reconciliation and offer restitution where appropriate.

Step 4: Defend against Spiritual Attacks

Now that you have repented and been set free from your sin, this freedom must be defended. You have to understand the tactics of your enemies and defend against them accordingly.

- The world tells you, "It's your body and you can do what you want with it." Overcome the world system by rejecting such a distorted value. Embrace the value God places on self-control and moderation over self-indulgence. Listen to Him and not to the world.
- Your flesh wants the gratifications of physical sensations. So when such desires arise, remember that your flesh is dead; you are now living by the Spirit. You do not have to do what your flesh wants.

> Those who live only to satisfy their own sinful nature will harvest decay and death from that sinful nature. However, those who live to please the Spirit will harvest everlasting life from the Spirit.
>
> —Galatians 6:8

- Satan will encourage you to satisfy your desires for excessive self-indulgence. Hold up the "shield of faith" to stop the fiery arrows of the devil (Ephesians 6:16), showing you realize that ungodly self-indulgence does not offer lasting satisfaction.

The temptation to overindulge oneself tends to be especially persistent in a person's life. Plan on remaining vigilant toward your enemies' attacks for the rest of your life. The battle is long, but in God's power you *can* be victorious.

Step 5: Flee Temptation

Take proactive measures if you wish to remain free from the sin of overindulgence. By reducing temptation, you can improve the chances of your success.

- Focus on your relationship with God.

  > Start every day with God. Give Him your attention and devotion instead of concentrating on the thing that once held you captive to your selfish desires. Consider fasting periodically as a reminder that "People do not live by bread alone, but by every word that comes from the mouth of God."
  >
  > —Mathew 4:4

- Latch on to God's promises.
  Find truths in Scripture that will encourage you in your resistance to the temptations of overindulgence. Memorize key verses for recall when you need them. Here is one verse we recommend:

  > The Holy Spirit produces this kind of fruit in our lives: love, joy, peace, patience, kindness, goodness, faithfulness, gentleness, and *self–control*. There is no law against these things!
  >
  > —Galatians 5:22–23, emphasis added

- Establish safeguards.
  What situations tend to encourage your excessive self-indulgence? Take decisive action to avoid those situations as much as possible. For example,

- If you are irresponsible in your eating, plan reasonable menus a week at a time and buy only what you will need.
- If you get drunk, remove all the alcohol from your house, ask your friends not to serve alcohol when you are around, and never go to an eating establishment that serves liquor.
- If you watch too much TV, get rid of your television set or put a timer on it.
- Ask a trusted Christian friend to hold you accountable in your commitment to not overindulge.

- Expect victory.
  You have the Spirit of God living in you and imparting to you everything you need to win this fight. Yield to Him daily in anticipation of total deliverance from your sin habit. When you do this, He will replace your self-indulgent desires with moderation and self-control.

Visit www.SoulPrescription.com for more insights and resources, and to download a free leader's guide for small group Bible studies.

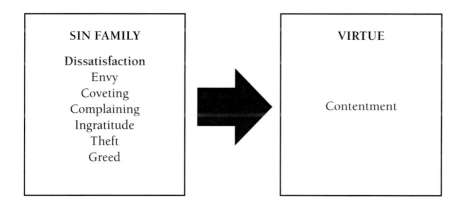

DISSATISFACTION:
THE RESTLESS HEART

SIN FAMILY	VIRTUE
Dissatisfaction Envy Coveting Complaining Ingratitude Theft Greed	Contentment

In his autobiography, *Just As I Am*, Billy Graham told the story of meeting two men on a Caribbean island he was visiting with his wife, Ruth.

> One of the wealthiest men in the world asked us to come to his lavish home for lunch. He was seventy-five years old, and throughout the entire meal he seemed close to tears.

> "I am the most miserable man in the world," he said. "Out there is my yacht. I can go anywhere I want to.

I have my private plane, my helicopters. I have everything I want to make me happy. And yet I'm miserable as hell."

We talked with him and had prayer with him, trying to point him to Christ, who alone gives lasting meaning to life.

Then we went down the hill to a small cottage where we were staying. That afternoon the pastor of the local Baptist church came to call. He was an Englishman, and he too was seventy-five. A widower, he spent most of his free time taking care of his two invalid sisters. He reminded me of a cricket—always jumping up and down, full of enthusiasm and love for Christ and for others.

"I don't have two pounds to my name," he said with a smile, "but I'm the happiest man on this island."[1]

One man rich and miserable, the other poor and joy-filled. Worldly values would tell us that the two men ought to have swapped attitudes. So what is the truth of the matter? Why are some people chronically dissatisfied, while others are content with the way things are? There must be something fundamentally flawed in the soul of one who is always dissatisfied. It must be a sin issue.

Having said that, we hasten to add that not all dissatisfaction is sinful. For instance, there is nothing wrong with dissatisfaction at sin and injustice. We *should* be dissatisfied with these wrongs and strive to correct them. (Your reading this book presumably reflects a godly dissatisfaction with habitual sin in your life.)

There is also nothing wrong with a dissatisfaction that exists because so much still remains to be done to build Christ's kingdom. If God has given you a vision for what He wants you to accomplish for Him, you certainly may let your dissatisfaction with your partial progress impel you to greater work in the future. Ambition and contentment are not necessarily opposed to one another.

The kind of dissatisfaction we are concerned with here is the kind that says, "I want more money, more stuff, more fun, more comfort in life—and I deserve it. I'd better take over the responsibility for myself; God isn't doing a good enough job."

But dissatisfaction is not only a slap in the face of God; it is also a way we rob ourselves of the joy we might have day by day, because we obsess about what we might have in the future instead of enjoying what we *do* have in the present. And as we become restless, resentful, and bitter, other people naturally prefer not to be around us.

Contentment ought to be the birthright (or rather, the new-birth right) of all Christians. However, not all enjoy contentment. What about you? Are you dissatisfied? Do you have a problem with envy or greed? Is your attitude marked by complaining and ingratitude? Are you prepared to steal and grab to get what you want?

Read on. From personal experience, we (Bill and Henry) know how strong the pull of greed or discontentment can be. But we also believe that the following scriptural truths will convict you of dissatisfaction. The soul prescription will help you root contentment in your soul like a vigorous new plant.

THE GRASS ON THE OTHER SIDE OF THE FENCE

One day years ago, I (Henry) was riding a horse across a ranch in Texas. The ranch property stretched over the horizon, with the only intrusion being the highway that ran through its middle. Now, you would think that the cattle on such a vast ranch would have all the grass they want, wouldn't you? But what did I see? I observed a cow stretching its neck through the barbed-wire fence to nibble grass on the highway's right-of-way.

Isn't that like us? We have so much, but we want more. If somebody else has got it and we do not, we want it. Even if we do not need it, and even if God has offered no indication that He wants to give it to us, we think it has got to be ours.

This attitude goes by the name of *envy* or *jealousy* or *covetousness*. (For our purposes, we'll use the words interchangeably.)

Are You Dissatisfied?

The following self-evaluation quiz will help you determine whether you have a tendency toward dissatisfaction.

- Do you dwell on what you would like to have more than on what you do have?
- Do you complain to others or God about what you are lacking?
- Do you neglect to thank God for the good things He has given you?
- Do you look at others' advantages in life and wish you had what they have?
- Do you scheme to gain more money and possessions than you really need?
- Are you tempted to take what belongs to others?
- Do you think of your possessions as belonging to you rather than to God?

Whatever you call this attitude, it is an improper craving for something another person possesses to such an extent that you cannot be happy unless you have it. It is a sinful desire for things that belong to your neighbor.

God condemned this attitude in the Ten Commandments, saying, "You must not covet your neighbor's house. You must not covet your neighbor's wife, male or female servant, ox or donkey, or anything else that belongs to your neighbor" (Exodus 20:17).[2] As the commandment suggests, the object of covetousness might be almost anything.

Most obviously, the object of coveting might be a material possession. In the Bible, for example, we read how King Ahab coveted Naboth's vineyard. (See 1 Kings 21.) We might want the new car our neighbor purchased or the big house our friend just acquired.

Also, we might be jealous over a person, perhaps someone else's attractive spouse. That was what happened when David spied Uriah's wife, Bathsheba, bathing in her yard. (See 2 Samuel 11:2–4.) Many a person today is similarly consumed with desire for another person's wife or husband.

We might also be envious of a personal quality or advantage that another person possesses. Jacob envied Esau's blessing and birthright as the older brother. (See Genesis 25:27). We might wish we had another person's good looks or social ease or singing ability.

It is not always wrong to want a possession, person, or quality. There is nothing necessarily blameworthy about wanting to have a new car or to be married or to be able to sing well. It is when we desire *someone else's* car or spouse or voice that we go wrong with envy. It is then that we sin and violate the tenth commandment.

Envy can become a habit as we brood over what we want.

Envy can become a habit as we brood over what we want. Our obsessive and misplaced desire can easily be compounded by other sins as we seek to get that which we lack from others. King Ahab murdered Naboth. David had an affair with Bathsheba. Jacob conned Esau out of his rightful blessing and birthright. All of these situations was the outworking of envy.

The message for us is simple: "Don't participate in...jealousy" (Romans 13:13).

Meanwhile, another form of dissatisfaction—greed—is just as bad for the Christian.

UNAPPEASABLE APPETITE FOR WEALTH

Early media mogul William Randolph Hearst invested a fortune in collecting art treasures from around the world. One day Hearst read the description of a valuable art item, which he then sent his agent abroad to locate. After months of searching, the agent reported that he had finally found the treasure. To the surprise of Hearst, the priceless masterpiece was stored in a warehouse belonging to none other than William Randolph Hearst.

Hearst had so much that he did not even know what he had. But that did not stop him from wanting more. Greed had set him to running in a circle. It is like a hunger that is never satisfied but only becomes more voracious as it is fed.

Greed is the inordinate love of money and what money can buy. It is a form of dissatisfaction with one's financial position that results in striving selfishly for more money rather than seeking after God. Thus, money may displace the Lord at the height of our affections.

"You can be sure that no...greedy person will inherit the Kingdom of Christ and of God," warned the apostle Paul. "For a greedy person is an idolater, worshiping the things of this world" (Ephesians 5:5).

Jesus likewise said, "No one can serve two masters. For you will hate one and love the other; you will be devoted to one and despise the other. You cannot serve both God and money" (Matthew 6:24). Notice that Jesus did not say we *should not* serve two masters but that we *cannot*. It is impossible to combine ultimate obedience to God while having ultimate obedience to any other person or thing, including wealth.

The Bible is consistent in condemning greed. We are warned, "Beware! Guard against every kind of greed. Life is not measured by how much you own" (Luke 12:15). And we are told, "Don't love money; be satisfied with what you have" (Hebrews 13:5). Nevertheless, greed is so widespread in our time that we might wonder if we live in the last days when "people will love only themselves and their money" (2 Timothy 3:2).

Greed, incidentally, is a temptation that affects rich and poor alike. Those of us with modest means cannot assume that greed is a failing that belongs only to the William Randolph Hearsts of the world. What matters is not how much you have but how badly you want more and what you are willing to do to get it.

It is possible to make a distinction between an acceptable desire for money and a sinful desire. Ask yourself these questions to test whether your desire for wealth is acceptable to God.

What is your motive for wanting more money? Is it because you are having trouble meeting the basic needs and wants that you and your family have? Is it because you want to give more generously to the work of God? These are good reasons for wanting more money.

What is your plan for acquiring more money? While working to acquire greater wealth, will you trust God to meet your needs and never forget that He is what you need most of all? Will you honor Him by pursuing financial gain in a just and ethical way, remembering to be generous to others along the way?

If your desire for money meets the requirements, work as hard at it as you like! If you fail the tests, on the other hand, you should be concerned about the kinds of wickedness you are being drawn into. A selfish desire for money that we do not really need is a soul crippler.

Paul made the same point, by observing, "True religion with contentment is great wealth."

> Yet true godliness with contentment is itself great wealth. After all, we brought nothing with us when we came into the world, and we can't take anything with us when we leave it. So if we have enough food and clothing, let us be content. But people who long to be rich fall into temptation and are trapped by many foolish and harmful desires that plunge them into ruin and destruction. For the love of money is the root of all kinds of evil. And some people, craving money, have wandered from the true faith and pierced themselves with many sorrows.
>
> —1 Timothy 6:6–10

Judas Iscariot's story bears out Paul's words in 1 Timothy. This man "was a thief, and since he was in charge of the disciples' money, he often stole some for himself" (John 12:6). In the end he went to the religious leaders and asked, "How much will you pay me to betray Jesus to you?" (Matthew 26:15). They offered him thirty pieces of silver and he took it.

Once Jesus was arrested, Judas was overcome by remorse. He threw the blood money back, but it was too late. He killed himself, and the thirty pieces of silver were used to buy a cemetery where, perhaps, Judas himself was buried. (See Matthew 27:3–10.) Thus greed ended up where it naturally will (unless repentance intervenes first): in death.

But before greed comes to an end, it contributes to all kinds of evil effects. One of these may be thievery.

HANDS THAT TAKE INSTEAD OF WORK

When greed and envy mate, they often produce the ugly offspring of stealing. This is the sin of taking money or possessions belonging to another. The Bible affirms the right to property, and so seizing what belongs to another rates God's condemnation. "You must not steal" (Exodus 20:15).[3]

To see the true extent of this sin, we need to define "stealing" widely enough. Failing to pay bills or taxes that we owe is stealing. Doing less work than we are being paid for is stealing. Using copyrighted material without the permission of the owner is stealing.

With such a definition, we can see that stealing is not so rare a problem as we might otherwise have thought. In fact, many people are willing to steal if they think they can get away with it. How quickly will normal law-abiding citizens resort to looting when the power goes out? How many "good" people download software or music files that belong to another?

The rule is this: if it is not yours, leave it alone. Never steal!

Paul was aware that stealing was a problem in the early church. He told new believers, "If you are a thief, quit stealing. Instead, use your hands for good hard work, and then give generously to others in need" (Ephesians 4:28). The same word applies to you if you steal. You may be pleasantly surprised by the changes it brings to your life.

Many years ago, a businessman approached me (Bill) and shared his desire to experience the blessing of the Spirit-filled life. But he said that every time he got down on his knees to pray to be filled with the Holy Spirit, he was convicted about what he had stolen from his employer.

I told him to confess his sin to God, then go to his employer and make restitution. He was terribly concerned that his employer would fire him, but he agreed to go.

When the man shared his dishonesty with his employer, he was shocked by his boss's response. His boss actually congratulated him for his honesty. Then the employer offered a plan that would take a small amount of what the man had stolen out of his paycheck each week until all had been repaid.

The result was that, not only did the formerly dishonest man learn a valuable lesson, but also two days later he was by faith filled with the Holy Spirit!

Trust God. Respect others' property. Do the right thing—stop stealing.

Also learn to stop complaining about what you do not have. We see the prevalence of such ingratitude in a story from the life of Jesus.

THE ATTITUDE OF INGRATITUDE

In ancient Israel the destiny of persons with infectious skin diseases was a hard one. They were required to quarantine themselves from the rest of society, leading to loneliness and a struggle for survival. But those shunned by others received the loving attention of our Lord.

> As Jesus continued on toward Jerusalem, he reached the border between Galilee and Samaria. As he entered a village there, ten lepers stood at a distance, crying out, "Jesus, Master, have mercy on us!"

> He looked at them and said, "Go show yourselves to the priests." And as they went, they were cleansed of their leprosy.

One of them, when he saw that he was healed, came back to Jesus, shouting, "Praise God!" He fell to the ground at Jesus' feet, thanking him for what he had done. This man was a Samaritan.

Jesus asked, "Didn't I heal ten men? Where are the other nine? Has no one returned to give glory to God except this foreigner?"

—Luke 17:11–18

Who are you more like: the grateful one or the ungrateful nine? If you have a problem with dissatisfaction, it is a safe bet that you are not as thankful to God as you should be, for a grateful attitude drives out dissatisfaction.

The ungrateful become complainers as soon as they put their regrets into words. To God and to others, they retail what is missing from their wish list for life. This is an insult to God—and it probably does not make them popular with their friends either. The Scriptures tell us, "Do everything without complaining and arguing" (Philippians 2:14). Instead of complaining, we should be praising God.

Paul declared, "All praise to God, the Father of our Lord Jesus Christ, who has blessed us with every spiritual blessing in the heavenly realms because we are united with Christ!" (Ephesians 1:3). If God gave us nothing but salvation through faith in His Son, along with salvation's spiritual blessings, that ought to be enough to silence our complaining tongues forever. But He gives us much more.

Stop for a minute and think about what you *do* have. You would like to have more money—but how much money *do* you have? There are some things you would like to own—but what *do* you own? Perhaps your physical health is limited—but what *can* you do? How are you blessed with abilities that enable you to create beauty, with friends who bring richness to life, or with good memories that warm your heart in moments of solitude?

Whatever is good and perfect comes down to us from God our Father.

—James 1:17

A Bible secret to banishing dissatisfaction is thanking our gift-giving God. "Pray about everything. Tell God what you need, and thank Him for all He has done" (Philippians 4:6). "Give thanks for everything to God the Father in the name of our Lord Jesus Christ" (Ephesians 5:20). The Bible even says, "Believers who are poor have something to boast about, for God has honored them" (James 1:9).

Gratitude is a like a lens that helps us refocus our attention from our perceived lacks to our actual blessings from God.

Gratitude is like a lens that helps us refocus our attention from our perceived lacks (which might not be good for us anyway) to our actual blessings from God. In this way, gratitude leads us to contentment and brings healing to our soul.

ALL IS WELL

The task of one with a dissatisfaction habit is not only to eliminate the sin of dissatisfaction from his or her life but also to cultivate the virtue of contentment. Contentment is a special benefit available to all followers of Jesus Christ. It is not something we can work up on our own. Rather, it *is* something we can receive as a gift while we cooperate with the Holy Spirit's work in our lives.

In *The Art of Divine Contentment*, Puritan Thomas Watson offered one of the best definitions of contentment: "It is a sweet temper of spirit, whereby a Christian carries himself in an equal poise in every condition." In other words, it is a kind of satisfaction that depends only on the presence of God in our lives, not on whether we are presently up or down in the changing mix of life's circumstances.

Contentment is not consistent with unrighteous desires, for unrighteous desires will always trouble our spirit. However, being content does not necessarily mean we give up wanting things that are legitimately good. Thomas Watson observed of Hannah in the Old Testament, "Hannah's spirit was burdened; 'I am,' says she, 'a woman of sorrowful spirit.' Now having prayed, and wept, she went away, and was no more sad; only here is the difference between a holy complaint and a discontented complaint; in the one we complain to God, in the other we complain of God."[4] We can pray to God for what we do not have even while we thank Him for what we do have.

The apostle Paul had discovered how to live with an equal poise in every condition.

> I have learned how to be content with whatever I have. I know how to live on almost nothing or with everything. I have learned the secret of living in every situation, whether it is with a full stomach or empty, with plenty or little.
>
> —Philippians 4:11–13

When Christ fills your heart and mind, you can be at peace and content with the things, people, and circumstances our sovereign God has placed in your life. The only thing that truly satisfies is knowing Jesus Christ. Striving, coveting, and spending our time wanting what is not available to us can leave us broken and bitter.

God is orchestrating life's circumstances leading us toward the fulfillment of His plans for our individual lives and for history as a whole. Contentment is a result of trusting the fact that God knows perfectly what is best to give us and when. It is saying yes to His blessings upon us. They are enough; we need no more.

Contentment is a result of trusting that God knows perfectly what is best to give us and when.

Someday God will share with us all the wealth of heaven. Our lifestyle then will be far greater than even that experienced by the rich man in the Caribbean whom Ruth and Billy Graham visited, with none of the emptiness in his soul. And in the meantime, each of us who knows the Lord can enjoy the "endless treasures available to them in Christ" (Ephesians 3:8).

SOUL PRESCRIPTION FOR DISSATISFACTION

Are you struggling with some type of dissatisfaction, such as envy, complaining, or greed? We have outlined a five-step process to help you repent and heal in this area of your life. Take all the time you need with each of the steps below.

Step 1: Adopt a Correct View of God

Flaws in your view of God can easily produce dissatisfaction in your life. For example, you may have made the mistake of looking to God as your own personal genie who should grant your every wish. On the other hand, you may see Him as some miserly old hermit who would not give a bone to a dog. Either viewpoint would greatly affect your ability to be content and satisfied.

- God is sovereign, and He is in control of your life.

    With my great strength and powerful arm I made the earth and all its people and every animal. I can give these things of Mine to anyone I choose.
    —Jeremiah 27:5

- God is faithful. He will always do what is best for us.

    So the LORD must wait for you to come to Him so He can show you His love and compassion. For the LORD is a faithful God. Blessed are those who wait for His help.
    —Isaiah 30:18

Through searching the Scriptures, learn more about God as Sovereign Lord. As you do so, consider how flaws in your view of God might be at the root of your problem of dissatisfaction. Ask God to help you understand Him as He really is.

Step 2: Revise Your False Beliefs

The belief that we deserve everything we want and more does not line up with God's Holy Word. The belief that happiness comes with possessions or position is in direct opposition to God's truth. Such examples of false beliefs about people and life can fuel dissatisfaction. Ask yourself the following questions:

- Do you believe you would be happy if you had more money?

    Don't love money; be satisfied with what you have. For God has said, "I will never fail you. I will never abandon you."
    —Hebrews 13:5

- Do you believe you would be happy if you looked different?

> Don't be concerned about the outward beauty of fancy hairstyles, expensive jewelry, or beautiful clothes. You should clothe yourselves instead with the beauty that comes from within, the unfading beauty of a gentle and quiet spirit, which is so precious to God.
>
> —1 Peter 3:3–4

- Do you believe you would be happy if you had a better job?

> Each of you should continue to live in whatever situation the Lord has placed you, and remain as you were when God first called you.
>
> —1 Corinthians 7:17

These questions reveal false beliefs that breed discontentment. Other such false beliefs are possible. Spend time searching the Word for its perspective on contentment. Ask the Holy Spirit to show you where your thinking has fallen off track and then to accept the truth.

Step 3: Repent of Your Sin

Are you ready to turn away from dissatisfaction? Begin by specifically identifying the way you tend to be dissatisfied (envy, ingratitude, or whatever). Next, pray a prayer of confession to God. If you wish, you may use the one below, inserting the name of your sin of dissatisfaction in the blank.

> God, I know that everything I have is a gift from You. Yet I have been dissatisfied through _____. I realize that my discontentment is born from a selfish and sinful heart, and I am truly sorry for my attitude. Please forgive me and wash all the discontentment out of my heart. Make me able to put _____ behind me for good and learn to be content. In the name of Jesus Christ, amen.

If you have harmed others with your sin, apologize to them. Seek reconciliation and offer restitution where appropriate.

Step 4: Defend against Spiritual Attacks

Remember, you must always be on your guard against attack from the three enemies of your soul: the world, the flesh, and the Devil. They will conspire to draw you back to your old habits of dissatisfaction.

- The world's value system perpetuates dissatisfaction as it preaches, "Always want more and better." Expose yourself to God's truth to the point that you have fully understood that a life of contentment is the best way to live.
- Your flesh, or sinful nature, will continue to crave its old objects of desire, whether it is more money, possessions, or people. Tell yourself every day, "My flesh is dead. I live by the Spirit now." Rely on the Holy Spirit for help in every temptation.
- Satan uses our neighbor's standard of living to breed discontent in our hearts. Put on "salvation as your helmet" (Ephesians 6:17) for protection from poisonous thoughts of envy.

Keep on the lookout for any temptation that would draw you back into your old ways of dissatisfaction. Seek God's strength to defend against spiritual attacks. His strength is sufficient.

Step 5: Flee Temptation

We are told in James 1:14 that the source of temptation lies in "our own desires." The desire for more, or for something different and new, is a catalyst for dissatisfaction. This desire must be kept under control over the long term by taking certain precautions.

- Focus on your relationship with God.
  Do not be satisfied with a brief quiet time in the morning and a trip to church once a week. Develop a devotional life

that spreads into your whole existence. As you keep your thoughts on God and His kingdom, instead of the things of this world, you will be less susceptible to temptations of dissatisfaction.

- Latch on to God's promises.
  Find verses in the Bible that are meaningful to you in your battle against dissatisfaction. Memorize these verses and re-call them whenever temptation strikes. Here are two verses for your consideration:

  > If God cares so wonderfully for wildflowers that are here today and thrown into the fire tomorrow, He will certainly care for you.
  > —Matthew 6:30

  > The LORD will withhold no good thing from those who do what is right.
  > —Psalm 84:11

- Establish safeguards.
  Make changes in your life that will keep you away from the most common temptations that have produced dissatisfaction for you. Be creative, and come up with as many changes as will help you. Then, don't forget to implement them! Consider these examples to spark your own ideas:

  - If you find yourself envying something another person possesses, immediately thank God for one blessing He has given you.
  - If you tend to be greedy, volunteer at a homeless shelter or some other ministry to the poor that will help you see how comfortable you really are.
  - Ask a trusted Christian friend to hold you accountable in your commitment to not be so dissatisfied.

- Expect victory.

   Remember that success in defeating the habitual sin of dissatisfaction can be found in the power and presence of the
   Holy Spirit. He is always working in you to make you more
   like Jesus, which includes being content. Yield to Him daily
   in anticipation of deliverance from the crippling habit of
   dissatisfaction.

Visit www.SoulPrescription.com for more insights and resources,
and to download a free leader's guide for small group Bible
studies.

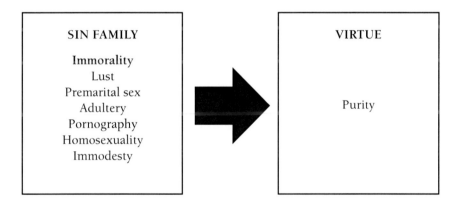

Chapter 14

IMMORALITY: SEX MISUSED

SIN FAMILY	VIRTUE
Immorality Lust Premarital sex Adultery Pornography Homosexuality Immodesty	Purity

Lust is the ape that gibbers in our loins," declares the character Godric in a novel by Frederick Buechner. "Tame him as we will by day, he rages all the wilder in our dreams by night. Just when we think we are safe from him, he raises up his ugly head and smirks, and there's no river in the world flows cold and strong enough to strike him down."

Godric concludes by crying out to heaven, "Almighty God, why dost thou deck men out with such a loathsome toy?"[1]

Many of us might nod along with Godric, having felt inside ourselves a lustfulness that would push us toward sexual immorality. But let us be clear about one thing from the start: it is lust, not sex itself, that is the "loathsome toy" and the "gibbering ape." Lust is unbridled sexual desire that is directed in the wrong way.

Sex per se is not loathsome at all. In fact, when properly expressed (that is, between a man and woman who are married to each other), sex is a great thing—one of God's best blessings to us. Sex without sin is a beautiful act of union, becoming "one flesh." (See Genesis 2:24–25 KJV). An entire book of the Bible, Song of Solomon, uses sexual imagery in a positive way. Only when this good gift of sex is perverted into an evil through lustful desires do we see the multiple expressions of immorality that mar our world.

Here are a few examples of perversion:

- The college student who "hooks up" with strangers at dorm parties.
- The homemaker who costars with a neighbor in her own romantic fantasies.
- The wayward husband who knows the numbers to call-girl services in every city where he travels on business.
- The girl who loves the attention she gets by dressing seductively.
- The man who logs on to immoral websites when his wife and kids have gone to bed.
- The woman who lets herself be led to the bed of another woman whom she once considered just a friend.
- The step-father who darkens the doorway of his step-daughter at night.

These are only a few of the types of sexual immorality that sadden the heart of God.

Counselors sometimes categorize sexual sins as "victimless" sins and "victimizing" sins.[2] Examples of "victimless" sins include calling a phone sex line, viewing pornography, and going to a strip show. Of course, these are not truly victimless activities. For example, someone who buys pornography helps to fund the porn industry, which goes on to ensnare other people with its immoral product. But other than indirectly, these activities involve no one who is participating unwillingly. In that sense, they are "victimless."

Victimizing sexual sins are more dangerous, even criminal. These include such actions as exposing oneself in public, molesting a child, and touching another person in a sexual way without his or her consent. If you or someone you know is involved in any of these kinds of victimizing sexual behaviors, more than just repentance is needed. Immediate intervention may be required to prevent someone from being seriously harmed. If you are connected with a situation like this, seek legal or professional help.

Whether the sexual immorality is "victimless" or "victimizing," it is a violation of God's will for human beings. And since sex is such a powerful "toy" (to use Godric's term), a pattern of sin can quickly set in. Some may call this a "sex addiction," but we prefer to call it a sexual sin habit needing healing.

Recently, I (Henry) was asked by a Christian couple to counsel their twenty-year-old son, who has started sleeping with his girlfriend. When I asked the young man about it, he said he knew his behavior was wrong but he had no desire to quit because he was having the most fun of his life. This is a person who has discovered the power of sex. This young man was caught in a sin habit but had no desire to break from the sin.

Sin habits must be broken. Time and again, Scripture warns us against misusing the gift of sex.

> Don't participate in…sexual promiscuity and immoral living.
>
> —Romans 13:13

> Have nothing to do with sexual immorality, impurity, lust, and evil desires.
>
> —Colossians 3:5

> You have had enough in the past of the evil things that godless people enjoy—their immorality and lust.
>
> —1 Peter 4:3

In another passage, the apostle Paul laid out the rationale for sexual purity among Christians. Since we are spiritually united

Are You Immoral?

The following self-evaluation quiz will help you determine whether you have a tendency toward sexual immorality.

- If you are single, will you be able to honestly say to your future spouse that you have saved yourself for him or her?
- If you are married, have you done (or thought about doing) anything sexually that you would want to hide from your spouse?
- Have you ever had an affair while married (or while the other person was married)?
- Have you ever engaged in sex with someone of your own gender?
- Do you ever choose what you will wear based on how effectively it will attract the attention of the opposite sex?
- Do you ever undress a person of the opposite sex with your mind?
- Do you ever look at pornography, whether "soft" or "hard"?
- Do you spend time fantasizing about sex with anyone other than your spouse?

with the Holy Spirit, we cannot be physically united with anyone other than our spouse.

> But you can't say that our bodies were made for sexual immorality. They were made for the Lord, and the Lord cares about our bodies....
>
> Run from sexual sin! No other sin so clearly affects the body as this one does. For sexual immorality is a sin against your own body. Don't you realize that your body is the temple of the Holy Spirit, who lives in you and was given to you by God? You do not belong to yourself, for God bought you with a high price. So you must honor God with your body.
>   —1 Corinthians 6:13, 18–20

Your body is the temple of the Holy Spirit.

We recognize that the causes for sexual immorality may be complicated. Childhood sexual abuse, for example, often predisposes its victims to making poor choices about their sexuality in later life. One's other sins, such as self-indulgence or deceit, may be related to improper sexual behavior. But regardless of these other factors, sin is still sin.

Let's look at some of the major types of sexual immorality. Do you have a problem with any of these?

SEX WITHOUT MARRIAGE

The older term for sex by unmarried persons is *fornication*. Today we are more likely to call it *premarital sex*. Either way, it is wrong in God's book. A young person (or an older one for that matter!) who is unmarried and tempted to have sex would do well to take to heart Solomon's speech to a young man about the temptation and costs of casual sex, recorded in Proverbs 6:24—7:27.

On the one hand, we are sympathetic to single people who are tempted to engage in premarital sex or who have already given in to that temptation. The sex drive is strong for most people, and without the acceptable outlet of marriage, people may be left with powerful feelings of sexual desire that they do not know how to manage. They consequently may allow their physical longings to override their moral standards and better judgment.

We are also aware that once a single person begins sleeping with a boyfriend or girlfriend, it is hard to quit. The powerful binding effect of physical intimacy makes it hard to break away from the sin habit of premarital sex. (Of course, the binding effect is also what causes much of the heartache that attends sex before marriage.) Desires for affection and security can lead to and reinforce premarital sexual behavior.

Because of the temptations facing single people today, an option that many (even some who profess Christ) would promote is a couple's cohabiting before marriage. This arrangement seems more acceptable than casual sex because it involves a "committed," quasi-married status. And so the practice of "living together" has become almost too commonplace for comment. Currently there are around 5 million unmarried couples living together in America. At least half of all marriages involve couples who have lived together before the ceremony.

But is a "trial marriage" good for the real marriage that follows? It seems not. Scott Stanley, co-director of the Center for Marital and Family Studies at the University of Denver, has found that "men who cohabit with the women they eventually marry are less committed to the union than men who never lived with their spouses ahead of time."[3] Not surprisingly, the divorce rate for those who cohabit and then marry is as much as 50 percent higher than for those who marry without living together first.[4]

In addition to increasing the risk of future divorce, premarital sex carries with it many other costs, including the danger of contracting a sexually transmitted disease, worry about creating an unwanted pregnancy, and the loss of the ability to give a future marriage partner the precious gift of one's virginity. It all adds up to a hefty price tag! But even if there were no practical drawbacks to premarital sex, it would still be wrong. Let's be frank here. Regardless of our sympathy for those tempted to engage in sex before marriage, we must agree with God in calling such behavior sin.

Many have remained chaste before marriage—or even for an entire lifetime. So regardless of how many times you hear that you "can't help" having sex, it *is* possible. No matter how powerful the desire to start or continue having sex before marriage may be, God is more powerful still.

A. C. Green is a former NBA player with the Los Angeles Lakers, as well as other NBA teams. He still holds the "Iron Man" of basketball record for most consecutive games played. Both during and after his basketball career, Green has been an outspoken advocate—especially to youth—of sexual abstinence and about putting an end to premarital sex once it has started. He was married in 2002, but prior to his marriage, he had this to say about sexual purity:

> God is the God of the second chance. I am a virgin by choice, and I hold that decision with honor and respect. But if you can't make that same claim, then God can help you reclaim the virtue of purity. He can enable you to regain self-control and self-respect and that desire to be a strong Christian.[5]

No matter how powerful the desire to start or continue having sex before marriage may be, God is more powerful still.

Regardless of your past sexual history, with God's help you can begin today to choose to remain pure. Every day you wake up alone will be a victory for you and a delight to God.

VIOLATION OF THE MARRIAGE BED

While fornication is sex between two unmarried persons, adultery is sex between two people who are not married to each other and when at least one of them is married to someone else. This violation of sex is called *infidelity* and *extramarital sex.*

One of God's top-ten commandments is "You must not commit adultery" (Exodus 20:14).[6] The author of the letter to the Hebrews offered one of several New Testament repetitions of the original ban on adultery when he wrote, "Marriage should be honored by all, and the marriage bed kept pure, for God will judge the adulterer and all the sexually immoral" (Hebrews 13:4 NIV).

Few people begin a marriage imagining they will ever cheat on their spouse. But time passes and temptations arise. Eventually a spouse finds himself or herself choosing to do what had previously seemed unimaginable.

For some adulterers, an affair can seem to restore the emotional intensity he or she has not felt since courtship before marriage. The intensity of the adultery serves to prolong the guilty relationship. Perhaps the adulterer likes the thrill of the chase. Serial conquests make him or her feel proud. Whatever the motivation, a pattern of destructive feelings, thoughts, and actions has developed.

Intimate relationships with the wrong people are not the only cause of adultery. In Matthew 19:9 the word usually translated "adultery" is *porneia*. It is a general term referring to any kind of sexual trespass. Therefore, such solitary behaviors as entertaining sexual fantasies and viewing pornography might qualify as adultery of a sort.

People caught in the habit of sexual sin keep on violating their marriage vows. They even think they will get away with it. Never! Adultery has subtle—and often not so subtle—destructive effects in this life. Certainly in the next life, adultery will come under divine judgment.

> Can a man scoop a flame into his lap and not have his clothes catch on fire? Can he walk on hot coals and not blister his feet? So it is with the man who sleeps with another man's wife. He who embraces her will not go unpunished....
>
> But the man who commits adultery is an utter fool, for he destroys himself. He will be wounded and disgraced. His shame will never be erased.
> —Proverbs 6:27–29, 32–33

For many unfaithful spouses, the attraction of adultery lies in its forbiddenness. This is nothing new. Solomon described a representative woman named Folly who called out to men, "Come home with me. Stolen water is refreshing; food eaten in secret tastes the best!"

Solomon had an answer for that kind of seduction.

> Drink water from your own well— share your love only with your wife. Why spill the water of your springs in the streets, having sex with just anyone? You should reserve it for yourselves. Never share it with strangers.

> Let your wife be a fountain of blessing for you. Rejoice in the wife of your youth. She is a loving deer, a graceful doe. Let her breasts satisfy you always. May you always be captivated by her love. Why be captivated, my son, by an immoral woman, or fondle the breasts of a promiscuous woman?
>
> —Proverbs 5:15–20

If you feel you do not love your spouse anymore and do love someone else, the answer is not to get involved with that other person; the answer is to yield to the love of God.

Adultery is often the last step in a series of sins that take place within a marriage. Disappointment or conflict in a marriage is never a justifiable cause for adultery. If you feel you do not love your spouse anymore and do love someone else, the answer is not to get involved with that other person; the answer is to yield to the love of God through repentance and obedience. Repentance will change your thoughts and actions so that you can love your spouse and reject all others who would come between you.

SAME-SEX SEX

Few special-interest groups in our society are as vocal and aggressive as the gay rights movement. If members of this movement get their way, they will have all of us believing that sex between persons of the same gender is as right as sex between a husband and a wife. But is it?

The Old Testament law plainly states, "Do not practice homosexuality, having sex with another man as with a woman. It is a detestable sin" (Leviticus 18:22). Male prostitution was a part of pagan worship in the Old Testament, so it had a doubly wicked appeal for some Israelite men. Sentencing guidelines for persons convicted of a homosexual act in ancient Israel decreed it to be a capital offense (Leviticus 20:13).

In New Testament times, the apostle Paul included gay and lesbian acts in his analysis of how the human race has gone astray.

> God abandoned them to their shameful desires. Even the women turned against the natural way to have sex and instead indulged in sex with each other. And the men, instead of having normal sexual relations with women, burned with lust for each other. Men did shameful things with other men, and as a result of this sin, they suffered within themselves the penalty they deserved.
> —Romans 1:26–27

Paul also included male prostitutes and homosexuals in his list of sinners who will not "inherit the Kingdom of God" (1 Corinthians. 6:9–10)—unless, of course, they repent.

It is important to realize that people make the choice to engage in homosexual acts. Some have touted genetic findings as proof that people are "born gay." But the truth is that if there *is* a genetic component to some people's homosexuality (and this is by no means finally settled), it at most opens the door to that behavior; it certainly does not *determine* that behavior. The decision to indulge in homosexual activity is a choice, and a sinful one.

It is also important to realize that people who have engaged in gay sex in the past can change. They do not have to believe the "once gay, always gay" propaganda of some gay and lesbian leaders.

In 1973, prominent psychiatrist Dr. Robert Spitzer led the movement to remove homosexuality from the *American Psychiatric Association's* manual of disorders. But a quarter century later he encountered some ex-gay protestors, and though he was skeptical, he decided to investigate the possibility of a person's changing from a homosexual orientation to a heterosexual one.

Spitzer's study results showed some remarkable results. He interviewed 200 subjects (143 men and 57 women) who claimed to have left homosexuality behind. "To Spitzer's surprise, good heterosexual functioning was reportedly achieved by 67 percent of the men who had rarely or never felt any opposite-sex attraction before the change process. Nearly all the subjects said they now feel more masculine (in the case of men) or more feminine (women)."[7]

We are not saying that breaking a homosexual sin habit is easy. But whether you have indulged in homosexual activity a little or a lot, or if you have just wanted to, God is more than able to help you escape the temptations you face. He loves gay people just the way He loves all sinners (that includes every one of us), and He can help you to have a chaste life as a single person or a satisfying marriage with a person of the opposite sex.

IMMODESTY: THE SEX APPEAL

Supermodel Kim Alexis appeared on over five hundred magazine covers, including those of *Vogue* and the *Sports Illustrated swimsuit edition*. Then in 1990 Alexis committed her life to Jesus Christ. This new spiritual relationship changed her perspective about the industry in which she participated.

In her 1998 book, *A Model for a Better Future*, Alexis says, "The worst part of this business is that you are constantly asked to compromise your moral standards. There are pictures I look back on today and think, *Oh, why did I let them talk me into that?* I made some choices I'm not proud of."

Based on her own experience, Alexis has advice for others. She says, "Many women are playing with fire in the way they dress. Dressing like a floozy tells the world, 'Look at me, want me, lust after me. I'm easy and you can have me.' Displaying intimate parts of the body is a form of advertising for sex—so if you dress to attract sexual attention, you can hardly blame anyone else if that kind of attention comes your way."

Dressing modestly tells the world, "I respect myself and I insist on being treated with respect."

On the other hand, "Dressing modestly tells the world, 'I respect myself and I insist on being treated with respect.'" Alexis adds, "It's possible to be stylish and attractive without wearing something that is too short, low-cut, or see-through."[8]

Of course, modesty is not all about covering up with clothes. Wendy Shalit is a young woman who got interested in the subject of modesty when she was forced to use coed bathrooms in her college dorm. She later wrote,

Many of the problems we hear about today—sexual harassment, date rape, young women who suffer from eating disorders and report feeling a lack of control over their bodies—are all connected, I believe, to our culture's attack on modesty. Listen, first, to the words we use to describe intimacy: what once was called "making love," and then "having sex," is now "hooking up"— like airplanes refueling in flight. In this context I was interested to learn, while researching for my book, that the early feminists actually praised modesty as ennobling to society.… Simone de Beauvoir…warned in her book, *The Second Sex*, that if society trivializes modesty, violence against women would result. And she was right. Since the 1960s, when our cultural arbiters deemed this age-old virtue a "hang-up," men have grown to expect women to be casual about sex, and women for their part don't feel they have the right to say "no." This has brought us all more misery than joy.[9]

God's prescriptions of sexual abstinence before marriage and of fidelity within marriage protect us from harm and at the same time offer married couples the freedom and enjoyment of sex as it was meant to be.

What Wendy Shalit, Kim Alexis, and other men and women have rediscovered is nothing more than a principle taught long ago in the New Testament. The apostle Paul wrote,

I want women to be modest in their appearance. They should wear decent and appropriate clothing and not draw attention to themselves by the way they fix their hair or by wearing gold or pearls or expensive clothes. For women who claim to be devoted to God should make themselves attractive by the good things they do.
—1 Timothy 2:9–10[10]

Let's be clear about a couple of things. First, a woman's immodesty in dress or behavior does not justify men in lusting after her or—certainly—in committing acts of sexual violence against her. Second, men can be just as guilty of immodesty as women. But regardless of who is behaving immodestly and why, that person is guilty of degrading himself or herself while tempting others to sin. As Paul said, let us make ourselves attractive through goodness, not sex appeal.

SEXUAL SINS OF MIND AND EYE

Not all sex involves two bodies coming together; sometimes the sin occurs with just the eye or the mind. For women, the problem is often one of sexual fantasy. They may read love stories or watch romantic movies and imagine themselves to be acting out the illicit situations that are portrayed. For men (who tend to be more visually stimulated), the problem more likely is ogling. An attractive woman passes by, and they do not merely notice and then glance away, but they keep on staring after her.

The Bible is realistic about the problems of ogling and sexual fantasy. And it does not downplay their seriousness, as we might do. Jesus said,

> You have heard the commandment that says, 'You must not commit adultery.' But I say, anyone who even looks at a woman with lust has already committed adultery with her in his heart. So if your eye—even your good eye—causes you to lust, gouge it out and throw it away. It is better for you to lose one part of your body than for your whole body to be thrown into hell.
>
> —Matthew 5:27–29

Jesus was using hyperbole, or exaggeration for effect. But His points are clear: intent is morally equivalent to action, and lustful looks require a radical response.

In a sermon, Minnesota pastor John Piper emphasized the importance of reacting quickly and aggressively when we have an immoral thought.

> We must not give a sexual image or impulse more than five seconds before we mount a violent counterattack with the mind. I mean that! Five seconds. In the first two seconds we shout, "NO! Get out of my head!" In the next two seconds we cry out: "O God, in the name of Jesus, help me. Save me now. I am Yours."
>
> Good beginning. But then the real battle begins. This is a mind war. The absolute necessity is to get the image

> and the impulse out of our mind. How? Get a counter-
> image into the mind. Fight. Push. Strike. Don't ease up.
> It must be an image that is so powerful that the other
> image cannot survive.

Piper suggested using an image of Christ dying on the cross as one's "counter-image."[11]

Another effective response might be to imitate Job, who said, "I made a covenant with my eyes not to look with lust at a young woman" (Job 31:1). No matter how deeply ingrained the habit has become, one who ogles can make a "covenant with his eyes," or establish a new commitment not to stare at women.

But there is more to the problem than just ogling. The wrong in staring lustfully at a woman applies equally to staring lustfully at the *picture* of a woman. We are talking here about pornography—a plague that has come to take a monstrous toll in our society.

Pornography is almost as old as human history. Archaeologists have found sexually titillating pictures molded on the lids of clay objects in Israel, glazed onto the sides of Grecian pottery, and painted on the walls of homes in Pompeii. What's new these days is the quantity and availability—not to mention the widespread acceptance—of pornography. When Hugh Hefner launched his *Playboy* magazine in 1953, pornography began to go mainstream in American culture. Dirty books, magazines, movies, and videos soon abounded. Then in the 1990s, when the world logged on to the Internet, porn proliferated like never before, with viewers able to access a seemingly endless supply of prurient images without ever leaving their homes.

When you look at pornography, it is as if you are filing away a photo in a photo album. From then on, the image remains buried in your unconscious and may surface to fill the eye of your mind even when you do not want it to, repeating its harm again and again. Why put pollution like that in your heart?

The argument goes on as to whether pornography contributes to incidences of sex crimes, and courts struggle to define what is "obscene." But we do not need to wait to declare pornography sinful. By encouraging lust, turning human beings into objects, and redirecting sexual desire outside of marriage, pornography is clearly wrong.

And if you have any doubts about the harm that pornography causes those who appear in it, willingly or unwillingly, you should consider the firsthand testimony of one of its victims, "Sandra." In her thirties today, in childhood Sandra was raped by her grandfather and was forced into posing for pornography when she was still in her early teens.

> The memories of posing for those pictures are so painful, more so than the physical and sexual abuse. At least then I was fighting with someone or I could get caught up in the pain of the struggle to distract myself. Posing was different. It was more vulnerable and exposed. I often prayed to God that he wouldn't look at me until it was over. I was so ashamed and didn't want him to see me like that. I also would worry about other people seeing the pictures and was terrified of what people would think of me. Having someone stare at me and judge me from ten feet away while taking pictures, as I stood there naked, cold, exposed, embarrassed and humiliated, made me wish I could be nothing. He [the photographer] would talk to me as if I was an object and was oblivious to my pain. I wanted to turn into an object but I couldn't, no matter how hard I tried I couldn't go that numb. My soul and heart just hurt so much every time the flash from the camera would go off. It felt like someone was knocking my worth down lower and lower, and by the time the roll of film was done I didn't have any worth. When it was over, getting dressed was like getting some dignity back. The worry of what would be done with those pictures would plague me from then on.[12]

Hardly a victimless crime, is it? Porn hurts both those who are featured in it and those who choose to view it.

If you are involved with porn, stop it now and stop it for good. Declare with David, "I will set before my eyes no vile thing."[13]

YOUR PURITY POTENTIAL

We have not dealt with all the possible forms of sexual immorality. There are also prostitution, incest, and other behaviors that frankly we do not even care to mention. However, our tour of sexual sins has been enough to demonstrate the many awful ways that the gift of sexuality can be perverted and turned into something degrading and shameful.

The bottom line is that the only place where sexual activity is acceptable is between a man and a woman who are married to each other. As hard as it may seem, sexual abstinence is the requirement for anyone who is not married. And for married couples, sexual attention can be directed only toward your spouse.

Harder than these restrictions are the costs of sexual misbehavior. Guilt. Shame. Abuse. Disease. Broken marriages. Even criminal charges.

God loves us and wants to preserve us from such suffering. His prescriptions of sexual abstinence before marriage and of fidelity within marriage protect us from harm and at the same time offer married couples the freedom and enjoyment of sex as it was meant to be.[14] Most of all, they show the way to holiness in relation to that important part of our life known as sexuality.

> We are instructed to turn from godless living and sinful pleasures. We should live in this evil world with wisdom, righteousness, and devotion to God.
> —Titus 2:12

> Run from anything that stimulates youthful lusts. Instead, pursue righteous living, faithfulness, love, and peace. Enjoy the companionship of those who call on the Lord with pure hearts.
> —2 Timothy 2:22

> God's will is for you to be holy, so stay away from all sexual sin. Then each of you will control his own body and live in holiness and honor— not in lustful passion like the pagans who do not know God and His ways.... God has called us to live holy lives, not impure lives.
> —1 Thessalonians 4:3–5, 7

Reading such scriptural passages, you may find yourself saying, "But I just can't! I've tried and I can't stop my compulsive immorality." You are right. You can't stop sinning in this way—on your own. It takes the supernatural intervention of God to control the "ape gibbering in your loins." And He is glad to give that intervention if you will ask for His help.

Need some encouragement that, through the power of God, you really can beat your immorality habit and become pure once more? Let us close with the story of "Jeff." He was formerly involved in pedophilia, often considered an intractable or even an incurable behavior. But by God's grace, and with the help of a ministry called Harvest USA, he is finding his way back to purity.

> God has brought me very low. I finally came to see that without Christ's work on the cross my own selfish desires would have me totally enveloped in my sin to the exclusion of my wife, my son, and everything I've ever cared for. I truly am nothing without his continuous grace in my life. After several months of being separated from my family, going through a court hearing in which God miraculously worked his sovereign grace, hearing in Harvest meetings how men are being transformed by God's power, and seeing the continued deep depravity of my own heart, God has begun his transforming work in my heart. I am seeing that the cross truly breaks the power of sin in my life—even my sin of pedophilia. I am seeing that God is faithful, even when we are faithless, and He is not limited by human institutions or people's opinions. It is his sovereign plan to set his children free from the law of sin and death and bring us into the eternal liberty to be shared with his Son.[15]

Purity is a beautiful thing. Its blessings exceed any brief pleasure that sexual immorality might offer. We pray that, like Jeff, you will take God's hand and let Him lead you into purity.

SOUL PRESCRIPTION FOR IMMORALITY

Are you struggling with a habit of sexual immorality? We have outlined a five-step process to help you repent and heal in this area of your life. Take all the time you need with each of the steps below.

Step 1: Adopt a Correct View of God

An incorrect view of God that sees Him as some kind of wishy-washy being who will simply look the other way when you sin will keep you in the vicious cycle of immorality.

- God is holy and cannot tolerate sexual immorality.

  God's will is for you to be holy, so stay away from all sexual sin.
  —1 Thessalonians 4:3

- God is present everywhere. There is no place you can hide your sin.

  Nothing in all creation is hidden from God. Everything is naked and exposed before His eyes, and He is the one to whom we are accountable.
  —Hebrews 4:13

Make no mistake about it: God sees your sexual sin for what it is. He does not look away, and you cannot hide it from Him. Pursue a study of God's holiness and justice in Scripture. Admit to yourself that He sees and judges what you are doing.

Step 2: Revise Your False Beliefs

The false ideas from the world, related to sexuality, are almost unending. The harm they produce in people's lives is almost unending as well. Just for starters, consider these self-evaluation questions:

- Do you believe your sexual immorality is acceptable?

  Some ungodly people have wormed their way into your churches, saying that God's marvelous grace allows us

to live immoral lives. The condemnation of such people
was recorded long ago, for they have denied our only
Master and Lord, Jesus Christ.

—Jude 1:4

- Do you believe your sexual desires are impossible to resist?

Dear brothers and sisters, you have no obligation to do
what your sinful nature urges you to do.

—Romans 8:12

Given the ease with which we can unknowingly adopt false beliefs about human sexuality, we need to work hard to understand
the truth about how God made us to be sexual beings. Using a
concordance or topical Bible, learn more about God's views on
sexuality. Ask the Holy Spirit to show you the truth about your sin
and to help you change your thinking.

Step 3: Repent of Your Sin

Do you use pornography? Have you been cheating on your spouse?
Have you been dressing immodestly to get attention? Whatever
your form of immorality has been, do not duck it—admit it to
yourself and name it.

Pray a prayer like the following, asking God to forgive your sin
and empower your obedience.

God, I am guilty of the sin of _____. I know that
my immoral behavior is wrong and that it causes You
great pain—I am truly sorry for that. Please forgive me
for my sin. Cleanse me now of this sin and of its effects
in my life. Fill me with the power of the Holy Spirit so
that I may never return to this sin again. In the name of
Jesus Christ I pray, amen.

If you have harmed others with your sin, apologize to them.
Seek reconciliation and offer restitution where appropriate.

Step 4: Defend against Spiritual Attacks

You will be attacked in your area of weakness—count on it. Every time you turn on your TV, log on to the Internet, or walk out your front door, the enemies of your soul will be there. Watch out for the world, the flesh, and the Devil.

The world's values about sexuality are not God's values. The world system tells you, "There is nothing wrong with two consenting adults finding pleasure in each other's bodies." But God says, "Your body was not created for sexual immorality. It does not belong to you; it belongs to Me." Become so familiar with God's values on sexuality that you can immediately see the error in the world's values.

Your flesh (your sinful nature) will seek the pleasure of the flesh (your body) in the same old sinful ways you have known. Remember that the flesh (as your old sinful nature) is dead, having been crucified with Christ. You have been raised as a new person by the Holy Spirit. Live by the Spirit and not by the flesh.

Satan will set out the bait of sexual immorality for you. Protect yourself from these darts of temptation with the "shield of faith" (Ephesians 6:16). Then the Devil's suggestions that you can find true happiness by doing something forbidden will fall harmless to the ground.

Most likely, you will need a defense against temptation for a long time. Prepare for a prolonged battle, yet keep up your hope, because God is stronger than all your foes.

Step 5: Flee Temptation

Sexual temptation can be hard to avoid. The roots of sexual desire run deep and feed off many different stimuli. If you are to remain free from this habitual sin, you must learn to avoid the things that feed it as much as possible.

- Focus on your relationship with God.
  Seek a rich spiritual relationship through regular worship of God. Physical stimulation through sinful means will then seem less appealing to you.

- Latch on to God's promises.

  Find biblical statements or stories that encourage you in your fight against sexual immorality. Commit at least one verse to memory so that you can use it in your fight against temptation, just as Jesus used Scripture against the Devil in the desert. Here is one verse to consider using:

  > You are not controlled by your sinful nature. You are controlled by the Spirit if you have the Spirit of God living in you.
  >
  > —Romans 8:9

- Establish safeguards.

  What sets off your lustful acts? Put a barrier between that sinful trigger and yourself if you can. Take as many practical precautions to guard yourself. For example,

  - Immediately break off any immoral relationship you have.
  - If you rent pornographic DVDs, get rid of your DVD player. Or if you go to sexually explicit websites, install filtering software.
  - If you tend to dwell on lustful thoughts, choose a substitute image to put in your mind.
  - If you have homosexual tendencies, seek a Christian counselor skilled in reparative therapy.
  - Ask a trusted Christian friend to hold you accountable in your commitment to remain sexually pure.

- Expect victory.

  You may have fallen to sexual immorality in the past, but that does not mean you cannot know sexual purity now. Believe in God and in the path toward holiness that only He can bring.

  Visit www.SoulPrescription.com for more insights and resources, and to download a free leader's guide for small group Bible studies.

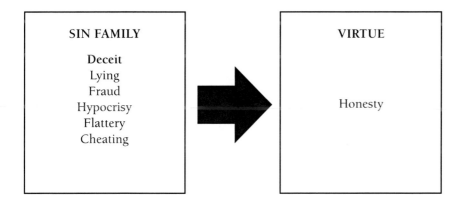

Chapter 15

DECEIT: SHOWING A FALSE FACE

SIN FAMILY		VIRTUE
Deceit Lying Fraud Hypocrisy Flattery Cheating	→	Honesty

You may remember the scandal from the 2002 Winter Olympics in Salt Lake City in which a French ice skating judge scored a Russian pair higher than the Canadians Jamie Salé and David Pelletier, who had turned in what was widely considered a superior performance. But do you know how the truth came out? With many tears and much loud wailing.

The French judge at the center of the scandal, Marie-Reine Le Gougne, was called into a meeting with the other judges just twelve hours after the skating event, on February 12, 2002. At one point the head referee, Ron Pfenning, passed around a sheet of paper that underscored the responsibility of judges to perform their duties with honesty and integrity. The French woman broke down.

Teary-eyed from the beginning, Le Gougne now began to cry out loud and to let loose an avalanche of words. "You don't understand," she said. "We're under an awful lot of pressure. My federation, my president Didier, I had to put the Russians first." She was referring to Didier Gailhaguet, then president of the French Figure Skating Federation, whom she alleged instructed her in advance how to score the event.

Le Gougne's wailing in the meeting went on for several minutes. Finally, it grew so loud that another person in the room covered the crack around the door with tape to keep people on the outside from hearing what was going on inside.[1]

And what *was* going on? The wailing was the sound of a conscience catching up with someone who was guilty of conspiring to cheat others. She was a deceiver found out.

To her credit, Le Gougne felt bad about what she had done. Others involved in various kinds of deceit seemingly do a better job of keeping their conscience pushed down and out of sight.

Of course, all persons are guilty of deceit to some extent. After all, we are told, "the human heart is the most deceitful of all things, and desperately wicked" (Jeremiah 17:9). Our race has participated in deception since Adam and Eve went along with the serpent's lies about the fruit God had placed off-limits. But some of us have a more serious problem in this area of deception. Some of us are serial deceivers.

Does that describe you? If so, where is your biggest problem with deception? Do you tell falsehoods when it serves your purpose? Do you pretend to be what you are not? Do you tell people what they want to hear about themselves, even when it is not true? Do you cheat to gain an advantage in a contest? Do you trick others for profit?

Watch out! Scripture tells us,

> You [God] will destroy those who tell lies.
> The LORD detests murderers and deceivers.
> —Psalm 5:6

Our race has participated in deception since Adam and Eve went along with the serpent's lies about the fruit God had placed off-limits.

We know how tempting it can be to shade the truth or present oneself in a false light for selfish reasons. Nevertheless, each of us must give up deception and learn the ways of honesty and integrity.

TRUTH DECAY

The image of the early Christian church in the opening pages of Acts is, for the most part, an attractive picture of faith, unity, and love. But in the midst of all this exemplary godliness, one event struck a jarring note, and it had to do with lying.

> But there was a certain man named Ananias who, with his wife, Sapphira, sold some property. He brought part of the money to the apostles, claiming it was the full amount. With his wife's consent, he kept the rest.
>
> Then Peter said, "Ananias, why have you let Satan fill your heart? You lied to the Holy Spirit, and you kept some of the money for yourself. The property was yours to sell or not sell, as you wished. And after selling it, the money was also yours to give away. How could you do a thing like this? You weren't lying to us but to God!"
>
> As soon as Ananias heard these words, he fell to the floor and died. Everyone who heard about it was terrified. Then some young men got up, wrapped him in a sheet, and took him out and buried him.
>
> About three hours later his wife came in, not knowing what had happened. Peter asked her, "Was this the price you and your husband received for your land?"
>
> "Yes," she replied, "that was the price."
>
> And Peter said, "How could the two of you even think of conspiring to test the Spirit of the Lord like this? The young men who buried your husband are just outside the door, and they will carry you out, too."

Are You Deceitful?

The following self-evaluation quiz will help you determine whether you have a tendency toward being deceptive.

- Do you look on truth as something you can mold rather than as an unchanging reality?
- Do you bend—or break—the truth when speaking with others?
- Do you use slyness, trickery, underhandedness, guile, or invention as a tool to get ahead?
- Are you a different person when you are alone than when others are watching?
- Do you leave the impression with others that you are a better person than you actually are?
- Do you say good things about other people insincerely, hoping to get on their good side?
- Do you cheat people out of what is rightfully theirs?
- Do you break the rules you had agreed to abide by?

Instantly, she fell to the floor and died. When the young men came in and saw that she was dead, they carried her out and buried her beside her husband. Great fear gripped the entire church and everyone else who heard what had happened.

—Acts 5:1–11

Fear, indeed, should be the reaction of anyone perpetrating dishonesty. God does not usually respond to lying by sending instant death. But lying is a form of deception that consistently earns His condemnation, for untruth interferes with justice and integrity in human relations.

One particular form of lying—perjury, or lying in a legal proceeding—made it into the Ten Commandments: "You must not testify falsely against your neighbor" (Exodus 20:16).[2] But both Testaments reflect how seriously God views the sin of lying. Consider this sampling:

> Keep your tongue from speaking evil and your lips from telling lies!
>
> —Psalm 34:13

The Devil is the sponsor of untruth.

> I will not allow deceivers to serve in my house, and liars will not stay in my presence.
>
> —Psalm 101:7

> A false witness will not go unpunished, nor will a liar escape.
>
> —Proverbs 19:5

> Stop telling lies. Let us tell our neighbors the truth, for we are all parts of the same body.
>
> —Ephesians 4:25[3]

> Don't lie to each other.
>
> —Colossians 3:9

When we lie, we are not motivated by God but rather by His enemy. The Devil is the sponsor of untruth. Jesus testified that

Satan "has always hated the truth, because there is no truth in him. When he lies, it is consistent with his character; for he is a liar and the father of lies" (John 8:44).

Reading all this, you may excuse your own dishonesty by calling it a "white lie"—a small, insignificant untruth that could not hurt a fly. Or, you may think you have escaped guilt through lying by implication instead of by telling a falsehood outright. And what about half-truths? Ananias and Sapphira discovered to their peril that a half-truth equates to a whole lie. Let us, then, always tell the truth, the whole truth, and nothing but the truth. We will be doing ourselves a favor.

The truth wants to be free. It has a way of escaping into daylight despite every attempt to keep it trapped under a lid—ask any politician who has tried to prevent a scandal from reaching public notice. Benjamin Franklin said, "A lie stands on one leg, truth on two." In the plain words of Scripture, "Truthful words stand the test of time, but lies are soon exposed" (Proverbs 12:19). Just as God knows every time we counterfeit the truth, so other people usually find out as well.

The practice of lying can easily develop into a habit over time. But truth telling can become a habit too. If your character has suffered from truth decay, resolve with Job, "As long as I live,… my tongue will speak no lies" (Job 27:3–4).

Equally as serious as lying is another form of deception— hypocrisy, or pretending to be better than we are.

THE MASK OF GOODNESS

Some years ago I (Henry) taught a college-age Sunday school class. One young man in the class often said, "I am very devoted to the Lord. Because my body is the Lord's, I want to take care of it. I don't stay up late; I'm careful what I eat; I exercise regularly; and I don't drink, smoke, or chase women."

We all listened and nodded. "Good for you," we would say.

Then one day, at an airport many miles from home, I saw this model student standing in front of the terminal building. Guess what? He had a cigar in his mouth and was puffing away as happy as could be. So much for taking good care of his body.

I walked up to chat with him. When he saw me coming, he did a strange thing. He stuck that cigar—still smoking—in his pocket!

Now, one would think that a young man would be glad to see his Sunday school teacher, especially so far from home. But the opposite was true in this case: my student seemed ill at ease and in a hurry to be off. A bit mischievously (that was *my* sin), I kept him talking as long as I could, until the smoke began curling up from his pocket.[4]

My student was a hypocrite. Are you? Do you act at church like your family gets along great, when in fact fighting is raging all the time at home? Do you pretend to have a profound relationship with God, when the truth is that your devotional life is about as substantial as a mirage? Do you let people assume that you are a highly moral being, even though you are sleeping with your boyfriend or girlfriend every weekend?

Hypocrisy is an add-on sin. If you are struggling with any other sin listed in this book, and then you lie about it through words or pretense, you have added hypocrisy to your burden of guilt. And even worse, if you have deluded yourself into believing that you are a godly person despite your sins, then you have let hypocrisy join hands with its favorite partner, self-righteousness.

Jesus reserved His harshest language for religious people who pretended to be holier than they were.

Jesus reserved His harshest language for religious people who pretended to be holier than they were. Matthew 23, in fact, is one long diatribe against the Pharisees for their hypocrisy. Christ said of these religious leaders, "They don't practice what they teach" and "Everything they do is for show" (verses 3, 5).

The Greek word used in the New Testament for "hypocrite" was originally applied to Greek and Roman actors. Following the convention of the day, these actors would play their parts while wearing large masks. In other words, the faces that theatergoers saw were not the real faces of the actors—those were hidden underneath.

So it is with hypocrites today: they put one face forward while hiding their real face from view. They "will act religious" but "reject the power that could make them godly" (2 Timothy 3:5). They "claim they know God" yet "deny Him by the way they live" (Titus 1:16).

Be honest about who you are. Authenticity puts you at a place where God may begin working with you to make things better. You might be surprised by how much people will still like you if you are honest about your failings. (There's a good chance they can smell the cigar smoke rising from your pocket anyway!)

"Get rid of all evil behavior." declared Peter. "Be done with all deceit, hypocrisy…" (1 Peter 2:1).

Hypocrisy is making yourself look better than you are. Flattery, on the other hand, is making *others* look better than *they* are. It is another form of deception.

BUTTERING UP

Darrin followed his boss into the conference room, and for a while the two of them were the only ones there.

"Is that a new jacket you're wearing, Mr. Gardner?" asked Darrin. "It's really stylish. I'd like to get one like that myself." Actually, Darrin considered the pattern in the sport coat to be way too busy.

Darrin's boss, Blaine Gardner, smiled and acknowledged the purchase of a new sport coat.

As Blaine started setting up his PowerPoint presentation, he passed the time by asking Darrin what Darrin thought about the proposal Blaine had circulated.

"It's great, Mr. Gardner!" said Darrin, even though he and all of his coworkers really believed the proposal would be far more costly to implement than management realized. "I think this will give us the market share we've been aiming for."

As Kirsten entered the room and overheard the final remarks, she rolled her eyes at Scott trailing behind her. Darrin was at it again, buttering up the boss.

The two-faced nature of deception is perhaps more evident in flattery than in any other form of deceit. Flattery is praising someone else untruthfully in the hope of gaining something by it, whether that gain is a promotion at work, mercy from a traffic cop, or even something as basic as attention from a friend. Flattery always has an ulterior motive.

Complimenting others is a neglected art form; we encourage praising the good in others. Flattery, however, goes beyond the honest compliment, using falsehood in an attempt to satisfy a selfish desire. As a result, it is destructive to relationships in the long run. "A lying tongue hates its victims, and flattering words cause ruin" (Proverbs 26:28).

The apostle Paul set an example of refusing to stoop to flattery. He told the congregation in Thessalonica, "Our purpose is to please God, not people. He alone examines the motives of our hearts. Never once did we try to win you with flattery, as you well know. And God is our witness that we were not pretending to be your friends just to get your money!" (1 Thessalonians 2:4–5).

Before praising another, stop and ask yourself: *Is what I am planning to say true? Why do I want to say it?* Taking time to evaluate your words carefully before saying them can help you keep your compliments within the bounds of truth. Your conscience will be your guide.

Your conscience will also guide you away from related forms of deception, fraud and cheating, if you will let it.

UNFAIR ADVANTAGE

Today, Frank W. Abagnale is sought after by governments and corporations as an expert on detecting forgery, embezzlement, and document falsification. But between the ages of sixteen and twenty-one, he was one of the world's most successful con artists. He cashed $2.5 million in fraudulent checks in all fifty states and twenty-six foreign countries. He also successfully posed as an airline pilot, an attorney, a college professor, and a pediatrician before being apprehended by the French police. His life of crime was portrayed in the 2002 movie *Catch Me If You Can*.

Like Abagnale, some people are frauds, impostors, and cheats. These people are practicing some of the most self-serving forms of deceptions out there. They are obscuring the truth while trying to gain an advantage at another's expense.

The problem of fraud in business came to public attention in recent years with a wave of corporate scandals. Enron's Ken Lay and Jeffrey Skilling were suspected of accounting fraud. WorldCom's

Bernard Ebbers was charged with securities fraud. Tyco boss Dennis Kozlowski was said to have used company money as his own. Such behaviors are hardly victimless crimes, as they have resulted in real losses to employees and small investors—not to mention the credibility of the US corporate world.

Do you think business fraud is a new problem? Think again. The Bible frequently takes on fraud in terms of businesspeople cheating their customers. For example, the prophet Amos railed against some of his fellow Israelites,

> You can't wait for the Sabbath day to be over and the religious festivals to end so you can get back to cheating the helpless. You measure out grain with dishonest measures and cheat the buyer with dishonest scales. And you mix the grain you sell with chaff swept from the floor. Then you enslave poor people for one piece of silver or a pair of sandals.
>
> —Amos 8:5–6[5]

What's so bad about fraud is that it frequently is a means for those with more wealth and power to oppress those who are less well-placed in society. God will always be on the side of the weak in such a situation.

Fraud is a perennial problem. Most are not committing fraud on the scale Amos mentions—or, certainly, on the scale of some modern-day CEOs lost to hubris. Instead, we commit fraud on the micro level. It goes by the label of "cheating."

Tim Schutt, crew chief for NASCAR driver Mike McLaughlin, became a Christian during a retreat for members of the racing world and shortly afterward ran up against the temptation to cheat. McLaughlin's car was not performing as Tim wished, and so Tim decided to add a small device that was outlawed by NASCAR. Tim justified his decision to himself on the basis that many of the cars McLaughlin would be up against already had the hard-to-detect device.

Tim crawled under McLaughlin's No. 20 car and started to install the device. "I got halfway through putting it on," recalled Tim, "and that verse 'Seek ye first the kingdom of God' came flashing in red in front of me, and whoa, that was it. I said, 'I'm leaving this up to you, God.'"[6] Schutt did not install the device.

As it turned out, McLaughlin won his next race anyway. When we choose to go against the trend of society and refuse to cheat, the outcome may not always be as positive for us. We may, in fact, lose whatever contest lies before us. But if we put God and His will first, determining to follow the rules no matter what, then in His eyes we will be winners every time. That's the virtue of honesty.

THE BEST POLICY

If we put God first, determining to follow the rules no matter what, then in His eyes we will be winners every time.

In 1948, while on my way to my wedding with Vonette Zachary, I (Bill) passed through the city of Okmulgee, Oklahoma, where my grandparents had lived for many years. Suddenly, I remembered my need to purchase gifts for the wedding party, and I stopped at a jewelry store.

Before looking for the items I wanted, I asked the owner if he would cash an out-of-state check.

"I'm sorry, sir." He shook his head courteously. "It's against our policy."

"I understand," I said and turned to walk out of the store.

He called after me, "Do you know anyone in this city?"

"No. My grandfather used to live here, but he's been dead for several years."

"What was his name?"

"Sam Bright."

"Sam Bright was the most honorable man I have ever known!" he exclaimed. "If you're anything like your grandfather, I will sell you anything in this store. And I'll take your check!"

I was moved by this experience. Although my grandfather had been gone for many years, he had left a legacy of integrity.

What legacy are we leaving? What reputation are we building for ourselves? One act of deceit can make others distrust us. A pattern of deceit is hard to overcome. But with God's help, any deceiver can begin to establish new patterns of honesty.

Shortly before his execution by the Nazis, the theologian Dietrich Bonhoeffer looked to the future. He said, "What the church will need, what our century will need, are not people of genius, not brilliant tacticians or strategists, but simple, straightforward, honest men and women." If anything, these words are more relevant today than at the time of World War II.

We deceive because we are worried about what will happen to us if we choose to tell the truth. What we find, though, is that when we practice deceit, we disappoint God, chip away at our own self-respect, and run the risk of a worse reaction from others when they find out the truth later. The proper response is to trust God to care for us as we honor His command to be truth tellers. There is, in fact, no peace to be had without truth.

When we practice deceit, we disappoint God, chip away at our own self-respect, and run the risk of a worse reaction from others when they find out the truth later.

A. W. Tozer said, "A guileless mind is a great treasure; it is worth any price." Are you willing to pay the price? It means forgoing the easy payoffs that deceit can seem to bring, choosing instead the slow and steady dividends of making your word your bond.

Give up the too-easy and too-costly habit of deceit. Embrace instead the policy of honesty at all times.

SOUL PRESCRIPTION FOR DECEIT

Are you struggling with being deceitful in some way? We have outlined a five-step process to help you repent and heal in this area of your life. Take all the time you need with each of the steps below.

Step 1: Adopt a Correct View of God

God is truth. To view Him in any other way will only serve to justify your deceitful behavior.

- God is absolute truth. He cannot lie and He does not change His standards.

    God is not a man, so He does not lie.
                                        —Numbers 23:19

- God is righteous, and He abhors dishonesty in every form.

> Because what you say is false and your visions are a lie, I
> will stand against you, says the Sovereign LORD.
> —Ezekiel 13:8

What is your view of God with respect to honesty and dishonesty? Go to Scripture and review every passage that talks about God's truthfulness. Don't fool yourself. God will not tolerate lies and deceitfulness.

Step 2: Revise Your False Beliefs

If you believe that your deceitfulness is justified or excusable for any reason, you are wrong. Perhaps mistaken views of yourself, other people, or how life works are making it harder for you to be truthful.

- Do you believe your "little white lies" do no harm?

  > Telling lies about others is as harmful as hitting them
  > with an ax, wounding them with a sword, or shooting
  > them with a sharp arrow.
  > —Proverbs 25:18

- Do you believe others are yours to "use"?

  > Do to others as you would like them to do to you.
  > —Luke 6:31

- Do you believe the end justifies the means and thus makes your deceitfulness okay?

  > Stop telling lies. Let us tell our neighbors the truth, for
  > we are all parts of the same body.
  > —Ephesians 4:25

Use scriptural truth about deceitfulness and honesty to expose errors in your thinking. Ask the Holy Spirit, who is the Spirit of truth, to help you first understand the truth and then speak the truth to others.

Step 3: Repent of Your Sin

In what way are you deceitful? Identify it specifically. Then if you are prepared to give up this sin, pray a prayer of confession. A model prayer is presented below for your use, or you can pray in your own words.

> God of truth, I have been deceitful by _____. This was a sin against You, and I am sorry for it. Please forgive me. Make me clean again, and fill me with Your power to help me remain clean of deceitfulness from this point on. In the name of Jesus Christ I pray, amen.

If you have harmed others with your sin, apologize to them. Seek reconciliation and offer restitution where appropriate.

Step 4: Defend against Spiritual Attacks

Your spiritual enemies—the world, the flesh, and the Devil—would like nothing better than to see you backslide into a pattern of deceitfulness. Beware of their wiles!

- The world system does not value honesty the way God does. The world's values would tell us to use deceitfulness if it will help us get ahead. We can overcome such an influence by immersing ourselves in God's value system. Develop the importance He places on honesty.
- Your flesh, or sinful nature, will tempt you to enjoy that self-reliant feeling that comes with trying to manipulate events through deceit. Do not give in to the craving! Your flesh is dead. You are a spiritual being now, living according to the Holy Spirit.
- Satan will make it as easy and as appealing for you to deceive others as possible. Put on the "belt of truth" (Ephesians 6:14) to help you discern true from false and remain committed to truth telling.

Be ever vigilant in defense against your spiritual foes. The attacks will not cease. Accessing the great power of God will empower you to be successful in every battle.

Step 5: Flee Temptation

You will never be able to completely avoid the temptation to return to your old deceitful ways. However, there are specific steps you can take to reduce your exposure and susceptibility to temptation.

- Focus on your relationship with God.

  Spend time regularly cultivating your relationship with God. In particular, make Bible study a consistent discipline in your life. Constant exposure to the truth will make you a more truthful person.

- Latch on to God's promises.

  Identify assurances in Scripture that make you more confident of winning over your sin of deceitfulness. Store assurances away in your mind as ammunition when the battle with temptation comes.

  > God has given both His promise and His oath. These two things are unchangeable because it is impossible for God to lie. Therefore, we who have fled to Him for refuge can have great confidence as we hold to the hope that lies before us.
  >
  > —Hebrews 6:18

- Establish safeguards.

  Why not make holiness more easy for yourself as possible? Think of ways you can cut off common temptations. Here are examples of the kinds of changes you can make for the better:

  - If you cheat on your taxes, hire a tax preparer next year and make all your records available to this person.

- If you defraud your employer by falsifying your time sheet, ask a friend on your work team to verify its accuracy each week.
- If you naturally resort to flattery, practice ahead of time what you can say in favor of a person without lying.
- Ask a trusted Christian friend to hold you accountable in your commitment to not deceive others.

- Expect victory.

  You are a new person in Christ Jesus. The Holy Spirit lives in you. He wants to create an honest heart in you. Seek His help as you eliminate deceit and adopt honesty in your life. As long as you are cooperating with Him, you cannot lose! Praise God!

Visit www.SoulPrescription.com for more insights and resources, and to download a free leader's guide for small group Bible studies.

Chapter 16

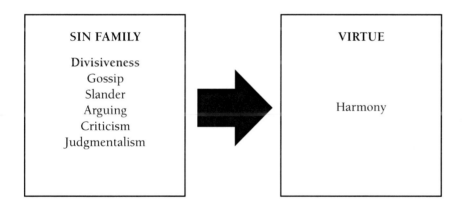

DIVISIVENESS: DISTURBING THE PEACE

SIN FAMILY		VIRTUE
Divisiveness		
Gossip		
Slander		Harmony
Arguing		
Criticism		
Judgmentalism		

V isitors to Castle Ward, a country estate near Strangford Lough in Ireland, are treated to the sight of a house divided against itself, literally. One façade is in the classical style, while the other is in the Gothic style. This difference in design extends to the interior of the house, where the rooms that were most frequented by females are adventurously decorated and the male preserves are more conservative and conventional.

The architectural discord is due to a difference of opinion between Bernard Ward (later Viscount Bangor) and his wife, Lady Anne Bligh, at the time the house was under construction in the 1760s. Apparently, the couple could not agree on a single style for their new house that would suit them both, so they "agreed to disagree." The house bears the marks of their disagreement to this day.

Like Lord and Lady Bangor, some people today have a history of being involved in disagreements. From fistfights on the playground, to power plays in the office, to arguments on a church committee, they are known for being at odds with others. They are quarrelsome, critical, and divisive.

In listing the acts of the sinful nature in Galatians 5, Paul included "divisions" and "the feeling that everyone is wrong except those in your own little group" (verse 20). He was describing what goes on in a body of people when its members don't agree. This is a type of "home divided against itself" and "kingdom at war with itself" (Matthew 12:25).

The sin of divisiveness raised its head early on among Paul's new congregation at Corinth. At one point in a letter to them, Paul had to say, "Now, dear brothers and sisters, I appeal to you by the authority of the Lord Jesus Christ to stop arguing among yourselves."

> I appeal to you, dear brothers and sisters, by the authority of our Lord Jesus Christ, to live in harmony with each other. Let there be no divisions in the church. Rather, be of one mind, united in thought and purpose. For some members of Chloe's household have told me about your quarrels, my dear brothers and sisters. Some of you are saying, "I am a follower of Paul." Others are saying, "I follow Apollos," or "I follow Peter," or "I follow only Christ." Has Christ been divided into factions? Was I, Paul, crucified for you? Were any of you baptized in the name of Paul? Of course not!
> —1 Corinthians 1:10–13

It is as we are all in one accord that we move ahead to the future that God has for us.

Divisiveness can be a problem in any type of team or group. But in a church group, particularly, unity is essential to bearing fruit. It is as we are all in one accord that we move ahead, under the Spirit's direction, to the future that God has for us. God bids us, as much as it is possible, to "live in peace with everyone" (Romans 12:18).

When an individual is picking a fight with someone else or setting one part of a group against another, he or she is at fault before God and the body.

Are you uncertain about whether this sin habit of divisiveness describes you? Keep your mind open as we look at different kinds of quarreling and ways of using words that lead to division.

THE MONSTER OF STRIFE

In a fable called "Hercules and Pallas," Aesop told a story that is instructive for people who find themselves embroiled in conflict.

It seems that Hercules, journeying along a narrow roadway, came across a strange-looking animal that reared its head and threatened him. Undaunted, the hero gave the animal a few powerful blows with his club.

Hercules would then have gone on his way. However, much to his astonishment, the monster grew three times as big as it was before and appeared still more threatening.

The hero redoubled his blows, striking fast and furiously at the monster. But the harder and quicker came the strokes of his club, the bigger and more frightful grew the monster. It now completely filled the road.

Just then Pallas appeared upon the scene. "Stop, Hercules. Cease your blows," she said. "The monster's name is Strife. Leave it alone, and it will soon become as little as it was at first."

Of course, every Aesop fable has its moral. What do you suppose is this one's? "Strife feeds on conflict."

Some people seem to have a knack for contributing to a conflict so that strife grows and grows. Maybe it is starting shouting matches with family members. Maybe it is alienating friends by talking about them behind their back. Maybe it is creating divisions in teams and groups. In any case, such people have a problem that calls for more than learning better social behavior; it is really a sin habit we are talking about.

These people need to know that in fact they are involved in a complex of sins. Certainly, sins of any sort rarely if ever stand on their own. But fighting, in particular, is a sin that tends to company with others of its kind. Sins like anger, bitterness, and

Are You Divisive?

The following self-evaluation quiz will help you determine whether you have a tendency toward conflict.

- Right now, are you engaged in a "hot" or "cold" war with anybody?
- How often do you argue and quarrel with others? Do you raise your voice?
- Do you tell stories about others that they would prefer not to be spread around?
- Do you ever make up (or exaggerate) stories to put your enemies in a bad light?
- Is it more important to you to get people on your side than it is to help reach agreement within a group you are a part of?
- Do you take delight in pointing out the faults of others?
- Do you condemn the piety or morality of others?
- Do you have a reputation as someone who is hard to get along with?

envy often erupt into visibility by means of the sin of quarreling. The apostle James explored this interaction of fighting and other sins.

"What is causing the quarrels and fights among you?" James asked a contentious bunch of early Christians. And then he answered his own question. "Don't they come from the evil desires at war within you? You want what you don't have, so you scheme and kill to get it. You are jealous of what others have, but you can't get it, so you fight and wage war to take it away from them. Yet you don't have what you want because you don't ask God for it" (James 4:1–2).

Due to the serious nature of its causes, conflict between individuals can be severe and bitter. And the closer the two people are, the more bitter the conflicts may become. This was well illustrated for me (Henry) in a true story about a man named Bert told to me by my friend Tim Daley.

BROTHERLY HATE

Bert was a Christian man and a successful insurance agent who had other agents working for him. Among these other agents was Bert's older brother, Allan, whom Bert had taken on with some trepidation because of the strain their working arrangement might put on their relationship. The trepidation Bert had felt proved to be prophetic.

All was fine at first, but then Allan refused to comply with some new procedures Bert established for all his agents to follow. Over the period of a full year, the two brothers had many strained and heated conversations about the issue. Finally, one day when they were throwing verbal bricks at each other, Allan cleaned out his office and left.

Feeling bad about what had happened, Bert called his brother on the phone a few days later. The verbal barrage started up again and ended only when Bert hung up on Allan. He was livid with rage.

There was no contact between the two for a month. Meanwhile, Bert consulted with biblical counselor Tim Daley about the situation.

After listening intently to the story, Tim leaned forward and said to Bert, "You are a bitter, angry man. The way you talked to your brother is unacceptable as a Christian example. You need to repent and then apologize to your brother for your bad attitude. You will not find peace until you do."

Bert was not prepared for that response. He was expecting some reassurance that he was justified in his response because of the problem Allan had created. Nevertheless, he pondered Tim's advice.

At first Bert did nothing. He was afraid to call his brother and did not want to admit he was wrong. In the end, though, he admitted his sin to God and asked to be cleansed and empowered to love his brother. To his surprise, his resistance to calling Allan turned into an urge to see him.

Bert managed to overcome Allan's reluctance and arranged a twenty-minute meeting. At the appointed time, as Bert looked at his brother, he sensed nothing but compassion for him in his heart; all the bitterness was gone. He proceeded to apologize for the attitude he'd had toward Allan and asked forgiveness. Both brothers had tears in their eyes.

Later, Bert would say to my friend Tim that at that moment it was as though a two-hundred-pound weight had been lifted from his shoulders.

As we see in the case of Bert and Allan, the unrighteous use of words plays a major role in our conflicts with others. Words can be tools to build up or they can be weapons to destroy.

WORDS AS WEAPONS

Interpersonal conflict usually occurs because of, and by means of, the words we use. "Harsh words make tempers flare" (Proverbs 15:1). With words, we quarrel, argue, and dispute. With words, we gossip, slander, and smear. With words, we mock and ridicule, taunt and deride. With words, we criticize and judge and curse and condemn. Certainly your authors can look back on times when we wish we could have taken back words we had spoken—but that's never possible.

The apostle James was right in saying that the tongue has a destructive power far beyond what its small size might suggest.

> We can make a large horse go wherever we want by means of a small bit in its mouth. And a small rudder makes a huge ship turn wherever the pilot chooses to go, even though the winds are strong. In the same way, the tongue is a small thing that makes grand speeches. But a tiny spark can set a great forest on fire. And the tongue is a flame of fire. It is a whole world of wickedness, corrupting your entire body. It can set your whole life on fire, for it is set on fire by hell itself.
>
> —James 3:3–6

We sometimes use our tongue like a weapon, to hurt and to maim others. Even if a part of us realizes that what we are doing is wrong, we cannot seem to stop ourselves. The tongue at such times, seems wild, unmanageable.

James, again, told us what this is like. "People can tame all kinds of animals and birds and reptiles and fish," he said, "but no one can tame the tongue."

If you have a divisiveness habit, it is almost guaranteed that you have a tongue like a poisonous snake that has gotten loose from its cage.

> People can tame all kinds of animals, birds, reptiles, and fish, but no one can tame the tongue. It is restless and evil, full of deadly poison. Sometimes it praises our Lord and Father, and sometimes it curses those who have been made in the image of God. And so blessing and cursing come pouring out of the same mouth. Surely, my brothers and sisters, this is not right!
>
> —James 3:7–10

Have you tried and failed to tame your tongue? If you have a divisiveness habit, it is almost guaranteed that you have a tongue like a poisonous snake that has gotten loose from its cage. The people nearby had better watch out!

You had better watch out too if you are prone to saying wicked things. Jesus explained, "A good person produces good things from the treasury of a good heart, and an evil person produces evil things from the treasury of an evil heart. And I tell you this, you must give an account on judgment day for every idle word you speak" (Matthew 12:35–36).

Two of the chief ways people hurt others are by gossiping about them and by slandering them.

TELLING TALES

One need only look at entertainment news to see how much we, as a society, love to know details from the lives of celebrities and other public figures—and the more intimate the detail, the better we like it. A similar dynamic is at work in our lives when we put gossip into circulation, or pass it on secondhand, and when we shoot out slander like a dart full of poison.

Gossip is passing around tales of an intimate nature about another. An example is telling Marilyn in Accounts Receivable that Phil in Marketing has separated from his wife. *Slander*, on the other hand, is telling a deliberate falsehood about someone else that damages that person's reputation. Here an example would be claiming that Phil has been embezzling from the company, when in fact, he has not. Both forms of talebearing are wrong.

If the tongue is a flame of destruction set on fire by hell itself, as James said, this is certainly true in the case of gossip. "Scoundrels create trouble; their words are a destructive blaze" (Proverbs 16:27).

Ramona Cramer Tucker tells a story about a friend of hers named Michelle, who learned too late the danger of gossip.

> While at a restaurant over lunch, Michelle and her coworker, Sharon, stopped in the restroom to fix their makeup before returning to their jobs. Their small talk turned to the subject of who drove them crazy. Immediately Michelle launched into a two-minute diatribe about Beth, a mutual coworker. As Michelle prepared to divulge more specifics, a stall door opened. Out walked Beth, red-faced and angry.
>
> In a split second, what had seemed like a pressure-relief session turned into an awkward mess. Michelle and Beth stared at each other in embarrassed panic. Michelle

knew she couldn't take her words back. In the instant
their eyes met, Beth fled out the door. That afternoon,
Beth didn't return to work, and the next day Michelle
heard through the grapevine that Beth had resigned.[1]

Michelle did not know Beth was listening and had no idea her
words would have such an effect. But it does not matter. She
should have been watching what she said about Beth anyway.

Gossip proceeds from an unkind spirit. Since gossip is rarely
about something that reflects positively on another, passing it on
may be an exercise in taking delight in another's error or misfortune. The desire to gossip is often connected with other sins,
such as idleness, gloating, and a desire for advantage (possessing
information makes one powerful).

The book of Proverbs reveals some of the wicked consequences
of gossip.

> Gossip makes people mad. "As surely as a north wind
> brings rain, so a gossiping tongue causes anger!"
> —Proverbs 25:23

> Gossip prolongs arguments. "Fire goes out without
> wood, and quarrels disappear when gossip stops."
> —Proverbs 26:20

> Gossip ruins relationships. "A troublemaker plants
> seeds of strife; gossip separates the best of friends."
> —Proverbs 16:28

*A gossip's mouth is
the Devil's mailbag.*

A Welsh saying states, "a gossip's mouth is the Devil's mailbag."
May none of us deliver any mail postmarked "Hell."

As devilish as gossip is, talebearing crosses a line to a new level
of seriousness when it becomes slander.

God's position on slander is clear enough. "Do not spread slanderous gossip among your people," He said (Leviticus 19:16). "I will
not tolerate people who slander their neighbors" (Psalm 101:5).
"Get rid of all...harsh words, and slander" (Ephesians 4:31).

Christians tell harmful untruths about others more often than
we would like to believe. Usually they are motivated by hate,

jealousy, or a thirst for revenge. We can be certain that something has gone seriously wrong in the spirit of a Christ follower who slanders another, especially if the slander is part of an ongoing pattern of behavior.

A. B. Simpson, an evangelical leader from a century back, spoke words we would be wise to take to heart today. He said, "I would rather play with the forked lightning, or take in my hands living wires with their fiery current, than speak a reckless word against any servant of Christ, or idly repeat the slanderous darts which thousands of Christians are hurling on others, to the hurt of their own souls and bodies."

But gossip and slander are not the only ways to hurt others with words. Criticism and judgmentalism are two more.

DESTRUCTIVE SPEECH

Russian theologian Alexander Schmemann and his fiancée were sitting in a Paris Métro subway train when a badly dressed and unattractive old woman got on and sat down across from them. Speaking in Russian, the couple began to talk about her and to laugh about her appearance, assuming all the while that she could not understand what they were saying. As the train pulled up to a station, though, the woman stopped in front of them and said in perfect Russian, "But I was not always so old or so ugly." Then without another word, she stepped onto the station platform, never to be seen by the couple again.

Schmemann reported later that he was not only shocked that he and his fiancée had been understood by the woman, but worse, he was shocked to realize that he, a follower of Christ, had so easily dehumanized another and ripped away some of her few, remaining shreds of dignity. He was driven to confession before the Lord.

Criticism is a kind of speech that tears down; it is not an expression of love that wants to build the other up. One biblical proverbialist said, "Love prospers when a fault is forgiven" (Proverbs 17:9). The apostle Paul warned, "If you are always biting and devouring one another, watch out! Beware of destroying one another" (Galatians 5:15).

Do you find fault with others? Do you point out their mistakes? Do you tease them about their weaknesses? Then remember what Paul said: "Don't use foul or abusive language. Let everything you say be good and helpful, so that your words will be an encouragement to those who hear them" (Ephesians 4:29).

If your criticism is tinged with self-righteousness, then you are likely guilty of judgmentalism—this is finding fault with others specifically, about their spiritual or moral condition. The New Testament is consistent in saying that God alone has the ability and right to judge others' standing before Him.

> Do not judge others, and you will not be judged. For you will be treated as you treat others. The standard you use in judging is the standard by which you will be judged. And why worry about a speck in your friend's eye when you have a log in your own? How can you think of saying to your friend, "Let me help you get rid of that speck in your eye," when you can't see past the log in your own eye? Hypocrite! First get rid of the log in your own eye; then you will see well enough to deal with the speck in your friend's eye.
> —Matthew 7:1–5

> Don't speak evil against each other, dear brothers and sisters. If you criticize and judge each other, then you are criticizing and judging God's law. But your job is to obey the law, not to judge whether it applies to you. God alone, who gave the law, is the Judge. He alone has the power to save or to destroy. So what right do you have to judge your neighbor?
> —James 4:11–12

If you see something that appears wrong in the spiritual life of another, do not presume that it is your job to flag the error for others. Instead, use it as a reminder that you need to examine yourself for similar flaws. Learn not to create conflict in this way but to set an example of harmony.

LEARNING TO GET ALONG

In his modern classic, the Lord of the Rings trilogy, author J. R. R. Tolkien tells the story of nine individuals who band together as "the fellowship of the Ring" to thwart the plans of the evil Sauron. During the course of their harrowing adventures, the nine often quarrel and disagree with one another—elf against dwarf, men against hobbits. But in the end, the fellowship holds together sufficiently for the group to succeed in rescuing Middle-earth from the perilous power of the Ring.

What was on Jesus' mind when whip, thorn, and nail were just hours away? Among other things, our getting along.

Tolkien was a Christian, and so maybe he had the church in the back of his mind as he developed his conception of the fellowship of the Ring. We are to be that body of people who overcome the human tendencies to fracture and fragment, such that others will look at us and know us by our "love for one another" (John 13:35). This goes even for Christians who have an ingrained habit of fighting with others.

What was on Jesus' mind when whip, thorn, and nail were just hours away? Among other things, He was concerned about our getting along. In His words to the Father, He said, "I pray that they will all be one, just as You and I are one—as You are in Me, Father, and I am in You. And may they be in us so that the world will believe You sent Me" (John 17:21).

Such unity and harmony are not ours just by choosing them; they are possible only through supernatural enabling. When Christ departed this world, He left behind the Holy Spirit to live in us and work in our hearts. He softens our hearts toward one another and quells our tendency toward conflict. For this reason, Paul could say, "Make every effort to keep yourselves united in the Spirit, binding yourselves together with peace" (Ephesians 4:3).

As we work through the soul-healing process, we should be seeking the virtue of harmony with others to take the place that was once filled by conflict. Our final word on the subject to you, then, is the same as that of the apostle Paul: "Live in harmony with each other" (Romans 12:16).

SOUL PRESCRIPTION FOR DIVISIVENESS

Are you struggling with a habit of being divisive? We have outlined a five-step process to help you repent and heal in this area of your life. Take all the time you need with each of the steps below.

Step 1: Adopt a Correct View of God

When we are constant sources of conflict and strife, it is obvious that we are not truly seeing God for who He is. What aspects of your view of God may be influencing your conflict problem? The points listed below will help you begin the process of self-analysis.

- God is love; there is no place in His kingdom for conflict.

> We don't need to write to you about the importance of loving each other, for God Himself has taught you to love one another.
>
> —1 Thessalonians 4:2

- God is merciful and He expects us to show mercy to others.

> Always be humble and gentle. Be patient with each other, making allowance for each other's faults because of your love.
>
> —Ephesians 4:2

When you view God as a loving and merciful being, you will respond in like manner to those around you. Undertake a survey on the Bible's passages on God's peaceable nature. Tools such as a concordance and a topical Bible can help you in this task.

Step 2: Revise Your False Beliefs

What erroneous beliefs do you have that justify your combative spirit? Chances are, you have some false beliefs about yourself, about other people, and about how life works. Ask yourself the following questions:

- Do you believe you must always correct others when they are wrong?

  > Starting a quarrel is like opening a floodgate, so stop before a dispute breaks out.
  >   —Proverbs 17:14

- Do you believe you have the right to say spiteful things about others because of something they have said about you?

  > Do all that you can to live in peace with everyone.
  >   —Romans 12:18

Continue your Bible study by examining what Scripture says about harmony and unity. As you do so, reconsider your beliefs, acknowledged or unspoken, that may have helped turn you into a fighter. Conform your thinking to God's truth.

Step 3: Repent of Your Sin

What type of conflict are you engaged in? Is it gossip? Quarreling? Judgmentalism? Something else? Identify it specifically.

After admitting your sin to yourself, admit it to God. Pray the following prayer of repentance (or pray in your own words):

> God, I am guilty of _____. It is sin, and I am sorry for it. Please forgive me for being a person of conflict and strife. Cleanse me of that sin, I pray. Then grant me some of Your power to keep from participating in conflict the next time the potential arises. And the next. And the next. In Christ's name, amen.

If you have harmed others with your sin, apologize to them. Seek reconciliation and offer restitution where appropriate.

Step 4: Defend against Spiritual Attacks

Beware the world, the flesh, and the Devil, who will want to goad you into fighting again. They want nothing better than to see you contradict your repentance by returning to a pattern of conflict. Do not be naive about these foes!

- In God's eyes, harmony among people is a high value. In the world system, though, conflict is seen as a way of getting what you want. Watch out for worldly values that would justify your sinful tendency toward conflict. Overcome the world by rejecting its values.
- God honors those who control their desires to say and do things that divide people. Your flesh, or sinful nature, however, still enjoys the feeling of power that comes from mixing it up with people. Do not forget that the sinful nature has been crucified and that you do not have to give in to its desires. Give in to the Spirit instead.
- God provides a way out of every situation where you would be tempted to spread strife. Satan, on the other hand, gladly points out each opportunity you have to fight, gossip, and judge. Resist his schemes with the "shoes of peace" and the rest of the spiritual armor (see Ephesians 6:10–18).

Remain alert to any temptation that would draw you back into your sin of conflict. Seek the resources offered by God to defend against the attacks when they come. Those resources are more than enough to beat back all attacks.

Step 5: Flee Temptation

If you do not want to give in to the temptation of conflict, get away from it as fast as you can!

- Focus on your relationship with God.
  You get into conflict when you focus on what others have done to upset you. So instead, keep your focus on God and His peace-loving nature. Learn to jump right into prayer when a situation arises that makes you want to fight.

- Latch on to God's promises.
  Find encouraging words in the Scriptures that you can learn from and memorize for times when you are inclined to jump into the fray. Psalm 133 is one eligible passage.

How wonderful and pleasant it is
       when brothers live together in harmony.
For harmony is as precious as the anointing oil
       that was poured over Aaron's head,
that ran down his beard and
       onto the border of his robe.
Harmony is as refreshing as the dew from Mount Hermon
       that falls on the mountains of Zion.
And the LORD has pronounced his blessing,
       even life everlasting.

- Establish safeguards.

  Are there certain things that trigger your tendency to sin through conflict? Of course there are. Take practical precautions to avoid those triggering situations. These are the kinds of things you can try:

  - If you like to gossip, avoid people who pass on juicy tidbits to you in the first place.
  - If you start arguments when your spouse criticizes something in your behavior, try harder to meet his or her expectations.
  - If you joined a committee and seem to always be the center of conflict, resign from the committee.
  - Ask a trusted Christian friend to hold you accountable in your commitment to not participate in conflict.

- Expect victory.

  Every day is a new day. Though you may have slipped into conflict regularly in the past, you can now become a peacemaker with the help of the Prince of Peace. Thank God in advance for the victory He will give.

Visit www.SoulPrescription.com for more insights and resources, and to download a free leader's guide for small group Bible studies.

Chapter 17

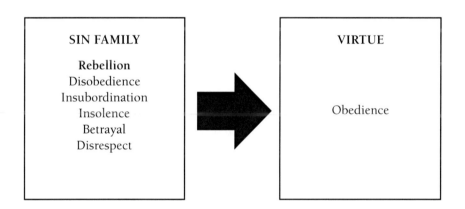

REBELLION: PLAYING AGAINST YOUR OWN TEAM

SIN FAMILY	VIRTUE
Rebellion Disobedience Insubordination Insolence Betrayal Disrespect	Obedience

In 1967, the ministry that Vonette and I (Bill) had started years earlier, *Campus Crusade for Christ*, was running smoothly and expanding steadily. But trouble was brewing on the inside. A half dozen regional directors had become disappointed with me as the CEO, and one day in October, they asked for a meeting with me. I agreed to hear them out.

These men had no complaints about my character or ethics. But they did have criticism to offer about my leadership style and philosophy and even one or two points of my theology. Furthermore, they thought my skills were not adequate for the challenges our ministry was then facing. In consequence, they asked me to resign.

I loved these men—I did then, and I do now. I had poured myself into them. I trusted them. So what they were saying was shocking to me. But it was as though God wrapped a protective shield around me. I did not feel as if I had to react out of anger, and I was able to listen to them patiently.

Finally I said, "Let's talk about this. I've got blind spots just like anybody else, and I'm very sorry I've disappointed you."

But then I added, "Gentlemen, there's one thing you need to know: Vonette and I started this movement by ourselves with the Lord. By the end of the day, there may be only the two of us left, but we started *Campus Crusade for Christ* and we will continue to direct it. God gave me this vision, and I'm going to be faithful to that vision."

When the meeting was over, I did not know what would happen. Perhaps my critics would be successful in pushing me out of my position. But what really happened was that over the next several months, the six disaffected regional directors all left *Campus Crusade* voluntarily.

Over the years since then, most of these former Crusade leaders have apologized to me. Meanwhile, I took steps to encourage constructive criticism within the organization's leadership structure. I matured as a result of this experience, and so did *Campus Crusade*.

One thing I learned from this episode, though, was just how painful rebellion can be. By God's choice, I was in charge of the ministry, and it was deeply hurtful to me when my subordinates would not accept my authority. I felt personally attacked and I was concerned that my position had been weakened.

To reject or undermine properly instituted authority is to rebel against the order God has established in human society.

The fact is that in life there are authority structures. In governments, in businesses, in churches, and in homes, some people are leaders over others. In different situations, indeed, each of us is a follower and a leader. Except in certain limited situations, to reject or undermine properly instituted authority is to rebel against the order God has established in human society.

Some people seem to be rebels and dissenters by nature. Using either passive or aggressive tactics (maybe both), they seek to overthrow the authority that others have over them. Obeying rankles with them, and so they do it as little as possible.

If this describes your behavior, you have a sin habit requiring repentance before God. Consider the types of rebellion as we describe them, keeping in mind the question *Am I willing to begin the healing process for my sin habit of rebellion?*

REBELLION AT HOME

Mary had rebelled against the preaching of her father, a godly pastor. This young woman lived with her boyfriend in open defiance of the biblical teaching she had received. She thought her new lifestyle would bring her happiness. Quickly, though, she became filled with hatred and resentment. When a mutual friend brought Mary to my office for counsel, I (Bill) had to explain that she was going through difficult times because she had rebelled against God and her father.

Mary and many others like her have violated the fifth commandment: "Honor your father and mother" (Exodus 20:12). This is one way rebellion can upset the natural order God has established in a family. It always produces harm, as in Mary's case. Compliance with the commandment, on the other hand, results in blessing.

The apostle Paul said as much when he reaffirmed the fifth commandment for Christian families.

> Children, obey your parents because you belong to the Lord, for this is the right thing to do. "Honor your father and mother." This is the first commandment with a promise: If you honor your father and mother, "things will go well for you, and you will have a long life on the earth."
>
> —Ephesians 6:1–3[1]

Even when we are grown up, we still have a responsibility to honor (though not necessarily obey) our parents. As adults, we can honor our parents by forgiving them when they have wronged us, respecting their God-given position, caring for their needs, and

Are You Rebellious?

The following self-evaluation quiz will help you determine whether you have a tendency toward rebellion.

- If your parents are still living, do they resent your attitude toward them?
- If you are a wife, does your husband feel that you work against him instead of with him?
- As a husband, do you expect compliance from your wife but resist those who have authority over you?
- Do you refuse to pursue the vision for your local church established by the church leaders?
- If you have a job, does your boss look upon you as an obstacle to getting the company where it is hoping to go?
- Do you set a poor example for your coworkers, bringing down morale?
- Do you disobey laws when you think you can get away with it?
- Do the people you know ever use words like *disloyal, disrespectful,* or *scornful* to describe your attitude toward people in authority?

loving them.[2] To refuse to do these things is to rebel against the order God has established between the generations of a family.

Another type of rebellion that can upset the family order is a lack of submission by a wife to her husband. We know this is a controversial subject these days. And most certainly we would not want wifely submission to be interpreted to mean that the wife becomes a doormat for her husband. But at the same time, we affirm the unequivocal teaching of Scripture.

> For wives, this means submit your husbands as to the Lord. For a husband is the head of his wife as Christ is the head of the church. He is the Savior of His body, the church. As the church submits to Christ, so you wives should submit to your husbands in everything.
> —Ephesians 5:22–24[3]

Though men and women are equal in importance, dignity, and ability, as well as in their relationship to God, He has granted to husbands the leadership in the home. As with all types of Christian leadership, however, the husband's leadership in the home is a servant leadership—he is to seek to understand his wife, meet her needs, and express love to her. Assuming she fulfills her duty of respecting her husband, their roles produce a complementary relationship between the two that ideally enables each to reach his or her full potential.

If there is discord between a husband and wife, the problem might be a failure in his leadership. But it also might be a failure in her followership. Some wives have fallen into a pattern of balking at their husbands' initiative, whittling away at their husbands' dignity, or openly scoffing at what the men suggest. This is rebellion within marriage, and it is wrong.

Paul used different words in his instructions to children and wives: children are to "obey" their parents, while wives are to "submit" to their husbands.[4] This difference reflects the fact that wives are equals with their husbands, whereas children are clearly subordinate to their parents.

Husbands and fathers also have a responsibility to model submission and obedience to God and other authorities in their life.

What example are they setting for their family? Do they demonstrate a desire to follow God wholeheartedly and live according to His ordained authority structure? If a man is living in rebellion, it is much more difficult for his wife to be submissive or his children to be obedient.

Rebellion can do much harm. Our families would not be in the sorry state they are in today if all of us would understand and fulfill our family roles better.

The same could be said for our churches.

REBELLION AT CHURCH

Arguably, 2 Corinthians is the most painful book of the New Testament to read. In these pages we listen to the anguish of a faithful apostle who was forced to defend his God-given position of authority over the church he had founded in Corinth, a city of Greece.

Some teachers had arrived in Corinth and were criticizing Paul in his absence. We are not sure who they were or exactly what they were teaching, but by reading between the lines we can conclude that these other leaders were accusing Paul of having inadequate authority, not being trustworthy, embezzling offerings, and being a braggart in his letters but a coward in person. Sadly, many of the Corinthian believers who should have known better were nodding along with these charges.

Paul wrote 2 Corinthians to defend himself. In it he said that he had been given a special call to be an apostle, as evidenced by how he had suffered for Christ. He had always taught the Corinthians the truth and acted in a selfless, aboveboard manner toward them. Given these truths, he deserved respect as their spiritual father. "We are not reaching beyond these boundaries when we claim authority over you," said Paul, "for we were the first to travel all the way to Corinth with the Good News of Christ" (2 Corinthians 10:14).

We do not know exactly how matters turned out within the congregation at Corinth, but since they preserved Paul's letters, they presumably continued to hold him in some esteem.

Our families would not be in the sorry state they are in today if all of us would understand and fulfill our family roles better.

What about in our churches today? Can the leaders count on the cooperation of the rest of the members? Let's say an elder board senses that God wants to do new things through the congregation by refocusing their efforts. Will the members go along with the changes, or will they cling to outmoded programs they have grown too comfortable with? Or consider a case where Dale is selected as teacher of the adult Sunday school class instead of Marvin. Will Marvin be a supporter of Dale's efforts, or will he make it subtly known that he would have done a better job?

The rule should be that all of us cooperate with those whom God has placed in positions of authority over us in the church.

Certainly, if church leaders are teaching false doctrine, we must try to correct their error. Or if we think they are making a strategic mistake, we may choose to raise the issue in an appropriate forum. But those are exceptions. The rule should be that all of us cooperate with those whom God has placed in positions of authority over us in the church. This rule is consistently taught in Scripture.

"Obey your spiritual leaders, and do what they say," ordered the writer to the Hebrews. "Their work is to watch over your souls, and they are accountable to God. Give them reason to do this with joy and not with sorrow. That would certainly not be for your benefit" (Hebrews 13:17).

Paul told the Thessalonians, "Dear brothers and sisters, honor those who are your leaders in the Lord's work. They work hard among you and give you spiritual guidance. Show them great respect and wholehearted love because of their work" (1 Thessalonians 5:12–13).

The young pastor Titus had a heart filled with love when the Corinthians "obeyed him and welcomed him with such fear and deep respect" (2 Corinthians 7:15). Our church leaders will feel the same toward us as we honor them for their shepherding over us.

A cooperative spirit seems appropriate to many when it comes to the church. But what about in secular society, particularly in that sphere of life where many of us spend so much of our time: our jobs?

REBELLION AT WORK

You have probably seen framed posters that feature beautiful nature images and inspirational slogans designed to motivate workers. But did you know that there is a line of products parodying these posters by inverting their messages? One company produces posters, notepads, and the like that feature beautiful pictures paired with cynical statements.

One poster features a tiger lying sleepily on a tree branch. The slogan says, "It takes 43 muscles to frown and 17 to smile, but it doesn't take any to just sit there with a dumb look on your face."

Another poster shows one hand passing a racer's baton to another. The slogan here? "The secret to success is knowing who to blame for your failures."

A third poster displays an eagle soaring above a mountain. "Leaders are like eagles. We don't have either of them here."[5]

We can laugh at such spoofs. And certainly these products expose some of the follies of the modern workplace. But imagine that you are a boss trying to do the best for your company, and then one day an employee of yours puts up a poster in his cubicle declaring, "Leaders are like eagles. We don't have either of them here." What would that do to *your* motivation?

Workplace insubordination comes in many forms. Sometimes it consists of flagrant backstabbing. Just as Judas betrayed Jesus to His enemies, so some employees will set their bosses up to take a fall. Perhaps they see it as a way of getting revenge or as aiding their own climb up the ladder.

Other times, insubordination is more subtle—but just as serious. Resisting change, criticizing the boss behind his back, dragging one's heels, neglecting to comply with the details of a plan, sabotaging an unpopular project—these and more are forms of rebellion against authority in the workplace. And these are unacceptable behaviors for Christians.

The Golden Rule applies here as in all interpersonal relationships: treat others as you would want them to treat you. And in fact, one day you may be elevated to the position that your boss now holds. How will you want your employees to react to you then? Set an example of cooperation with company leadership now.

The apostle Paul wrote on this subject to some early Christians who were slaves. While the slave/master relationship does not exactly parallel our modern employee/employer relationship, Paul's words are, nevertheless, instructive to those of us with jobs today.

> Slaves, obey your earthly masters with deep respect and fear. Serve them sincerely as you would serve Christ. Try to please them all the time, not just when they are watching you. As slaves of Christ, do the will of God with all your heart. Work with enthusiasm, as though you were working for the Lord rather than for people. Remember that the Lord will reward each one of us for the good we do, whether we are slaves or free.
> —Ephesians 6:5–8[6]

That's the opposite of demotivating, isn't it? If you have been insubordinate on the job, replace "slaves" with "employees" and "masters" with "bosses," then make Paul's words your motto to live by.

But there is still one more major realm of life in which we must consider the dangers of rebellion: our role as citizens of the land.

REBELLION IN SOCIETY

During the period when Moses was leading the Hebrews in the Sinai desert, a tribal leader named Korah instigated a rebellion with 250 other Hebrew leaders. These men approached Moses and his brother, Aaron, and asked them, "What right do you have to act as though you are greater than the rest of the LORD's people?" (Numbers 16:3).

Here was the authentic voice of rebellion. It has been echoed down through the ages as individuals, with whatever mixture of selfish and altruistic motives, have sought to take away the power of those in authority over them in the community. Sometimes they are successful; sometimes they are not. In the case of Korah versus Moses, God passed sentence by opening up the earth to swallow the conspirators. It seems God did not appreciate it when people tried to replace the leader He had picked.

But few of us would ever consider starting a coup. We are more likely to register our disappointment in our civil leaders by criticizing, whining, and complaining. That happened in ancient Israel too. "The whole congregation of the children of Israel murmured against Moses and Aaron in the wilderness" (Exodus 16:2 KJV). The King James version uses the word "murmur" that fits the noise we collectively make when we grumble about what is happening in government instead of taking constructive steps for change—or just holding our tongue.

We can learn an important lesson from the case of the "murmuring" Hebrews. As the apostle Paul wrote, "Don't grumble as some of them did, and then were destroyed by the angel of death. These things happened to them as examples for us. They were written down to warn us who live at the end of the age" (1 Corinthians 10:10–11).[7]

The New Testament is quite definite on the point that Christians are to be obedient to civil authorities. The clearest exposition of this point occurs in the letter to the Romans, where Paul said, "Obey the government, for God is the one who put it there."

> Everyone must submit to governing authorities. For all authority comes from God, and those in positions of authority have been placed there by God. So anyone who rebels against authority is rebelling against what God has instituted, and they will be punished. For the authorities do not strike fear in people who are doing right, but in those who are doing wrong. Would you like to live without fear of the authorities? Do what is right, and they will honor you. The authorities are God's servants, sent for your good. But if you are doing wrong, of course you should be afraid, for they have the power to punish you. They are God's servants sent for the very purpose of punishing those who do what is wrong. So you must submit to them, not only to avoid punishment, but also to keep a clear conscience.

Pay your taxes, too, for these same reasons. For government workers need to be paid. They are serving God in what they do. Give to everyone what you owe them: Pay your taxes and government fees to those who collect them, and give respect and honor to those who are in authority.

—Romans 13:1–7[8]

Paul was writing about the government in Rome. The Roman Empire, while being an agent of civil order in many ways, had, nevertheless, forcibly occupied many of its neighboring lands, including the Holy Land. Israel had no more chance of being allowed its independence than an Eastern Bloc nation had of being set free by the Soviet Union at the height of the Cold War. Paul himself would eventually be executed by officers of the Roman government.

This shows us that we must not wait for our government to be all that we wish before we will give it our proper obedience as citizens. Even if our leaders are less than perfect (and who is not?), we should show respect to them. David offers us a beautiful example of this.

When David was a young man, the king of Israel, Saul, became jealous of David and wanted to kill him. Though David had done nothing wrong, he had to go on the run. At one point while Saul was searching the wilderness for David, the younger man had an opportunity to assassinate the king. But he did not do it. He even felt badly about his decision to cut off a piece of Saul's robe. "The LORD knows I shouldn't have done that to my lord the king," he said to his men. "The LORD forbid that I should do this to my lord the king and attack the LORD's anointed one, for the LORD Himself has chosen him" (1 Samuel 24:6). Even after Saul died in battle and David himself became king, David continued to honor his predecessor's memory.

Our first reaction to any requirement placed upon us by duly instituted authorities in our society should be to obey. As Jesus Himself said, we should "give to Caesar what belongs to Caesar" (Matthew 22:21). Caesar was head of the much-hated Roman government.

Of course, Jesus also said, "Everything that belongs to God must be given to God." What does that mean for us?

REBELLION AGAINST GOD

Rebellion against human authority figures is always rebellion against God in an indirect sense because it means refusing to accept the order He has established. But there is also such a thing as direct rebellion against God. Some people refuse to obey His commands in Scripture or His individual leading in their lives.

The truth is, the most unhappy people in the world are not unbelievers, many of whom are ignorantly and blissfully happy in their sin, albeit temporarily; the most unhappy people in the world are Christians who resist the will of God for their lives. The Christian who refuses to do the will of God must be prepared to pay the price of disobedience. "You will always harvest what you plant" (Galatians 6:7).

A man in Sweden stubbornly resisted God's call to ministry— even through the death of his wife and daughter. He went into business and prospered, only to be robbed by his own son. In his older years, he languished with cancer. He said, "I know that I am saved, but, oh, the loss, for I know that I soon will be ushered into His presence only to give an account of a whole life of disobedience."

Did this man really know Christ? Consider the Bible's words:

> And we can be sure that we know Him if we obey His commandments. If someone claims, "I know God," but doesn't obey God's commandments, that person is a liar and is not living in the truth. But those who obey God's word truly show how completely they love Him. That is how we know we are living in Him. Those who say they live in God should live their lives as Jesus did.
> —1 John 2:3–6

Whether the Swedish man was a true Christian or not, we can say we have never met a happy disobedient Christian or an unhappy obedient one.

R. A. Torrey, a famous educator and evangelist, told the story of a woman who came to him and said she did not believe in the Bible anymore. When he asked her why, she replied, "Because I have tried its promises and found them untrue. The Bible says, 'Whatsoever ye ask believing, ye shall receive.' Well, I fully expected to get things from God in prayer, but I did not receive them, so the promise failed."

Dr. Torrey then turned her to 1 John 3:22: "We will receive from Him whatever we ask because we obey Him and do the things that please Him." Then he said, "Were you keeping His commandments and doing those things pleasing in His sight?"

She confessed she was not.

Her trouble was not that the Bible's promises were not true; it was her own disobedience that was the problem. May that never be the case with any of us. As the fifteenth-century religious writer Thomas à Kempis is said to have prayed every day, let us say to God, "As Thou wilt; what Thou wilt; when Thou wilt."

This brings us to an interesting question. What do we do when our obedience to God would seem to conflict with our obedience to human authority figures? Is it ever acceptable to disobey earthly authority, whether that be of government, business, church, or home?

DISOBEDIENCE—WHEN AND HOW

Certainly our normal response to authority should be obedience. But if a human leader is calling us to do something that would require us to disobey God, then we can and should refuse to obey the human leader. Actually, in such a case, we are still being obedient, only it is to the higher authority (God) when there is a conflict with a lesser authority (some human leader).

We see a clear example of this in the history of the early church. When Peter and the other apostles were hauled up before the Jewish high council, the Sanhedrin, for preaching about Jesus after they had been told not to, they boldly declared to the council members, "We must obey God rather than any human authority" (Acts 5:29). Complying with the Sanhedrin's restriction would have meant violating the Great Commission, given to them by Jesus not long before. That the disciples could not do.

Neither can we disobey God in order to obey someone else.

- If a parent urges his teenager to cheat on a test, the teen should say no.
- If a husband suggests that he and his wife watch a pornographic movie "to spice things up," she should refuse.
- If a pastor preaches that faith in Jesus is not the only way to acceptance with God, a church member should object.
- If a boss tells an employee to do something unethical, the employee should not comply.
- If a government official seeks a bribe to do a favor, a citizen should blow the whistle.

These responses are not rebellion. They are not a refusal to accept authority per se, but rather they are a considered reaction to a specific injustice. Such a reaction is more akin to civil disobedience than to rebellion. One can remain the "loyal opposition" while disobeying on ethical grounds.

Of course, there are poor ways and better ways to disobey when the need arises. Here are a few guidelines to remember:

- Raise objections respectfully.
- Continue to love the other, making sure your objection does not turn into a personal attack.
- Choose the right time and place, working through proper channels to the extent that it is possible.
- State your reasons logically and do not let your emotions run away with you.
- Seek justice but at the same time be ready to forgive.

These legitimate responses to errors by those in authority are in keeping with a general pattern of obedience to authority. For those of us who have a habit of rebellion, obedience is a virtue to ask the Lord to build into our lives instead of sin.

GET YOURSELF IN LINE

We want to be clear about one thing. In authority relationships, responsibility goes both ways. Possessing authority is never the same thing as having a license for tyranny. The misuse of power is as great a sin, perhaps greater, than rebellion.

The same New Testament passages that speak about children's submission to their parents, wives' submission to their husbands, and slaves' submission to their masters also speak about the responsibilities of those in authority. In fact, Christians are all to "submit to one another out of reverence for Christ" (Ephesians 5:21). Leaders submit by serving righteously, while followers submit by cooperating willingly. In this way order and love may coexist.

As we said earlier, at different times and in different circumstances, all of us are both leaders and followers. For example, a woman may be a follower in relation to her boss at work and a leader to her child at home. When we are in positions of following, obedience should be our habitual practice.

When the troops scatter, the war is lost.

The Greek word used for "submit" in Ephesians 5 came out of military experience. It referred to soldiers lining up in ranks under their officers. So when we are called to submit, we should get in line under the authority of our leaders. To do otherwise is to risk failure, even disaster, in the family or organization of which we are a part. For when the troops scatter, the war is lost.

If obedience is a virtue that does not come easily to you, you can learn it with God's help. Even though Jesus was God's Son, "He learned obedience from the things He suffered" (Hebrews 5:8). Seek the Holy Spirit for the ability to eliminate the ugliness of rebellion from your life and replace it with the beauty of obedience.

Begin now to heal the sin of rebellion in your life.

SOUL PRESCRIPTION FOR REBELLION

Are you struggling with a form of rebellion against authority? We have outlined a five-step process to help you repent and heal in this area of your life. Take all the time you need with each of the steps below.

Step 1: Adopt a Correct View of God

If you have a tendency toward rebellion, chances are good that your view of God has become skewed in some way. Perhaps you see God as a tyrant, selfishly wanting everything His own way. Your reaction to Him, then, could spill over to your relationships with other authority figures. Consider these points:

- God's commandments are fair and good.

    > He is the Rock; His deeds are perfect.
    >   Everything He does is just and fair.
    > He is a faithful God who does no wrong;
    >   how just and upright He is!
    > —Deuteronomy 32:4

- God will hold us accountable for our rebellion.

    > The LORD is slow to anger and filled with unfailing love, forgiving every kind of sin and rebellion. But He does not excuse the guilty. He lays the sins of the parents upon their children; the entire family is affected—even children in the third and fourth generations.
    > —Numbers 14:18

Embark on a study of the justice and sovereignty of God as reflected in Scripture. Keep an open mind as you encounter biblical truth, asking God to change your view of Him to make it more nearly conformed to the truth.

Step 2: Revise Your False Beliefs

If you have mistaken ideas about people and the world, you will rebel against authority figures and especially the greatest Authority Figure of them all–God. Evaluate your beliefs with the following questions:

- Do you believe you are not subject to properly instituted authorities?

   Those in positions of authority have been placed there by God.

                                                          —Romans 13:1

- Do you believe you can defy authority without consequences?

   You will say, "How I hated discipline! If only I had not ignored all the warnings!"

                                                          —Proverbs 5:12

- Do you believe God's commandments and will are unreasonable?

   I will walk in freedom, for I have devoted myself to Your commandments.

                                                          —Psalm 119:45

Trace the theme of obedience through Scripture. In the process, test your beliefs about how families, businesses, churches, and society should operate. Choose to accept the principle of obedience to proper authority.

Step 3: Repent of Your Sin

Where does your rebellion usually manifest itself? At home? In church? At work? In society at large? Toward God? Is your problem disobedience, insubordination, lawlessness, insolence, scoffing, or disrespect? Pinpoint your sin habit. Admit it to yourself. Own it.

When you are ready, pray the following prayer in faith, trusting that God will forgive your sin and empower your obedience.

   God, You have established structures of authority to make things work better for Your children. Yet I have sometimes strived not to support but to break down

those structures. In particular, I am guilty of _____.
It is a sin, and I am sorry for it. Please forgive me now.
Cleanse me entirely of my sin of _____. Then fill
me with Holy Spirit power to enable me to resist the
temptation of rebellion from now on. In the name of
Christ the King, amen.

If you have harmed others with your sin, apologize to them.
Seek reconciliation and offer restitution where appropriate.

Step 4: Defend against Spiritual Attacks

Don't breathe too big a sigh of relief after repenting of rebellion.
Attacks from the world, the flesh, and the Devil are all but inevi-
table now. These spiritual enemies want to draw you back into
disobedience to God.

- The world system tells us, "The way to a good life is to have
  total freedom and do whatever you want." Would God agree?
  Of course not. He says, "True freedom comes from submitting to proper authorities, especially Mine." Overcome the
  world by rejecting its values and embracing God's.
- Your flesh, or sinful nature, has always enjoyed the sense
  of power and autonomy that comes from rebelling against
  authority. It craves to get that feeling back. What you need
  to do is remember that your flesh is already dead; you have
  no need to obey its dictates. Obey the Spirit and not the
  flesh.
- The Devil is hatching schemes to tempt you to rebel again,
  doing damage to you and others in the process. Among the
  other pieces of spiritual armor listed in Ephesians 6, put on
  the helmet of salvation to protect your mind from Satan's
  poisonous thoughts.

The attacks of the world, the flesh, and the Devil are formidable,
but not impossible to defeat. With God acting in your life, you are
more than able to repel each assault thrown at you.

Step 5: Flee Temptation

Take practical steps to avoid sliding back into rebellion and to cement an attitude of obedience in your heart.

- Focus on your relationship with God.

  In your devotional and worship times, focus on God as King over all the universe. Learning to be obedient to this Sovereign will help you be obedient in all areas of life.

- Latch on to God's promises.

  Find helpful verses in Scripture and then commit them to memory to help you in your struggles against the temptation to rebel. One such verse for you may be the following:

  > The commandments of the LORD are right,
  >   bringing joy to the heart.
  > The commands of the LORD are clear,
  >   giving insight for living.
  > —Psalm 19:8

- Establish safeguards.

  Think about the usual sources of temptation for you to rebel. Identify precautions you can take to protect yourself from those sources. Let the following examples spark your imagination:

  - If you tend to be insubordinate to your boss, start calling this person "sir" or "ma'am" as a reminder of the respect you owe.
  - If you are inclined to scoff at church leaders' direction, take the lowliest position of service in the church you can find—and fulfill it without complaint.
  - If you tend to be critical of government officials, send a card of thanks to your congressional representative the next time he or she does something honorable.
  - Ask a trusted Christian friend to hold you accountable in your commitment to not rebel against authority.

- Expect victory.

  Developing a submissive spirit is not easy, but you have the Holy Spirit living in you and producing in you a spirit of obedience. Be confident and rejoice in every sign of progress.

Visit www.SoulPrescription.com for more insights and resources, and to download a free leader's guide for small group Bible studies.

IRRESPONSIBILITY: THE UNDISCIPLINED LIFE

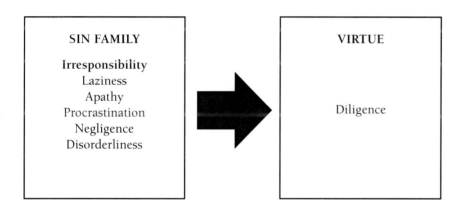

SIN FAMILY	VIRTUE
Irresponsibility Laziness Apathy Procrastination Negligence Disorderliness	Diligence

A bout to open wide, with the drill lowering toward his mouth, a man humorously pleaded with his dentist, "Careful, Doc. I can stand anything but pain."

By nature, every one of us is inclined to take the path of least resistance. The dentist usually injects us with Novocain to keep us from feeling any pain. We do not like the injection needle because of its momentary sting. We look for easy exercise programs that are perspiration free and tireless. Students shortcut their assigned reading by reviewing study notes.

And diets? There always seems to be a new fad for shedding weight without hunger or exercise. Liquid diets, banana diets, grapefruit diets, carbohydrate diets, protein diets.... The list goes on and on.

When it comes right down to it, we do not like hard work. Areas that we recognize are in our best interest, such as with exercise, diet, and study, are avoided even though we know they will help us.

For most of us, the irresponsibility is merely occasional, cropping up only when a particularly hard chore stands before us. Others, though, are chronically irresponsible, rarely doing more than enough to get by at work, frequently arriving late for appointments, or so disorderly that their houses are a perpetual mess. Filled with lethargy and indifference, they go through life earning a reputation for being undependable. They have grown used to accomplishing little.

Does any of this describe you? Are you troubled in your conscience about your indolence, negligence, tardiness, apathy, or passivity? Are you aware that you only fulfill your responsibilities when it is clear that there is something in it for you? Our Lord would not have you so live.

I (Bill) have been inspired since my early Christian years by something the evangelist D. L. Moody said: "The world has yet to see what God can do with a man fully consecrated to Him." Sticking close to God, working hard to fulfill His will for me in every facet of life—that is what I have strived to do, not for my own glory, but for God's.

A life of working hard at one's pursuits is a glorious adventure when we do it in tune with God's Spirit.

To what degree I have succeeded in my objective is for God to judge. But I can testify that a life of working hard at one's pursuits is a glorious adventure when it is done in tune with God's Spirit. It is the way we are meant to live.

If you have a sin habit of irresponsibility, it is not too late to seek the Lord's help for change. You can become a responsible and hardworking member of His kingdom if you will face up to your problem and seek to heal this area of your life according to His principles.

Let us begin our exploration of the sins of irresponsibility with laziness. No other sin in this family is so frequently addressed or so roundly criticized in Scripture. "Never be lazy, but work hard and serve the Lord enthusiastically" (Romans 12:11).

A LESSON FROM THE ANTS

The book of Proverbs is about how to live skillfully, from a godly perspective. Given the frequency with which laziness is condemned in this book of the Bible, it is easy to see that sloth can have no place in a well-lived life. What can we learn about the causes and costs of laziness from the book of Proverbs?

1. In the worst cases, laziness can reach ridiculous proportions.

    Lazy people don't even cook the game they catch, but the diligent make use of everything they find.
    —Proverbs 12:27

    Lazy people take food in their hand but don't even lift it to their mouth.
    —Proverbs 19:24

2. Laziness is on a par with other serious sins.

    A lazy person is as bad as someone who destroys things.
    —Proverbs 18:9

3. Lazy people sleep too much.

    As a door swings back and forth on its hinges, so the lazy person turns over in bed.
    —Proverbs 26:14

(If you were not already convinced that the Bible has a sense of humor, this image should help to change your mind.)

4. The lazy make excuses for their laziness.

    The lazy person claims, "There's a lion on the road! Yes, I'm sure there's a lion out there!"
    —Proverbs 26:13

Are You Irresponsible?

The following self-evaluation quiz will help you determine whether you have a tendency toward irresponsibility.

- Do you sleep more than you need to?
- At work, do you watch the clock and worry more about looking busy than about being productive?
- Does your boss feel that he or she must keep an eye on you?
- Do you often forget appointments or show up late without any good reason for it?
- Do you put things off that you know you need to do?
- Do you start projects and then leave them undone?
- Do you have trouble finding what you need in your home or workspace?
- Do other people criticize you for carelessness?
- At night, do you ever look back on your day and wonder what you accomplished?
- Has it been a while since you were excited about anything you were doing?

(Now are you convinced that the Bible can be funny?)

5. The lazy delude themselves.

> Lazy people consider themselves smarter than seven
> wise counselors.
> —Proverbs 26:13–16

(If they are that smart, why aren't they, instead of others, serving as trusted counselors to the mighty? If they were half as smart as they think they are, they would know better than to be so lazy.)

6. The lazy grow unhappy because they have *wants* but do not have the *willingness* to work to fulfill those wants.

> Lazy people want much but get little, but those who
> work hard will prosper.
> —Proverbs 13:4

> Despite their desires, the lazy will come to ruin, for
> their hands refuse to work.
> —Proverbs 21:25

7. The lazy are unpopular, especially among those whom they let down.

> Lazy people irritate their employers, like vinegar to the
> teeth or smoke in the eyes.
> —Proverbs 10:26

8. Laziness leads to poverty and to a menial position in society.

> Lazy people are soon poor; hard workers get rich.
> —Proverbs 10:4

> Work hard and become a leader; be lazy and become a
> slave.
> —Proverbs 12:24

Those too lazy to plow in the right season will have no
food at the harvest.

—Proverbs 20:4

9. The tendency of the lazy to oversleep is a key reason why
   they grow poor.

Take a lesson from the ants, you lazybones. Learn from
their ways and become wise! Though they have no
prince or governor or ruler to make them work, they
labor hard all summer, gathering food for the winter.
But you, lazybones, how long will you sleep? When will
you wake up? A little extra sleep, a little more slumber,
a little folding of the hands to rest—then poverty will
pounce on you like a bandit; scarcity will attack you
like an armed robber.

—Proverbs 6:6–11

*The man or woman of
God is expected to be
diligent in all areas
of life.*

Lazy people sleep soundly, but idleness leaves them
hungry.

—Proverbs 19:15

Too much sleep clothes them in rags.

—Proverbs 23:21

10. Laziness actually makes life harder, not easier.

A lazy person's way is blocked with briers, but the path
of the upright is an open highway.

—Proverbs 15:19

It seems, from all this, that the man or woman of God is expected to be diligent in all areas of life. We should be working
hard at doing our jobs or studies, taking care of home chores, rais-
ing our children, serving in our churches and communities, and
most importantly, cultivating our relationship with God through
spiritual disciplines. One who is chronically lazy is a person with
a serious sin habit.

Of course, while saying this, we do not mean to imply that taking it easy is always wrong. In fact, rest has its proper place in a well-lived life.

THE PROPER PLACE OF REST

Jesus said, "My Father never stops working, so why should I?" Talk about a work ethic!

The rhythm of labor and rest goes all the way back to the beginning, as the Creator Himself rested on the seventh day. That was the example God offered when instructing His nation Israel to set aside one day of the week as a day of rest.

> Remember to observe the Sabbath day by keeping it holy. You have six days each week for your ordinary work, but the seventh day is a Sabbath day of rest dedicated to the LORD your God. On that day no one in your household may do any work. This includes you, your sons and daughters, your male and female servants, your livestock, and any foreigners living among you. For in six days the LORD made the heavens, the earth, the sea, and everything in them; but on the seventh day He rested. That is why the LORD blessed the Sabbath day and set it apart as holy.
>
> —Exodus 20:8–11

Based on this and other observations in Scripture, we affirm the need for periodic rest. Obviously, since God made the human body, He knows we need regular times for rest and recuperation. We should obey the Bible and see that our body gets its required rest.

I (Bill) was raised on a ranch where we grew crops and raised cattle. We worked between ten and fifteen hours a day, six days a week. But as important as work was during the Depression years, we did not work on Sunday.

Today, Sabbath keeping is still vitally important to me. I instruct my associates who arrange my travel not to book a flight that will require me to travel on Sunday unless it is absolutely necessary. I ask them to help me avoid situations where I would go out to eat in restaurants on Sunday, because that would cause others to work.

So Henry and I recognize that Sabbath rest is important. But what we are talking about in this chapter are the other six days of the week. We are talking about people who are idle when they should be working. We want to say that getting *too much* rest is wrong.

According to Hebrews 4, we can all look forward to a time of ultimate rest in the eternal state. But that time is not yet. Paradoxically (or so it would seem), we are bid to "labour…to enter into that rest" (Hebrews 4:11 KJV). In this life we have much to do. Let us get on with it.

A WORKING SAVIOR

The Bible is full of examples of men and women who labored diligently at their tasks. There was Jacob, who worked fourteen years for his two wives. There were Joseph and Daniel, two Israelites whose hard work and ability raised them to near the pinnacle of power in pagan nations. But if we are looking for a hard worker, we can find no better example than that of the carpenter turned rabbi, Jesus.

Let us consider a single day in the course of our Lord's earthly ministry. (See Mark 1:21–39.)

One Saturday morning, Jesus attended a worship service at the synagogue in the village of Capernaum. There He gave the sermon and also expelled an evil spirit from one of the men attending the service. In the afternoon He visited the home of a pair of His disciples and healed a member of their family who was ill with a high fever. In the evening a crowd sought Him out, and "Jesus healed many people who were sick with various diseases, and he cast out many demons" (verse 34).

If we had such a day, we might want to sleep in. But did Jesus? No. Rather, "Before daybreak the next morning, Jesus got up and went out to an isolated place to pray" (verse 35). He would not let His outer (ministry) duties interfere with His inner (devotional) duties. His prayer time was interrupted by His disciples seeking Him out and saying, "Everyone is asking for you" (verse 37). And so the round of service to others began all over again.

Jesus expressed the divine attitude when He said on one occasion, "My Father is always working, and so am I" (John 5:17). Talk about a work ethic! This work ethic is passed down to us via the apostle Paul.

SACRED WORK

Paul told his readers (including us), "You should imitate me, just as I imitate Christ" (1 Corinthians 11:1). A part of that has to do with labor. Like Jesus, Paul was a hard worker.

Even though the apostle had a right to expect his converts to support him financially (1 Corinthians 9:3–19), he chose to support himself with a textile trade (Acts 18:3). And because of this practice, he was in a moral position to lecture some others who were idle.

> Dear brothers and sisters, we give you this command in the name of our Lord Jesus Christ: Stay away from all believers who live idle lives and don't follow the tradition they received from us. For you know that you ought to imitate us. We were not idle when we were with you. We never accepted food from anyone without paying for it. We worked hard day and night so we would not be a burden to any of you. We certainly had the right to ask you to feed us, but we wanted to give you an example to follow. Even while we were with you, we gave you this command: "Those unwilling to work will not get to eat."

> Yet we hear that some of you are living idle lives, refusing to work and meddling in other people's business. We command such people and urge them in the name of the Lord Jesus Christ to settle down and work to earn their own living. As for the rest of you, dear brothers and sisters, never get tired of doing good.
> —2 Thessalonians 3:6–13

"Settle down and get to work." Is that a command you need to hear? Jesus set the example for hard work. Paul followed it. We must follow both of their examples.

Our work matters to God. It does not merely improve our economic position; it also has spiritual significance. As Henry David Thoreau said, "You cannot kill time without injury to eternity."

But you may say, "You don't know how dreary my job is. You don't know the way my work around the house is overlooked by my spouse. You don't know the difficult people I have to work with on that committee I volunteered for."

True, we do not. But no one ever said work would always be easy or enjoyable, just that it is the right thing to do. The Bible, however, describes a change of perspective that can affect our attitude about our work. And it comes out of a context that was worse than anything any of us has to deal with.

Our work does not merely improve our economic position; it also has spiritual significance.

BOSS OF BOSSES

Slavery was widespread in the Roman world, and consequently, many of the early Christians were slaves. No doubt Paul wanted all Christian slaves freed from their servitude, just as he did Onesimus.[1] But since that was not possible, he instead helped them understand how they should act in their circumstances.

Were they to slack off whenever they got a chance, like most slaves, since someone else was unjustly reaping the benefits of their labor? No. Instead, Paul told the slaves, "Try to please them all the time, not just when they are watching you. As slaves of Christ, do the will of God with all your heart. Work with enthusiasm, as though you were working for the Lord rather than for people" (Ephesians 6:6–7).[2]

No matter how bad your job is, at least it is not slavery! But did you catch Paul's change of perspective? It can be useful to us in our own situations. We are to do our work as if we were working for the Lord rather than for people. That enables us to be consistent, diligent, reliable—and even happy—in our work.

And do you know what is most amazing? We *really are* doing our work for the Lord. When we earn an honest paycheck for honest labor, when we take care of our children, when we cultivate our personal relationship with the Lord, or contribute to the life of our local church, we are doing it out of obedience to God because we know it is what He wants us to do. Our work is for Him.

It should go without saying that this means we should strive for excellence, not just to put in our time. The Lord deserves the best, and so the Bible says, "Whatever you do, do well" (Ecclesiastes 9:10). As Martin Luther King Jr. once preached, "If a man is called to be a streetsweeper, he should sweep streets even as Michelangelo painted, or Beethoven composed music, or Shakespeare wrote poetry. He should sweep streets so well that all the hosts of heaven and earth will pause to say: 'Here lived a great streetsweeper who did his job well.'"

Work is worship.

Work is worship, if we will see it as such.

THE UNDEPENDABLE

Laziness may be the most common type, but not the only type, of irresponsibility.

Some people are irresponsible with time. They are habitually late for engagements, causing other people inconvenience as a result. Or they procrastinate, putting off doing what they know they ought to do.

Others are irresponsible with material objects. They borrow things from others and either forget to return them or else let them become damaged while in their possession. Or they may take poor care of their own possessions, letting their homes and workplaces get messy or rundown. They forget that "God is not a God of disorder but of peace" and that we are to "be sure that everything is done properly and in order" (1 Corinthians 14:33, 40).

Some people seem to be negligent, careless, and inconsistent in every area of life. Should you depend on them to fulfill what they promised? You had better not. Should you trust them to help you out if you are not keeping an eye on them? Certainly not.

What's behind all this is usually an attitude problem, whether it goes by the name of apathy, boredom, or lethargy. Theologian J. I. Packer analyzed such attitudes when he said,

The world today is full of sufferers from the wasting disease that Albert Camus focused as absurdism ("life is a bad joke"), and from the complaint that we may call Marie Antoinette's fever, since she founded the phrase that describes it ("nothing tastes"). These disorders blight the whole of life: everything becomes at once a problem and a bore, because nothing seems worthwhile.

But Packer also suggested the response to absurdism and Marie Antoinette's fever:

What makes life worthwhile is having a big enough objective, something that catches our imagination and lays hold of our allegiance; and this the Christian has in a way that no other person has.[3]

What is the "big enough objective"? It is knowing God—a task that is like penetrating ever deeper into the interior of a land that is infinite in size and so accommodates an eternity of exploration. Do you sense that your life is a part of the great story God is writing in history? Do you understand that by obeying Him in your duties and relationships you are helping to build an everlasting kingdom?

With the right perspective, your attitude can change from apathy to enthusiasm. And your sin habit of irresponsibility can be replaced by the virtue of diligence.

GET GOING!

Every year in January, health clubs around the country report a surge in membership. Can you guess why? It is because of the New Year's resolutions people make to lose weight and become more fit.

But by the end of February, attendance at the clubs is back to normal. In weeks, or even just in days, most people have broken their resolution to exercise. They are sitting at home, eating a snack or watching TV, when they could be working out for the good of their bodies.

If you have an ongoing problem with some type of irresponsibility, what we are *not* asking of you is a New Year's type of resolution to do better. We are not asking you to *force* yourself to do better on the job, at home, or wherever you tend to be irresponsible. If we asked this kind of self-effort from you, you would likely be no more successful than the people who show up at the gym with brand-new exercise clothes in January.

What we are asking of you is that you begin praying for help and committing yourself, in the grace of God, to fulfill the responsibilities He has laid on your heart. Seek the Lord, repent of your sin, and rely on the Spirit's empowering. Only in this way will you be able to acquire the virtue of diligence—and keep it.

When ejection seats for jet fighters were first invented, the pilot was supposed to push a button, clear the plane, and then roll out of his seat so that his parachute could deploy. The problem was that, under the intense conditions of a high-speed ejection, most pilots would hold on to their seat like it was their last link with safety. Their parachutes, consequently, could not open.

What did jet designers do in response to this unexpected problem? They invented a device that would force ejected pilots out of their seats, enabling them to correctly operate their parachutes—where their real safety came from.

If a responsibility is lying before you and you are hesitating to do anything about it, what will it take for you to get out of your seat? Get help now. Begin the healing process by embodying the virtue of diligence in every responsibility the Lord gives you. It is a privilege to serve Him with all that lies within us.

SOUL PRESCRIPTION FOR IRRESPONSIBILITY

Are you struggling with being irresponsible? We have outlined a five-step process to help you repent and heal in this area of your life. Take all the time you need with each of the steps below.

Step 1: Adopt a Correct View of God

A poor conception of God may well lie behind your problem with irresponsibility. For example, if you see God as an uncaring and detached deity, you will likely have the same attitude toward life. Are the following points ones you need to take to heart?

- God is absolutely concerned about every aspect of our lives.

  > What shall we say about such wonderful things as these?
  > If God is for us, who can ever be against us?
  > —Romans 8:31

- God uses His power on our behalf.

  > The eyes of the LORD search the whole earth in order to strengthen those whose hearts are fully committed to Him.
  > —2 Chronicles 16:9

In your Bible, read a sampling of some of the key events in salvation history, such as creation, the call of Abram, the exodus, and so on. Examine these events from the perspective of God's activity in the world. Begin to develop a picture of God as a deity who is far from apathetic or irresponsible toward His creation.

Step 2: Revise Your False Beliefs

Irresponsibility is fed by erroneous beliefs about life and one's place in it. How might your false views have helped to make you irresponsible? Ask yourself the following questions:

- Do you believe you cannot make any real changes in your world?

  > I can do everything through Christ, who gives me strength.
  > —Philippians 4:13

- Do you believe that the needs of others are none of your concern?

> Suppose you see a brother or sister who has no food or clothing, and you say, "Good–bye and have a good day; stay warm and eat well"—but then you don't give that person any food or clothing. What good does that do?
>
> —James 2:15–16

Use a concordance to help you trace the themes of laziness and diligence through the Scriptures. Seek God's help to correct your unbiblical views of life as they apply to irresponsibility.

Step 3: Repent of Your Sin

What type of irresponsibility is your downfall? Name it and disclaim it. Pray a simple prayer of repentance, and ask God to supernaturally motivate you into action.

> God, I have been guilty of _____. I know it is sinful, and I am sorry for the way I have let You down. Forgive me now, I pray. Wash away the stain of this sin. Make me over into a person who uses Your power to reject irresponsibility and embrace a diligent lifestyle— one that pleases You. I ask these things in Christ's name, amen.

If you have harmed others with your sin, apologize to them. Seek reconciliation and offer restitution where appropriate.

Step 4: Defend against Spiritual Attacks

Now that you have repented, watch out for demotivating spiritual attacks. They are certain to occur.

* In the world system, responsibility is not a high value in itself. The world would tell you to only do what you need to in order to get by—everything else is a waste. But God's values in this area are quite different. He wants diligence to be a regular part of your nature. You can overcome the world by rejecting its values and embracing God's values instead.

- Laziness and other types of irresponsibility are pleasurable to your flesh (sinful nature)—they are easy and comfortable. The flesh will desire to get that kind of pleasure back. But you must recall that your flesh is really dead now, because of Christ. You are a new person and are to obey the Spirit and not the flesh.

- The Devil is scheming to draw you back to your old ways of irresponsibility. Put on all the armor of God to defend against him (Ephesians 6:10–18). If you will resist the Devil in God's power, you can defeat him.

The quickest way to become irresponsible in life again is to be irresponsible about defending against spiritual attacks. Such attacks will come, and you should be ready for them. But remember that God will be empowering you and helping you be successful every time.

Step 5: Flee Temptation

The best way to avoid being tempted to lie on the couch and watch the world go by is to just do something. Take these active steps to be a more active person.

- Focus on your relationship with God.
  Begin your new, more disciplined life by maintaining your spiritual disciplines with God. He has something for you to do; ask Him what it is.

- Latch on to God's promises.
  Find Bible verses that speak encouragement to you in your struggle against irresponsibility. Commit the verses to memory and use them when temptation arises. Here is one you may find valuable:

> He gives power to the weak and strength to the powerless.
> —Isaiah 40:29

- Establish safeguards.

  What inspires you to be irresponsible? Do whatever it takes to block such influences from your life. These are examples of the kinds of things you can do:

  - If you are lazy, make a "to do" list of the things you ought to accomplish.
  - If you tend to procrastinate, create a calendar with all the deadlines for the things you are supposed to do.
  - If you typically leave your bedroom a mess, set your alarm a few minutes earlier so you can straighten it up every morning.
  - Ask a trusted Christian friend to hold you accountable in your commitment to not be irresponsible any longer.

- Expect victory.

  The Holy Spirit will motivate you into action if you will yield your heart to Him. Trust Him to make you a diligent person. Look forward to the victory He will give.

Visit www.SoulPrescription.com for more insights and resources, and to download a free leader's guide for small group Bible studies.

CONCLUSION

A young friend of mine (Bill's) found that his life had become a nightmare of addiction, promiscuous living, brushes with the law, and loneliness. One night he called out to God for help—he was not seeking salvation, just deliverance.

In reply to his prayer, he sensed the Father's reply: "You don't want Me in your life; you just want Me to get you out of a jam."

The truth cut through this man's heart like a knife. He prayed, "Then do whatever You have to do to bring me home."

The next twelve months of this man's life were a virtual replay of the previous year. Finally, though, the reality of his situation came crashing down on him and he prayed to God, "Take my life, Lord. It is Yours' to do with as You wish. Just please set me free." He kept seeking God and seeking holiness, and today he is free from his sin problem.

I tell this story to underscore how much of a struggle it can sometimes be, and how long it can sometimes take, to be healed of a habitual sin problem. The soul prescription we have written for you—adopting a correct view of God, revising your false beliefs, repenting of your sin, defending against spiritual attacks, and fleeing temptation—is able to bring you to spiritual well-being. But that does not mean the healing is easy.

We all know the reality. We mean not to repeat a sin; we think we will not commit the sin again—and then we do it! The apostle Paul agonized, "I don't really understand myself, for I want to do what is right, but I don't do it. Instead, I do what I hate" (Romans 7:15). The same experience is familiar to us. We have to expect difficulty and spiritual opposition in doing what God wants. Nevertheless, the five steps represent a natural progression that can help us defeat sin.

We hope that today you are praising God for the victory He has given over your sin problem. But if it has proved more stubborn than you thought, you may need to work through the five steps more than once. That's okay. As you repeat the process, you will be ingraining biblical truths of holiness in your spirit and drawing nearer to freedom. Over time, with God's help, the five steps will move you toward complete freedom from your sin problem.

And of course, that is what you want: to be able to say in all honesty that you *used to* have a problem with a particular sin. You will repeat the five-step process if you have to, but you do not want to be on a treadmill of sinning and recovering from sin forever. Eventually you want to get off the treadmill entirely by putting your habitual sin behind you. It is possible to do this by being honest with yourself and trusting in God.

Don't be overconfident, but don't be discouraged either. God is capable of curing your sin sickness. Like my young friend, many have practiced the principles embodied in our five steps and can testify of the victory they have achieved through the Spirit. You, too, can be free of your troublesome sin—permanently.

Remember, the definition of victory for you includes not only being freed from your habitual sin but also having the opposing virtue established firmly in your life. You not only get rid of pride but also embrace virtue; you not only give up anger but also practice forgiveness; and so forth. As God deals with your habitual sins, the whole garden of Christian virtues blooms in your life. Most of all, you are filled with love, the mark of a Christian.

Will you permit us to pray a prayer of blessing upon you as you go out to live a life of love and holiness in the Spirit?

> Heavenly Father, we pray for this dear child of Yours who loves You and wants to be holy as You are holy. Honor this child's attempts to follow the path toward holiness laid out in Your Word, and respond with grace and power to every plea for help. Once and for all, break the hold that a habit of sin has had over this one, so that every temptation to renew the sin may be rendered ineffective. Crown this child's virtues with a love inspired by Your own immeasurable love shown to us by Christ. And in the end, bring this child home to the place our Lord has prepared, glorified and shining with a purity that can never be tarnished again.

"Now may the God of peace make you holy in every way, and may your whole spirit and soul and body be kept blameless until our Lord Jesus Christ comes again" (1 Thessalonians 5:23). Amen.

HOW TO KNOW GOD PERSONALLY

J ust as there are physical laws that govern the physical universe, so there are spiritual laws that govern your relationship with God.

Law 1: *God loves you and created you to know Him personally.*

God's Love

> God so loved the world that he gave his only Son, so that everyone who believes in him will not perish but have eternal life.
>
> —John 3:16

God's Plan

> This is the way to have eternal life—to know you, the only true God, and Jesus Christ, the one you sent to earth.
>
> —John 17:3

What prevents us from knowing God personally?

Law 2: *People are sinful and separated from God, so we cannot know Him personally or experience His love.*

Human Beings Are Sinful

> All have sinned; all fall short of God's glorious standard.
>
> —Romans 3:23

The human race was created to have fellowship with God. But because of our own stubborn self-will, we chose to go our own independent way, and fellowship with God was broken. This self-will, characterized by an attitude of active rebellion or passive indifference, is an evidence of what the Bible calls sin.

Human Beings Are Separated

> The wages of sin is death [spiritual separation from God].
>
> —Romans 6:23

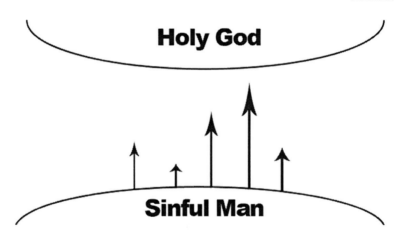

This diagram illustrates that God is holy and humanity is sinful. A great gulf separates the two. The arrows illustrate that people are continually trying to reach God and establish a personal relationship with Him through their own efforts, such as a good life, philosophy, or religion—but they inevitably fail.

The third principle explains the only way to bridge this gulf.

Law 3: *Jesus Christ is God's only provision for human sin. Through Him alone we can know God personally and experience God's love.*

He Died in Our Place

> God showed his great love for us by sending Christ to die for us while we were still sinners.
>
> —Romans 5:8

He Rose from the Dead

> Christ died for our sins, just as the Scriptures said. He was buried, and he was raised from the dead on the third day, as the Scriptures said. He was seen by Peter and then by the twelve apostles. After that, he was seen by more than five hundred of his followers at one time.
>
> —1 Corinthians 15:3–6

He Is the Only Way to God

> Jesus told [Thomas], "I am the way, the truth, and the life. No one can come to the Father except through me."
>
> —John 14:6

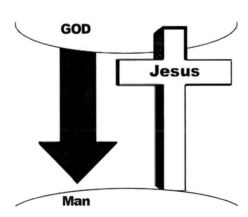

This diagram illustrates that God has bridged the gulf that separates us from Him by sending His Son, Jesus Christ, to die on the cross in our place and pay the penalty for our sins.

It is not enough just to know these truths.

Law 4: *We must individually receive Jesus Christ as Savior and Lord. Then we can know God personally and experience His love.*

We Must Receive Christ

To all who believed him and accepted him, he gave the right to become children of God.

—John 1:12

We Receive Christ through Faith

God saved you by his special favor when you believed. And you can't take credit for this; it is a gift from God. Salvation is not a reward for the good things we have done, so none of us can boast about it.

—Ephesians 2:8–9

When We Receive Christ, We Experience a New Birth

After dark one evening, a Jewish religious leader named Nicodemus, a Pharisee, came to speak with Jesus. "Teacher," he said, "we all know that God has sent you to teach us. Your miraculous signs are proof enough that God is with you."

Jesus replied, "I assure you, unless you are born again, you can never see the Kingdom of God."

"What do you mean?" exclaimed Nicodemus. "How can an old man go back into his mother's womb and be born again?"

Jesus replied, "The truth is, no one can enter the Kingdom of God without being born of water and the Spirit. Humans can reproduce only human life, but the Holy Spirit gives new life from heaven. So don't be surprised at my statement that you must be born again. Just as you can hear the wind but can't tell where it comes from or where it is going, so you can't explain how people are born of the Spirit."

—John 3:1–8

We Receive Christ by Personal Invitation

[Christ said,] "Look! Here I stand at the door and knock. If you hear me calling and open the door, I will come in, and we will share a meal as friends."

—Revelation 3:20

Receiving Christ involves turning to God from self (repentance) and trusting Christ to come into our lives to forgive us of our sins and to make us what He wants us to be. Just to agree intellectually that Jesus Christ is the Son of God and that He died on the cross for our sins is not enough. Nor is it enough to have an emotional experience. We receive Jesus Christ by faith, as an act of our will.

These two circles represent two kinds of lives.

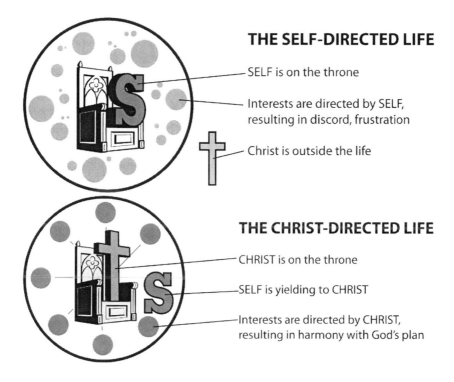

THE SELF-DIRECTED LIFE

— SELF is on the throne

— Interests are directed by SELF, resulting in discord, frustration

— Christ is outside the life

THE CHRIST-DIRECTED LIFE

— CHRIST is on the throne

— SELF is yielding to CHRIST

— Interests are directed by CHRIST, resulting in harmony with God's plan

Which circle best represents your life?
Which circle would you like to have represent your life?

You Can Receive Christ Right Now by Faith through Prayer

Prayer is talking with God. God knows your heart and is not so concerned with your words as He is with the attitude of your heart. The following is a suggested prayer:

> Lord Jesus, I want to know You personally. Thank You for dying on the cross for my sins. I open the door of my life and receive You as my Savior and Lord. Thank You for forgiving me of my sins and giving me eternal life. Take control of the throne of my life. Make me the kind of person You want me to be.

Does this prayer express the desire of your heart? If it does, pray this prayer right now, and Christ will come into your life, as He promised.

How to Know That Christ Is in Your Life

Did you receive Christ into your life? According to His promise in Revelation 3:20, where is Christ right now in relation to you? Christ said He would come into your life and be your friend so you can know Him personally. Would He mislead you? On what authority do you know that God has answered your prayer? (The trustworthiness of God Himself and His Word.)

The Bible Promises Eternal Life to All Who Receive Christ

"This is what God has testified: He has given us eternal life, and this life is in his Son. So whoever has God's Son has life; whoever does not have his Son does not have life. I write this to you who believe in the Son of God, so that you may know you have eternal life."

—1 John 5:11–13

Thank God often that Christ is in your life and that He will never leave you (Hebrews 13:5). You can know on the basis of His promise that Christ lives in you and that you have eternal life from the very moment you invite Him in. He will not deceive you.

An important reminder...

Do Not Depend on Feelings

The promise of God's Word, the Bible—not our feelings—is our authority. The Christian lives by faith (trust) in the trustworthiness of God Himself and His Word. This train diagram illustrates the relationship among fact (God and His Word), faith (our trust in God and His Word), and feeling (the result of our faith and obedience). (Read John 14:21.)

The train will run with or without the caboose. However, it would be useless to attempt to pull the train by the caboose. In the same way, we as Christians do not depend on feelings or emotions, but we place our faith (trust) in the trustworthiness of God and the promises of His Word.

Now That You Have Received Christ

The moment you received Christ by faith, as an act of your will, many things happened, including the following:

- Christ came into your life (Revelation 3:20; Colossians 1:27).
- Your sins were forgiven (Colossians 1:14).
- You became a child of God (John 1:12).
- You received eternal life (John 5:24).
- You began the great adventure for which God created you (John 10:10; 2 Corinthians 5:17; 1 Thessalonians 5:18).

Can you think of anything more wonderful that could happen to you than entering into a personal relationship with Jesus Christ? Would you like to thank God in prayer right now for what He has done for you? By thanking God, you demonstrate your faith.

Suggestions for Christian Growth

Spiritual growth results from trusting Jesus Christ. "The righteous man shall live by faith" (Galatians 3:11). A life of faith will enable you to trust God increasingly with every detail of your life and to practice the following:

G   Go to God in prayer daily (John 15:7).
R   Read God's Word daily, beginning with the gospel of John (Acts 17:11).
O   Obey God moment by moment (John 14:21).
W   Witness for Christ by your life and words (Matthew 4:19; John 15:8).
T   Trust God for every detail of your life (1 Peter 5:7).
H   Holy Spirit—allow Him to control and empower your daily life and witness (Acts 1:8; Galatians 5:16–17).

Fellowship in a Good Church

God's Word admonishes us to "not neglect our meeting together" (Hebrews 10:25). Several logs burn brightly together, but put one aside on the cold hearth and the fire goes out. So it is with your relationship with other Christians. If you do not belong to a church, do not wait to be invited. Take the initiative; call the pastor of a nearby church where Christ is honored and His Word is preached. Start this week and make plans to attend regularly.

HOW TO BE FILLED WITH
THE HOLY SPIRIT

Every day can be an exciting adventure for the Christian who knows the reality of being filled with the Holy Spirit and who lives constantly, moment by moment, under His gracious direction.

The Bible tells us there are three kinds of people:

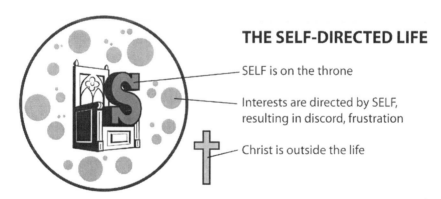

THE SELF-DIRECTED LIFE

SELF is on the throne

Interests are directed by SELF, resulting in discord, frustration

Christ is outside the life

1. **The Natural Person:** One who has not received Christ

People who aren't Christians can't understand these truths from God's Spirit. It all sounds foolish to them because only those who have the Spirit can understand what the Spirit means.

—1 Corinthians 2:14

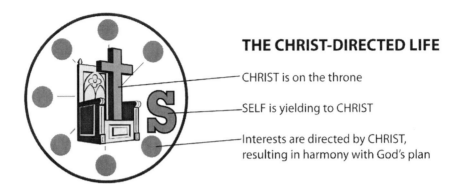

THE CHRIST-DIRECTED LIFE

CHRIST is on the throne

SELF is yielding to CHRIST

Interests are directed by CHRIST, resulting in harmony with God's plan

2. **The Spiritual Person:** One who is directed and empowered by the Holy Spirit

> We who have the Spirit understand these things.... We have the mind of Christ.
>
> —1 Corinthians 2:15–16

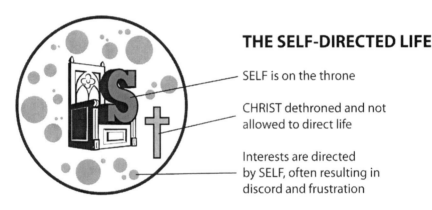

THE SELF-DIRECTED LIFE

SELF is on the throne

CHRIST dethroned and not allowed to direct life

Interests are directed by SELF, often resulting in discord and frustration

3. **The Worldly (Carnal) Person:** One who has received Christ but who lives in defeat because the person is trying to live the Christian life in his or her own strength

> Dear brothers and sisters, when I was with you I couldn't talk to you as I would to mature Christians. I had to talk as though you belonged to this world or as though you were infants in the Christian life. I had to feed you with milk and not with solid food, because you couldn't handle anything stronger. And you still aren't ready, for you are still controlled by your own sinful desires. You are jealous of one another and quarrel with each other. Doesn't that prove you are controlled by your own desires? You are acting like people who don't belong to the Lord.
>
> —1 Corinthians 3:1–3

The following are four principles for living the Spirit-filled life:

1. God has provided for us an abundant and fruitful Christian life.

[Jesus said,] "My purpose is to give life in all its fullness."

—John 10:10

[Jesus said,] "I am the vine; you are the branches. Those who remain in me, and I in them, will produce much fruit. For apart from me you can do nothing."

—John 15:5

When the Holy Spirit controls our lives, he will produce this kind of fruit in us: love, joy, peace, patience, kindness, goodness, faithfulness, gentleness, and self-control. Here there is no conflict with the law.

—Galatians 5:22–23

When the Holy Spirit has come upon you, you will receive power and will tell people about me everywhere—in Jerusalem, throughout Judea, in Samaria, and to the ends of the earth.

—Acts 1:8

The following are some personal traits of the spiritual person that result from trusting God:

Christ-centered
Empowered by the Holy Spirit
Introduces others to Christ
Effective prayer life
Understands God's Word

Understands God's Word
Trusts and obeys God
Experiences love, joy, peace, patience, kindness, faithfulness, gentleness, goodness, and self-control

The degree to which these traits are manifested in the life depends on (1) the extent to which the Christian trusts the Lord with every detail of life and (2) his or her maturity in Christ. One who is only beginning to understand the ministry of the Holy Spirit should not be discouraged if he or she is not as fruitful as more mature Christians who have known and experienced this truth for a longer period.

Why is it that most Christians are not experiencing the abundant life?

2. Worldly Christians cannot experience the abundant and fruitful Christian life.

Worldly (carnal) people trust in their own efforts to live the Christian life:

- They are either uninformed about, or have forgotten, God's love, forgiveness, and power (Acts 1:8; Romans 5:8–10; Hebrews 10:1–25; 2 Peter 1:9; 1 John 1; 2:1–3).
- They have an up-and-down spiritual experience.
- They cannot understand themselves—they want to do what is right but cannot.
- They fail to draw on the power of the Holy Spirit to live the Christian life (Romans 7:15–24; 8:7; 1 Corinthians 3:1–3; Galatians 5:16–18).

Some or all of the following traits may characterize the worldly person—the Christian who does not fully trust God:

Unbelief

Disobedience

Poor prayer life

No desire for Bible study

Legalistic attitude or critical spirit

Impure thoughts, jealousy, guilt

Worry, discouragement

Loss of love for God and others

(Those who profess to be Christians but who continue to practice sin should realize that they may not be Christians at all, according to Ephesians 5:5 and 1 John 2:3; 3:6–9.)

The third truth gives us the only solution to this problem.

3. Jesus promised the abundant and fruitful life as the result of being filled (directed and empowered) by the Holy Spirit.

The Spirit-filled life is the Christ-directed life by which Christ lives His life in and through us in the power of the Holy Spirit (John 15).

- One becomes a Christian through the ministry of the Holy Spirit, according to John 3:1–8. From the moment of spiritual birth, the Christian is indwelt by the

Holy Spirit at all times (John 1:12; 14:16–17; Colossians 2:9–10). (Though all Christians are indwelt by the Holy Spirit, not all Christians are filled—that is, directed and empowered—by the Holy Spirit on an ongoing basis.)

- The Holy Spirit is the source of the overflowing life (John 7:37–39).
- The Holy Spirit came to glorify Christ (John 16:1–15). When one is filled with the Holy Spirit, he or she is a true disciple of Christ.
- In His last command before His ascension, Christ promised the power of the Holy Spirit to enable us to be witnesses for Him (Acts 1:1–9).

How, then, can one be filled with the Holy Spirit?

4. We are filled (directed and empowered) by the Holy Spirit by faith. Then we can experience the abundant and fruitful life that Christ promised.

You can appropriate the filling of the Holy Spirit right now if you:

- Sincerely desire to be directed and empowered by the Holy Spirit (Matthew 5:6; John 7:37–39).
- Confess your sins. By faith, thank God that He has forgiven all of your sins—past, present, and future—because Christ died for you (Colossians 2:13–15; Hebrews 10:1–17; 1 John 1; 2:1–3).
- Present every area of your life to God (Romans 12:1–2).
- By faith claim the fullness of the Holy Spirit, according to

His command: Be filled with the Spirit.

> Don't be drunk with wine, because that will ruin your life. Instead, let the Holy Spirit fill and control you.
> —Ephesians 5:18

His promise: He will always answer when we pray according to His will.

> We can be confident that he will listen to us whenever we ask him for anything in line with his will. And if we know he is listening when we make our requests, we can be sure that he will give us what we ask for.
> —1 John 5:14–15

Faith can be expressed through prayer.

How to Pray in Faith to Be Filled with the Holy Spirit

We are filled with the Holy Spirit by faith alone. However, true prayer is one way of expressing our faith. The following is a suggested prayer:

> Dear Father, I need You. I acknowledge that I have sinned against You by directing my own life. I thank You that You have forgiven my sins through Christ's death on the cross for me. I now invite Christ to again take His place on the throne of my life. Fill me with the Holy Spirit as You commanded me to be filled and as You promised in Your Word that You would do if I asked in faith. I pray this in the name of Jesus. As an expression of my faith, I now thank You for directing my life and for filling me with the Holy Spirit.

Does this prayer express the desire of your heart? If so, bow in prayer and trust God to fill you with the Holy Spirit right now.

How to Walk in the Spirit

Faith (trust in God and His promises) is the only way a Christian can live the Spirit-directed life. As you continue to trust Christ moment by moment,

- Your life will demonstrate more and more of the fruit of the Spirit (Galatians 5:22–23) and will be more and more conformed to the image of Christ (Romans 12:2; 2 Corinthians 3:18).
- Your prayer life and study of God's Word will become more meaningful.
- You will experience His power in witnessing (Acts 1:8).
- You will be prepared for spiritual conflict against the world (1 John 2:15–17), against the flesh (Galatians 5:16–17), and against Satan (1 Peter 5:7–9; Ephesians 6:10–13).
- You will experience His power to resist temptation and sin (Romans 6:1–16; 1 Corinthians 10:13; Ephesians 1:19–23; Philippians 4:13; 2 Timothy 1:7).

Appendix C

SPIRITUAL BREATHING

If you become aware of an area of your life (an attitude or an action) that is displeasing to the Lord, even though you are walking with Him and sincerely desiring to serve Him, simply thank God that He has forgiven your sins—past, present, and future—on the basis of Christ's death on the cross. Claim His love and forgiveness by faith and continue to have fellowship with Him.

If you retake the throne of your life through sin—a definite act of disobedience—breathe spiritually. Spiritual breathing (exhaling the impure and inhaling the pure) is an exercise in faith that enables you to experience God's love and forgiveness.

1. *Exhale:* Confess your sin—agree with God concerning your sin and thank Him for His forgiveness of it, according to 1 John 1:9 and Hebrews 10:1–25. Confession involves repentance—a change in attitude and action.

2. *Inhale:* Surrender the control of your life to Christ, and receive the fullness of the Holy Spirit by faith. Trust that He now directs and empowers you, according to the command of Ephesians 5:18 and the promise of 1 John 5:14–15.

ENDNOTES

Chapter 1

1. See Genesis 3:12–13.
2. In this book we use "cure" and "healing" interchangeably. Using either word, we are referring to a process that does not lead to sinless perfection (we all struggle with temptation) but most definitely can put an end to a sin habit.
3. The list went through some modification over time, but it ended up with these seven elements. The list was not meant to identify the worst sins but rather the basic sins from which others arise—similar to our concept of sin families.

Chapter 2

1. In this book, when we refer to "cooperating" with God, we mean acknowledging that He provides the answers in His Word, the Bible, and then submitting to those commands.
2. John Ortberg, "True (and False) Transformation," *Leadership* (summer 2002): 104.
3. The biblical words for the Spirit, *ruach* and *pneuma,* both mean "wind" or "breath."
4. We recognize that God's kindness does not mean that He never allows suffering to enter the lives of His children. See Bill Bright, *Why Do Christians Suffer?* (Orlando, FL: New Life, 2000).
5. Kay Arthur, *As Silver Refined: Learning to Embrace Life's Disappointments* (Colorado Springs: WaterBrook, 1997), 3.

6. For more on the five prayers of repentance, see Henry R. Brandt and Kerry L. Skinner, *The Heart of the Problem* (Nashville: Broadman & Holman, 1997), 73–83; Henry R. Brandt and Kerry L. Skinner, *The Word for the Wise: Making Scripture the Heart of Your Counseling Ministry* (Nashville: Broadman & Holman, 1999), 102–106; Kerry L. Skinner, *The Joy of Repentance* (Mobile, AL: KLS LifeChange Ministries, 2006).

Chapter 3

1. A. W. Tozer, *The Knowledge of the Holy: The Attributes of God: Their Meaning in the Christian Life* (Lincoln, NE: Back to the Bible, 1961), 6–7.
2. Barna Research Group, press release, "American Faith Is Diverse, as Shown among Five Faith-Based Segments," January 29, 2002, http://www.barna.org/, accessed September 2003. An atheist is one who believes there is no God. An agnostic is one who is undecided about the existence of God.
3. Bill Bright, *God: Discover His Character* (Orlando, FL: New Life, 1999). See also the related website at http://www.discovergod.org.

Chapter 4

1. See also John 14:16 and John 15:26.
2. See the King James Version, Acts 17:11.

Chapter 5

1. For more on the five prayers of repentance, see Henry R. Brandt and Kerry L. Skinner, *The Heart of the Problem* (Nashville: Broadman & Holman, 1997), 73–83; Henry R. Brandt and Kerry L. Skinner, *The Word for the Wise: Making Scripture the Heart of Your Counseling Ministry* (Nashville: Broadman & Holman, 1999), 102–106; Kerry L. Skinner, *The Joy of Repentance* (Mobile, AL: KLS LifeChange Ministries, 2006).
2. As you are reading about the five prayers, notice how the first three correspond to exhaling guilt, while the remaining two correspond to inhaling grace. (See appendix C: "Spiritual Breathing.")
3. We are not sure what the "thorn" was, though it may have been a persistent temptation.

Chapter 6

1. Martin Luther, *Works of Martin Luther*, 6 vols. (Philadelphia: Holman, 1915–1932), 3:279.

2. That misunderstanding has led to the unfortunate belief by many that the body is bad in itself.
3. In Romans 8, Paul was circling back to the same point he had made in Romans 6. We have died to sin.

Chapter 7

1. See chapters in part 2 for verses related to specific sins.
2. Quoted in Famous Sports Quotes, http://ktornado.tripod.com/khs/id13.html, accessed September 2003.
3. For more about supernatural thinking, see Bill Bright, *The Joy of Supernatural Thinking* (Colorado Springs: Victor, 2005).

Chapter 9

1. The pride of the king of Babylon (Isaiah 14:3–23) and the king of Tyre (Ezek. 28:1–19) may reflect Satan's overweening pride and desire to supplant God.
2. C. S. Lewis, *Mere Christianity* (New York: Macmillan, 1952), 112–13.
3. Frederica Mathewes-Green, "Pride: The Anti-Self-Esteem," Beliefnet (http://www.beliefnet.com/story/110/story_11056_1.html), accessed November 2003.
4. See also 1 Timothy 2:9.
5. Lewis, *Mere Christianity*, 95.
6. Esther de Waal, *Living with Contradiction: Reflections on the Rule of St. Benedict* (San Francisco: Harper & Row, 1989), 96.
7. Benjamin Franklin, *The Autobiography of Benjamin Franklin and Selections from His Other Writings*, Modern Library (New York: Random House, 2001), 101.

Chapter 10

1. Evelyn Underhill, *The Spiritual Life* (New York: Harper & Row, n.d.), 103–104.
2. If you want to look at a few more Bible verses on courage, try Psalms 27:14; 46:1–2; 118:6; Proverbs 29:25; Isaiah 35:3–4; 51:12–13; John 14:27; 16:33; and 1 Corinthians 16:13.
3. Neil T. Anderson and Rich Miller, *Freedom from Fear: Overcoming Worry and Anxiety* (Eugene, OR: Harvest House, 1999), 203.
4. Joyce Meyer, *Be Anxious for Nothing: The Art of Casting Your Cares and Resting in God* (Tulsa, OK: Harrison House, 1998), 27.
5. Anderson and Miller, *Freedom from Fear*, 100.

6. John Edmund Haggai, *How to Win over Worry: Positive Steps to Anxiety-Free Living* (Eugene, OR: Harvest House, 2001), 46–47.

Chapter 11

1. Adapted from Henry R. Brandt and Kerry L. Skinner, *The Heart of the Problem* (Nashville: Broadman & Holman, 1997), 123–125.
2. Paul was quoting Psalm 4:4.
3. Adapted from Henry R. Brandt and Kerry L. Skinner, *The Heart of the Problem* (Nashville: Broadman & Holman, 1997), 140–145.
4. See also Proverbs 12:16 and 14:29.
5. Frederick Buechner, *Wishful Thinking: A Theological ABC* (New York: Harper & Row, 1973), 2.
6. Adapted from Henry R. Brandt and Kerry L. Skinner, *The Heart of the Problem* (Nashville: Broadman & Holman, 1997), 149.
7. Paul was quoting Deuteronomy 32:35.
8. Stephen Leon Alligood, "American Profile," June 14, 2003, CBS News, www.cbsnews.com, accessed November 2003.
9. Even when someone is angry at an impersonal event, such as a hurricane that swept away his house, he is really angry at a person—namely, God.
10. Tim LaHaye and Bob Phillips, *Anger Is a Choice* (Grand Rapids, MI: Zondervan, 2002), 122.

Chapter 12

1. Adapted from David Slagle, "Doctor Calls Man's Overeating Sin," *Preaching Today*, http://www.preachingtoday.com, accessed October 2003.
2. American Obesity Association, http://www.obesity.org/, accessed September 2003.
3. Cornelius Plantinga Jr., in *The Reformed Journal* (November 1988), as quoted in *Christianity Today* 33, no. 2.
4. Quoted in Chuck Green, "Sound Salvation," *The Reader's Guide to Arts and Entertainment*, February 28, 2003, 6.
5. Other proverbs underscore the way drunkenness can lead to poverty and prevent the acquisition of wisdom. (See Prov. 20:1; 21:17; 23:20–21.)
6. See also Romans 13:13 and Galatians 5:21.
7. Quoted in Steve Beard, "Johnny Cash Approaches Judgment Day with Faith," *Relevant*, http://www.relevantmagazine.com, accessed August 2003.

8. William Law, *A Serious Call to a Devout and Holy Life*, chapter 7, Christian Classics Ethereal Library, http://www.ccel.org/l/law/serious_call/cache/serious_call.html3, accessed December 2003.

Chapter 13

1. Billy Graham, *Just As I Am: The Autobiography of Billy Graham* (San Francisco: HarperSanFrancisco, 1997), 697.
2. For more on the tenth commandment, see Bill Bright, *Written by the Hand of God: Experience God's Love and Blessing through the Liberating Power of His Ten Commandments* (Orlando, FL: New Life, 2001), chap. 15.
3. For more on the eighth commandment, see Bright, *Written by the Hand of God*, chap. 13.
4. Thomas Watson, *The Art of Divine Contentment: An Exposition of Philippians 4:11* (1653; reprint, Glasgow: Free Presbyterian Publications, 1885), chap. 6. For Hannah's story, see 1 Samuel 1—2.

Chapter 14

1. Frederick Buechner, *Godric* (New York: Harper & Row, 1980), 153.
2. The language used here has been popularized in Harry W. Schaumburg, *False Intimacy: Understanding the Struggle of Sexual Addiction*, rev. ed. (Colorado Springs: NavPress, 1997).
3. Quoted in *Karen S. Peterson,* "Cohabiting Can Make Marriage an Iffy Proposition," *USA Today*, July 8, 2002, D1.
4. Larry L. Bumpass, James A. Sweet, and A. Cherlin, "The Role of Cohabitation in Declining Rates of Marriage," *Journal of Marriage and the Family* 53 (1991): 913–927.
5. Quoted in Will Greer, "A. C. Green: Man Enough to Wait," *Breakaway*, http://www.family.org/teenguys/breakmag/features/a0009929.html, accessed November 2003.
6. For more on the seventh commandment, see Bill Bright, *Written by the Hand of God: Experience God's Love and Blessing through the Liberating Power of His Ten Commandments* (Orlando, FL: New Life, 2001), chap. 12.
7. Joseph Nicolosi and Linda Ames Nicolosi, *A Parent's Guide to Preventing Homosexuality* (Downers Grove, IL: InterVarsity, 2002), 141.
8. Kim Alexis, "Supermodel Kim Alexis: Kim Shares Her Thoughts on Self-Respect, Sex, Life, Abortion & Marriage," Love Matters, http://www.lovematters.com/kimalexis.htm, accessed November 2003.

9. Wendy Shalit, "Modesty Revisited," Imprimis, http://www.hillsdale.edu/imprimis/2001/march/article_1.asp, accessed November 2003. Shalit is the author of *A Return to Modesty: Discovering the Lost Virtue* (New York: Free Press, 1999).

10. See also 1 Peter 3:3–5.

11. John Piper, "A Passion for Purity vs. Passive Prayers," November 10, 1999, Desiring God Ministries, http://www.desiringgod.org/library/fresh_words/1999/111099.html, accessed November 2003.

12. Sandra, "Child Pornography: What Happens When They Grow Up," National Coalition for the Protection of Children and Families, http://www.nationalcoalition.org/sandra.phtml, accessed November 2003. Used by permission.

13. See Psalm 101:3 NIV.

14. William Mattox, in a magazine article, summarized how "a 1940s Stanford University study, a 1970s *Redbook* magazine survey of 100,000 women and at least one other study from the early 1990s all found higher levels of sexual satisfaction among women who attend religious services." Mattox speculated on the reasons as including (1) a lack of "sexual baggage" from promiscuity before marriage; (2) the confidence that comes from a mutual commitment to marriage; (3) an absence of sexual anxiety because the couples do not fear sexually transmitted diseases and other ill effects of out-of-wedlock intercourse; and (4) an ability to enjoy the spiritual dimension of sexuality. William R. Mattox Jr., "Revenge of the Church Ladies," Plain Truth, July–August 2001, http://www.ptm.org/01PT/JulAug/revenge.htm, accessed November 2003.

15. "Coming out of Pedophilia: Jeff's Story," Harvest USA, http://www.harvestusa.org/articles/jeffstory.htm, accessed November 2003. Used by permission.

Chapter 15

1. Selena Roberts, "Olympics: The Pivotal Meeting. French Judge's Early Tears Indicated Controversy to Come," *New York Times*, February 17, 2002, sect. 8, p. 1.

2. For more on the ninth commandment and lying in general, see Bill Bright, *Written by the Hand of God: Experience God's Love and Blessing through the Liberating Power of His Ten Commandments* (Orlando, FL: New Life, 2001), chap. 14.

3. Paul was quoting Zechariah 8:16.

4. Adapted from Henry R. Brandt and Kerry L. Skinner, *The Word for the Wise* (Nashville: Broadman & Holman, 1999), 192–193.

5. For God's commandments against fraud, see Leviticus 19:35–36 and Deuteronomy 25:13–16. Proverbs 20:23 says, "The LORD despises double standards; he is not pleased by dishonest scales."

6. Quoted in Victor Lee, "Wrenching the Rules," *Men of Integrity,* May–June 2002, May 20 devotional.

Chapter 16

1. Ramona Cramer Tucker, "Loose Lips," *Christian Reader,* March–April 2002, 38–39. Michelle tried to get in touch with Beth to apologize but was never able to.

Chapter 17

1. For a similar statement by Paul, see Colossians 3:20.
2. For more on the fifth commandment, see Bill Bright, *Written by the Hand of God: Experience God's Love and Blessing through the Liberating Power of His Ten Commandments* (Orlando, FL: New Life, 2001), chap. 10.
3. For more about a wife's submission to her husband, see 1 Corinthians 11:3; Colossians 3:18; and 1 Peter 3:1–6.
4. The word for "submit" is *hupotass* , meaning to make oneself subject to another. The word for "obey" is *hupakou* , meaning to listen and to obey.
5. See online at http://www.despair.com. The products are called "Demotivators."
6. For more about slaves' duty to their masters, see Colossians 3:22–25; 1 Timothy 6:1–2; Titus 2:9–10; and 1 Peter 2:18–20.
7. For a description of the death that came to the "murmuring" Hebrews, see Numbers 14.
8. For more on obedience to civil authorities, see Titus 3:1 and 2 Peter 2:13–14, 17.

Chapter 18

1. See the book of Philemon.
2. For the whole context, see Ephesians 6:5–8. For similar discussions in Paul's letters, see also Colossians 3:22–25; 1 Timothy 6:1–2; and Titus 2:9–10. The importance of slaves doing their work well was a consistent teaching of the apostle.
3. J. I. Packer, *Knowing God* (Downers Grove, IL: InterVarsity, 1993), 34, 106.

ABOUT THE AUTHORS

DR. HENRY BRANDT

Henry was awarded his Ph.D. in Marriage and Family Relations at Cornell University in 1952, his Master of Arts Degree in Clinical Psychology from Wayne State University in 1949, and his Bachelor of Arts Degree in Psychology and Sociology from Houghton College in 1947.

After completing his doctorate at Cornell, Henry accepted what he thought would be his life's vocation—serving as Dean of Men at his alma mater, Houghton College. After two years, he realized God had other plans. Subsequently, Henry was invited to take a one-year sabbatical replacement position teaching speech at North American Baptist Seminary. The experience taught him far more than he had anticipated: it set the course of his career in public speaking.

In 1955, following his pivotal year at North American Baptist Seminary, Henry moved to Michigan. He worked for three years as a full-time staff member for the Clare Elizabeth Fund, not only to develop further some of the key teaching principles behind the Lamaze Program, but also to supervise twelve children's nurseries! Henry served for over a decade (1955–65) as a licensed psychologist in the area of individual, marriage, and family counseling in private practice in Michigan. During this time his call to ministry and his gifts in public speaking led him to host a popular family radio program aired over the Moody Bible Institute's station WMBI from 1961 to 1971.

From the earliest days of Henry's vocation, he trained missionaries at home and ministered to them abroad. At his own expense, he reached out to countless men and women stationed in extreme and isolated locations. He was the first counseling psychologist to meet with the missionary wives after the Auca massacre in the Amazon.

Throughout Henry's career, he taught in a number of institutes, colleges, and seminaries, including the General Motors Institute, Houghton College, North American Baptist Seminary, Trinity Evangelical Divinity School, Christian Heritage College, and Palm Beach Atlantic University. He was instrumental in founding departments of psychology for both Christian Heritage College and Palm Beach Atlantic University.

Henry rightly has been honored with the title "The Father of Modern-Day Biblical Counseling." For decades he has counseled individuals to evaluate their heart attitudes and behavior in the light of biblical teaching and to guide them to a godly solution. In 2003, the American Association of Christian Counselors honored Henry with their "Care Giver Award" for a lifetime of outstanding achievements.

Known as a communicator of communicators, Henry has an uncanny ability to understand his audience and to deliver just the right message. His use of Scripture, combined with his unique sense of humor, has reached the "inner person" of many to help facilitate genuine change. Over the decades, Henry's wisdom and skill as a communicator have enabled him to author numerous books with a focus on individual development and marriage and family living. His work, which has been translated into many languages, has circulated the globe.

Henry was married for forty-two years to Eva (d. 1979), with whom he had three children—Dick, Beth, and Suzanne. He has four grandchildren and five great-grandchildren.

Henry was married to Marcy (d. 1982) for three years. Then Henry married Jo in 1987. Jo has three children—Chris, Juliette, and Will (d. 2001)—and four grandchildren.

Henry Brandt died on November 25, 2008 from complications related to Parkinson's disease. He was 92.

For more information about Henry Brandt go to HenryBrandtFoundation.org

DR. BILL BRIGHT

Dr. William R. ("Bill") Bright was born in Coweta, Oklahoma, on Oct. 19, 1921. He graduated from Northeastern State University in Oklahoma with a Bachelor of Arts degree in economics and a minor in sociology. While a student, Dr. Bright served as editor of the university yearbook, was student body president, was chosen as a member of Who's Who in American Colleges and Universities, and was selected by students and faculty as the year's outstanding graduate. After graduation, he joined the extension faculty of Oklahoma State University. He later moved to Los Angeles where he launched a successful business career.

While in California, Dr. Bright attended the First Presbyterian Church in Hollywood. Largely through the influence of his mother's prayers and that church, he became a Christian in 1945 and then began an intensive study of the Bible. His studies led him to almost five years of graduate work at Princeton and Fuller theological seminaries, while still continuing his business interests. It was while a seminary student at Fuller that the young Bright felt the call of God to help fulfill Christ's Great Commission (Matthew 28:18-20). He began by sharing Christ with students on campus at UCLA, an activity that soon became a full-time calling, and which gave birth to the present worldwide ministry of Campus Crusade for Christ International.

From a small beginning in 1951, the organization he began now has more than 25,000 full-time staff and over 553,000 trained volunteer staff in 196 countries in areas representing 99.6 percent of the world's population. What began as a campus ministry now covers almost every segment of society with more than 70 special ministries and projects which reach out to students, inner cities, governments, prisons, families, the military, executives, musicians, athletes, and many others.

Each ministry is designed to help fulfill the Great Commission, Christ's command to carry the gospel to the entire world. The film, JESUS, which Bright conceived and funded through Campus Crusade for Christ, is the most widely viewed film ever produced. It has been translated into more than 730 languages and viewed by more than 4.5 billion people in 234 countries, with 300 additional languages currently being translated. More than 148 million people have indicated making salvation decisions for Christ after viewing it live. Additional tens of millions are believed to have made similar decisions through television and radio versions of the JESUS Film.

Dr. Bright holds six honorary doctorate degrees: a Doctor of Laws from the Jeonbug National University of Korea, a Doctor of Divinity from John Brown University, a Doctor of Letters from Houghton University, a Doctor of Divinity from the Los Angeles Bible College and Seminary, a Doctor of Divinity from Montreat-Anderson College, and a Doctor of Laws from Pepperdine University. In 1971, he was named outstanding alumnus of his alma mater, Northeastern State University. He is listed in Who's Who in Religion and Who's Who in Community Service (England), and has received numerous other recognitions. In 1973, Dr. Bright received a special award from Religious Heritage of America for his work with youth, and in 1982, received the Golden Angel Award as International Churchman of the Year.

Together with Mrs. Bright, he received the Jubilate Christian Achievement Award, 1982-1983, for outstanding leadership and dedication in furthering the gospel through the work of Campus Crusade and the Great Commission Prayer Crusade. In addition to many other responsibilities, Bright served as chairman of the Year of the Bible Foundation, and he also chaired the National Committee for the National Year of the Bible in 1983, with President Ronald Reagan serving as honorary chairman. Bill Bright was the 1996 recipient of the $1 million Templeton Prize for Progress in Religion. He dedicated all of the proceeds of the award toward training Christians internationally in the spiritual benefits of fasting and prayer, and for the fulfillment of the Great Commission. Bright was also inducted into the Oklahoma Hall of Fame in November 1996.

Dr. Bright also received the first Lifetime Achievement Award from his alma mater, Northeastern State University, as well as a co-recipient with his wife of the Lifetime Inspiration Award from Religious Heritage of America Foundation. In addition, he received the Lifetime Achievement Award from both the National Association of Evangelicals and the Evangelical Christian Publishers Association, which also bestowed on him the Chairman's Award. He was inducted into the National Religious Broadcasters Hall of Fame in 2002.

Dr. Bright has authored more than 100 books and booklets as well as thousands of articles and pamphlets that have been distributed by the millions in most major languages. His books include: *Come Help Change the World, The Secret, The Holy Spirit, A Man Without Equal, A Life Without Equal, The Coming Revival, The Transforming Power of Fasting & Prayer, Red Sky in the Morning* (co-author), *God: Discover His Character, Living Supernaturally in Christ, Written by the Hand of God, Blessed Child* (co-author), *and more recently Beyond All Limits: The Synergistic Church For A Planet In Crises* (co-author), *and First Love.* He and Mrs. Bright co-authored *Building a Home in a Pull-Apart World,* and he is the editor of *The Greatest Lesson I've Ever Learned,* a compilation of input from 38 prominent Christian men. His booklet, *Have You Heard of the Four Spiritual Laws?,* has a distribution of more than 2.5 billion, and has been translated into more than 200 languages.

Bill Bright died on July 19, 2003 from complications related to pulmonary fibrosis. He was 81.

Dr. Bright's wife, Vonette, cofounder of Campus Crusade for Christ, lives in Orlando, Florida. They have two grown sons: Zachary, who is pastor of Divine Savior Presbyterian Church in California, and Brad, who is President and CEO of Bright Media Foundation.

Buy the Authorized Biography of Bill Bright at NewLifePubs.com
For more information about Bill Bright go to BillBright.com

More Resources From
Henry Brandt Foundation

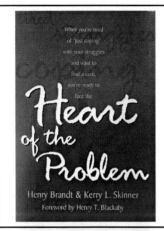

The Heart of the Problem
By Henry Brandt, Kerry L. Skinner

The Heart of the Problem: How to Stop Coping and Find the Cure for Your Struggle–This helpful work gives encouragement to everyone who has ever faced a situation they felt was insurmountable. Pride, anger, and denial separate people from the solutions and comfort they long for. By seeking God's answer, even the most complex problems can be solved once and for all.

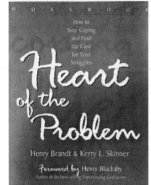

The Heart of the Problem Workbook
By Henry Brandt, Kerry L. Skinner

An interactive, Scripture-based workbook that shows readers how to fight sin effectively and live a more problem-free life.

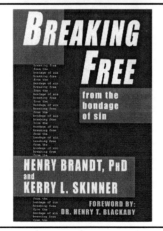

Breaking Free From the Bondage of Sin
By Henry Brandt, Kerry L. Skinner

A human approach to dealing with sin does indeed relieve symptoms. But there is no human remedy for the problem of sin. The cure is out of this world. Only God can help. Hopefully this book will help to illuminate the barriers [sins] that come between a person and the resources available from God through Jesus Christ.

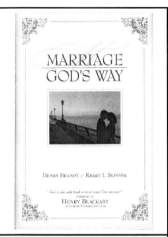

Marriage God's Way
By Henry Brandt, Kerry L. Skinner

Tragic but true: couples who follow the world's models of marriage end up in divorce. This problem is growing more and more prevalent even in the church. But Marriage-God's Way takes a fresh and frank new look at how to ease marital strife by considering marriage from a biblical perspective.

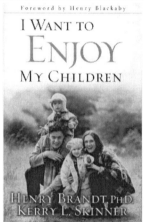

I Want To Enjoy My Children
By Henry Brandt, Kerry L. Skinner

If you didn't plan for them — or, even if you did — having kids may threaten to spoil the fun of marriage. Henry Brandt and Kerry Skinner's book shows how to make parenting a fascinating, pleasant journey, wherever it may lead. This biblical, practical guide is based on the truth that parents need help from a resource outside themselves.

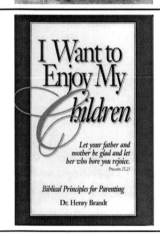

I Want To Enjoy My Children Workbook
By Henry Brandt, Kerry L. Skinner

Based on the book, I Want to Enjoy My Children, 11 chapters are divided into five daily lessons to help a parent focus on God's plan for parenting. To qualify as a Godly parent, you need to be a person of inner peace evidenced in the unexpected, unprepared for, unwanted twists and turns of life. This inner peace makes life a fascinating, pleasant journey, wherever it may lead.

The Word For the Wise
By Henry Brandt, Kerry L. Skinner

Worldly solutions offer people only temporary relief from their problems, but biblical counseling offers a trustworthy and lasting cure. This book shows ministers and other counselors how to help angry, broken, confused people look at their lives from a biblical perspective.

The Power of the Call
By Henry Blackaby, Henry Brandt, and Kerry L. Skinner

Whether you find yourself on the verge of burnout or simply need someone to fan the flames of your faith, take time to experience afresh The Power of the Call. This practical and uplifting guide takes a biblically sound and realistic look at how God provides fully for every need a pastor.

Available online at: www.HenryBrandtFoundation.org

More Resources From
Bright Media Foundation

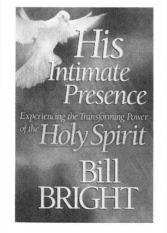

His Intimate Presence
Experiencing the Transforming Power of the Holy Spirit
By Bill Bright

Do you daily experience the glorious presence of God in a loving, intimate relationship? Or, like many Christians, do you experience frustration and despair as you struggle to live a joyful, fruitful life?

Perhaps the missing link in your spiritual walk is the presence and work of the Holy Spirit. In this book, Dr. Bill Bright explores what the Holy Scriptures teaches about the amazing presence and power of God's Spirit. Discover the marvelous, supernatural results of drawing close to God and inviting His Holy Spirit to live through you as your teacher, motivator, comforter, peacemaker, protector, counselor and intimate friend.

In this inspirational, informative book, Dr. Bright distills the essence of a lifetime of teaching and experience. Whatever your situation, these chapters will encourage you to live in greater dependence on the magnificent Holy Spirit who indwells you and you will be eager to allow the Spirit to have greater control in your life. Practical "Life Application" sections will help you not only learn the truths of these chapters, but live them and experience an intimate relationship with God.

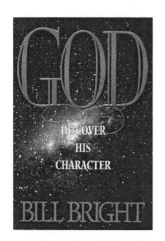	## God: Discover His Character By Bill Bright "Everything about our lives is determined and influenced by our view of God", writes Bill Bright, founder of Campus Crusade for Christ. But most of us have misguided perceptions about the nature of God. How we view God and His involvement touches every facet of our lives -- our family, work, and ministry. In this timeless treasure, you will discover how you can develop an intimate relationship with God as you uncover the truth about God and His marvelous character.
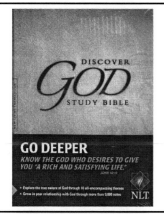	## Discover God Study Bible Every problem in life is based on an incorrect view of God. The Discover God Study Bible is the first study Bible specifically designed to address this issue. Every note and feature draws the reader to a deeper understanding of who God is and how He can transform their life. It features an easy-to-use TopicGuide to every major topic and teaching of the Bible.
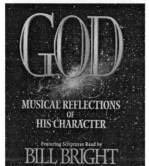	## God: Musical Reflections of His Character (CD) Come join Bill Bright in an intimate time of worship focusing on the true character of God. Heartfelt to majestic, poignant to triumphant, this CD is perfect for personal quiet times, Bible Studies, even as a gift to someone seeking comfort or the knowledge of God.

Available online at: www.DiscoverGod.com and www.CampusCrusade.com

CPSIA information can be obtained at www.ICGtesting.com
Printed in the USA
BVOW060923160812

297925BV00004B/116/P